ICE & OIL

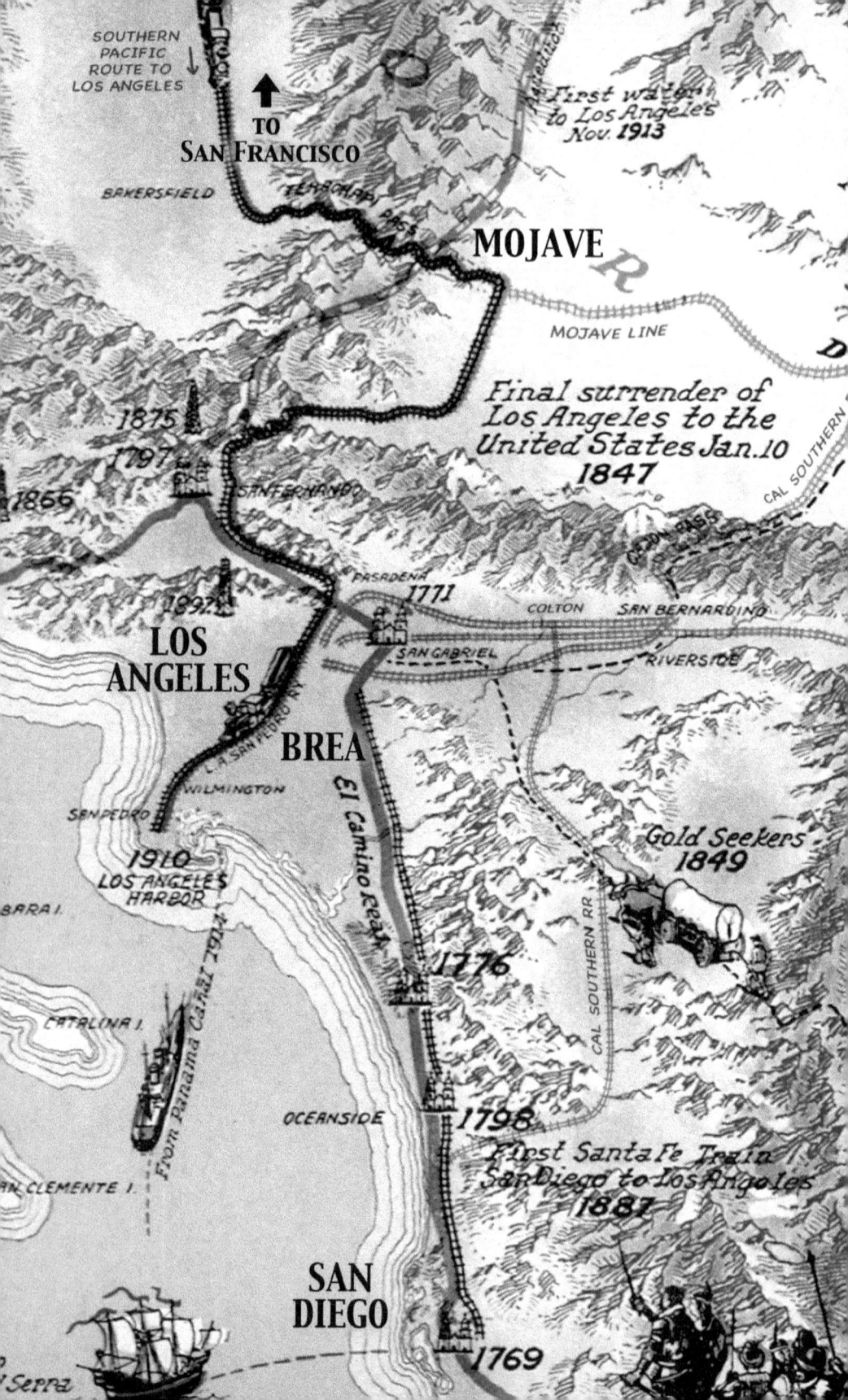

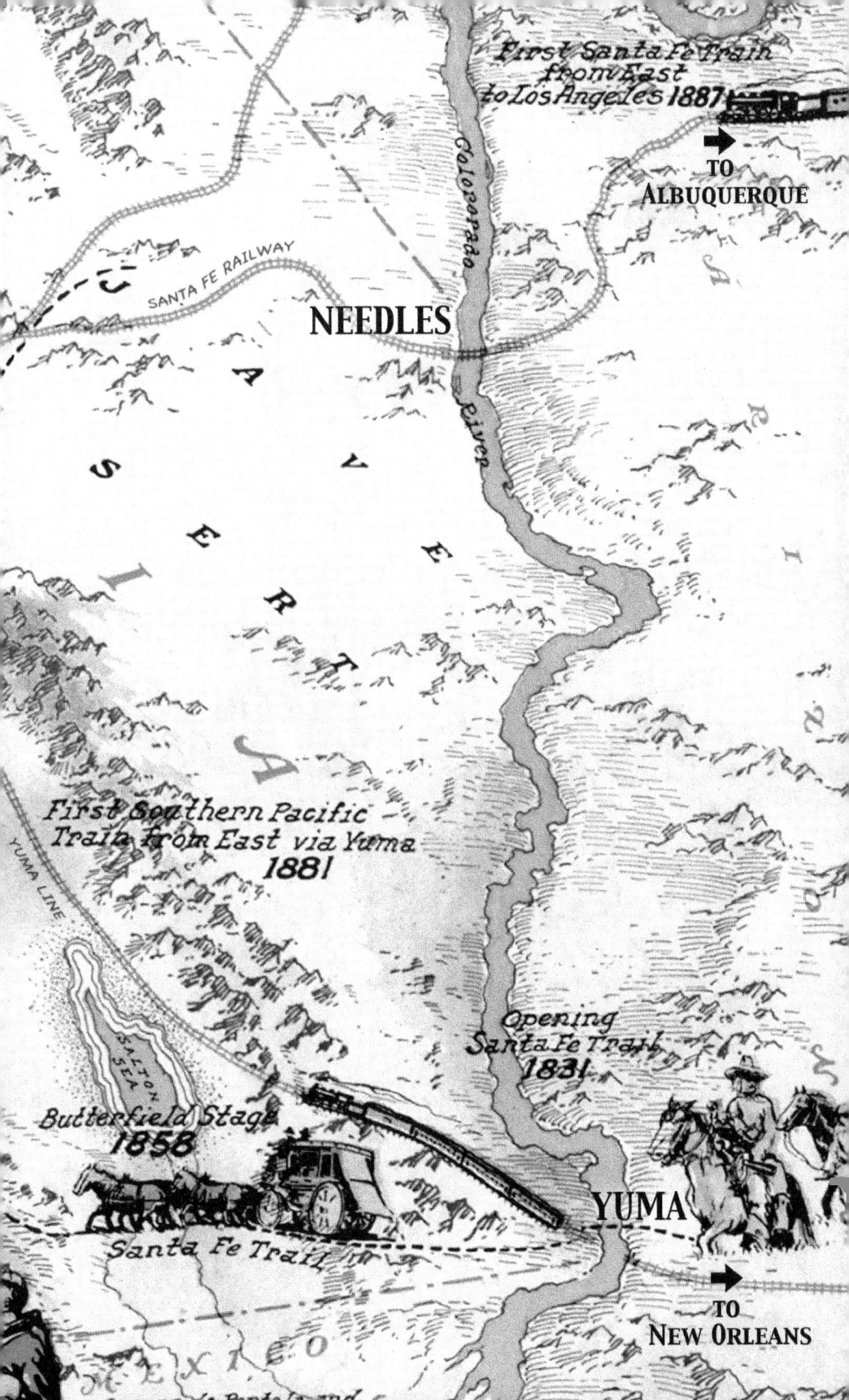

The Life and Legacy of Dan Murphy
California's Unlikely Titan

JOSEPH FRANCIS RYAN

Foreword by Tom Sitton

Ice & Oil:
The Life and Legacy of Dan Murphy, California's Unlikely Titan

By Joseph Francis Ryan
Foreword by Tom Sitton

Copyright © 2020 Joseph Francis Ryan

Design by J. Eric Lynxwiler, Signpost Graphics

10 9 8 7 6 5 4 3 2 1

www.iceandoil.com

Images in this book, unless otherwise noted, are from the author's and other private collections.

All rights reserved. No part of this book may be reproduced or transmitted in any form or by any means, electronic or mechanical, including photocopying, recording, or by an information storage and retrieval system, without express written permission from the publisher. "Angel City Press" and the ACP logo are registered trademarks of Angel City Press. The names and trademarks of products mentioned in this book are the property of their registered owners.

Library of Congress Cataloging-in-Publication Data is available.

Published in association with Angel City Press, www.angelcitypress.com

To my life partner
Chuck

In memory of my sister
and co-researcher
Pat Ryan

and

To those people whose
names are often lost
in history, but whose
lives have meant so
much to the future.

Contents

	Foreword by Tom Sitton	11
	Introduction	15
1.	Hanover	21
2.	Atlantic & Pacific	35
3.	Night Train	47
4.	Mojave Line	59
5.	Murphy and the Mojave	71
6.	Godfrey Holterhoff	87
7.	Screams in the Dark	95
8.	Leadville	101
9.	Great White City	109
10.	Ahvote	127
11.	It's A Gusher	135
12.	We Ask Your Blessing	143
13.	Indian Territory	153
14.	Champs-Elysees	161
15.	"Aunt" Sue	169
16.	Got Nerve	181
17.	A Showplace	185
18.	Dust and Oranges	195
19.	West Adams	201
20.	The Good Life	207
21.	War Ships	215
22.	My Warriors Fell Around Me	223
23.	The Pump Is Busted	237
24.	Gentleman In Question	243
25.	Knight Commander	249
26.	Our Dan	255
	Epilogue	261
	Appendices	266
	Endnotes	269
	Acknowledgments	293
	Bibliography	297
	Index	304

Deacon Dan's Birthday

What care I whether Standard Oil
    Goes up—or down—or out,
What care I whether more gray hairs
    Come in or new ones sprout,
I want you just to live some more
    To be the same next year
    And radiate that Irish smile
    So redolent of cheer.

To one whose life has been so full
    Of good deeds done to others,
    The charity of kindly acts
    To children and to mothers,
The blessings of mankind go out
    A thousandfold old man,
To make more sweet the birthday
Of my good friend Deacon Dan.

The wish that's in my heart today
    Is that the coming years
    May be enshrined in happiness
    And be undimmed by tears,
And that the love of wife and friends
    Will be so strong and true
That you will be just middle age
When you are ninety-two.[1]

                      September 21, 1916.
                            T.C. Stevens
On the occasion of Dan Murphy's fifty-eighth birthday

Foreword
by Tom Sitton

California has long been known as a land of opportunity for budding entrepreneurs dedicated to making their mark in the economy and society through various business ventures, participation in civic and social circles, and in philanthropy. Many came to the state with few dollars in their pockets, some hit a jackpot, and some lost everything.

Many who retained their fortunes made sure that their actions and status were publicized—or at least they left considerable evidence of their work and victories, so future historians could ponder their legacies. And it's probable that almost none of them disregarded those legacies, or even their social status, during their lifetimes. In fact, maybe there was just one man in the early days of Southern California who was satisfied to make a huge impact and not make headlines.

Author Joe Ryan discovered him—Daniel Murphy, or just "Dan" as he preferred. Dan came to California as a young man to seek his fortune. Over the next six decades, he accumulated a vast fortune through his numerous enterprises and played an important role in the development of Southern California and the American Southwest. And few history books have ever even mentioned him. Not even when the subject is ice or oil.

Dan Murphy departed the Midwest for the West while in his early twenties and soon went to work for the Southern Pacific Railroad. He arrived in Los Angeles in 1878, when it was just a generation removed from its Mexican pueblo past. By that time, the cattle economy of Southern California had given way to the expansion of agriculture tended by Midwestern and Southern immigrants, many of them being the families of soldiers from both the Union and Confederate armies who had battled in the Civil War. Tradesmen and professionals also arrived to service the farmers, and the population of Los Angeles rose to 12,000 by 1880.

When the number of these newcomers had surpassed the existing population, one observer noted "Mexican civilization all but vanished" and the Anglo presence dominated. The same person, who visited the city in 1867 and again seven years later, raved about the transformation. For him, Los Angeles had become "...an American city. Adobe has given way to elegant and substantial dwellings and stores," as the downtown architecture changed. Such was the tenor of the times. Civic leaders such as Phineas Banning and Benjamin D. Wilson had been active in bringing a Southern Pacific Railroad connection to the city by 1876, and worked to gain federal support to expand the nearby San Pedro harbor. Since Los Angeles was the county seat of Los Angeles County, its board of supervisors and the city's municipal representatives generously supported such expansion, economic growth, and infrastructure, as well as increasing agricultural production.

Gaining a major railroad connection became a critical objective in modernizing Los Angeles, as well as California and the rest of the US in the nineteenth and early-twentieth centuries. Railroads connected communities and far-flung regions throughout the nation, made travel more convenient, and opened many areas to opportunities for economic growth by reaching new markets for agricultural and manufactured goods, spurring urbanization and industrialization. The railroads helped to standardize manufacturing by demanding consistency when it came to their equipment, and even made accurate timekeeping crucial by setting definite departure and arrival schedules.

When Dan Murphy arrived in Los Angeles, Southern Pacific (formerly the Central Pacific) was the major railroad in California and an important factor in the state's growth. He soon worked for Charles Crocker, one of the SP's "Big Four" leaders, the man responsible for directing some of its key initiatives. These included developing and protecting state resources and its environment, encouraging California agriculture and public irrigation, attracting industries, and expanding the SP transportation system. At the same time, other SP executives and its political agents protected its interests by lobbying the US Congress, the California state legislature and some of the state's local governments, as well as nearby territorial representatives. There would be plenty to defend as the railroad forged eastward through Arizona Territory and Texas to New Orleans and other destinations.

By the 1880s, Southern Pacific faced major competition from the Atchison, Topeka & Santa Fe Railway. Santa Fe was heading through Southern California toward Los Angeles in 1883, when Dan Murphy and a business partner, at Crocker's behest, established a general store in the new town of Needles on the state's eastern border, where Murphy soon sold ice for refrigerated railroad boxcars and invested in gold and silver mining. Santa Fe would reach Los Angeles in 1885 and launch a rate war with SP that triggered the population explosion of the late 1880s.

During its expansion, Southern Pacific absorbed smaller railroads in Southern California, and if a town or city was to be on the route, there was a price to pay—be it big or small. In 1872, Los Angeles had to ante-up its own short-lived railroad to the San Pedro harbor *and* pay a huge price to get its connection to northern California completed in 1876. SP would fight local boosters and others in the 1890s by trying to win a federal subsidy to establish a new harbor where most of the land was controlled by the SP. Its leaders heavily lobbied US senators for support, but SP met defeat in the contest. Despite this and other conflicts with Los Angeles city and county governments—as well as other cities in California—the SP network became a major force in the development of the state.

After 1900, Los Angeles continued to grow as the city fathers moved to bring in an additional water source and urban transportation networks for more development. By 1930, residents in the municipality surpassed one million and Los Angeles became the fifth most populous city in the nation.

Dan Murphy must have anticipated all this expansion when he added oil to his businesses in 1899, at the very moment that the demand for petroleum increased dramatically. In a similar fashion, he took control of the California Portland Cement Company, just when Los Angeles would require tons of concrete for its industrial, commercial, and residential infrastructure. In the 1930s, his cement was used in the colossal Boulder (later Hoover) Dam. That dam would bring water and electrical power from the Colorado River to serve the essential needs of Southern California, whether that meant irrigating its huge agricultural business, watering the lawns of its suburbs, or eventually powering our computers. Could Dan Murphy have foreseen it all?

Joe Ryan is certainly right that Dan Murphy was a major player in the regional economy, but one we knew so little about—Dan was a self-made entrepreneur, not a self-promoter seeking to advance his reputation for future generations. Inspired by Dan Murphy, an unpretentious "Everyman," and a desire to learn more about Los Angeles in Dan's era, Ryan has worked diligently for over a decade to research and compose Dan's fascinating story. In his first book, Ryan has now established Dan's reputation and given us the details of Dan's life, his family, and his philanthropy, and his many contributions to Southern California and the larger Southwest. Another important piece of California history has emerged.

Introduction

Dan (never Daniel) Murphy is a man you probably have never heard of. He is not of this age, but harkens to the twilight of Westward Expansion and the closing of the American Frontier. He actualized numerous industries, institutions, and partnerships that shaped the megalopolis of Los Angeles. Although Murphy was well-known and respected in his day, his impact on the nascent city has been overlooked in the city's history. The reason for this is that he purposely did not want publicity—something almost impossible to comprehend in our current narcissistic culture. Murphy avoided all publicity, granted no interviews, and declined almost all photographers—that kind of humility characterized his entire life. His contemporaries in industry, commerce, and education sought his views and judgment as evidenced by the numerous boards of directors in which he was engaged. His life could be an inspiration—and a tonic—for the postmodern world.

Dan Murphy's biography dates from the days when Los Angeles was still a remote western adobe town to its pre-World War II building boom. Throughout Murphy's life, he engaged with prominent individuals of his day and great effort has been made in this story to delineate several lives, those individuals from the city's past who have been similarly neglected. Traditional history usually mentions only the celebrated masters of the California universe—the Big Four of the Southern Pacific Railroad, the Dohenys, the Mulhollands, the Gianninis—and overlooks the people who made less-heralded events happen, but whose collected actions molded all facets of the state.

Murphy lived an extremely diverse life. He went from being a brakeman on the Yuma, Arizona, train to adventures with the Mojave Indians, discovering gold, and being showered with untold wealth from his gushing oil derricks. In retirement, he conversed with popes, princes, and nobility, while traveling through Belle Epoch European spas and resorts. It is a wild and fascinating story of a man who made a substantial contribution to the creation of modern-day California and the greater Southwest. Few historians are aware of this man's profound influence which has largely been unrecorded until now. Yet, this is not the traditional rags-to-riches story.

Murphy never wanted anyone to know his worth—he was never caught up in his wealth. Murphy always avoided reporters and photographers, and he opposed the use of his name in any publication. Vanity biographies published in encyclopedia-sized tomes and "Who's Who" publications were popular at the time, but by Murphy's choice, they never involved him. This voluntary exclusion was eminently illustrated when the Los Angeles Catholic Archdiocese celebrated its centennial with a commemorative book. Murphy, the largest donor to the archdiocese, was not even mentioned. Instead, the publication featured a multipage article about Murphy's California Portland Cement Company and how it had been used in the erection of numerous ecclesiastical buildings throughout the archdiocese. The cumulative effect of his avoiding publicity has resulted in his near anonymity in the history of the Southwest, a history in which he played an extraordinary role.[1]

At the age of twenty-five Murphy founded the town of Needles that is located on the Colorado River and is also the site of the native home to the Mojave tribe that numbered more than one thousand individuals at the time. This book brings to light several examples of Murphy's benevolent interactions with these indigenous people. His treatment sharply contrasts with the cruelty Native Americans typically received at the time. His adventures also delve into the Southwest's mining territories, and discover the obstacles these rugged individuals faced as they hauled millions of dollars of gold, silver, and copper from their claims. Murphy and his partner Frank Monaghan were at the center of the excitement— in Needles on the Colorado River—at first running the only mining supply store within five hundred miles of barren desert. The Monaghan & Murphy General Merchandise Store was known "far and wide" and its two proprietors were "legends in their own day."

As a resident of Needles and the holder of free railroad passes, Murphy directed most of his attention eastward to Chicago, St. Louis, and New York City. As a young man in the 1870s, he had worked in St. Joseph, Missouri, a prosperous, vibrant, and cosmopolitan city where Mississippi riverboats traversed between St. Louis and New Orleans. Murphy always identified with the east and considered pueblo Los Angeles to be a frontier town. He came to the southwest to explore its untapped resources, not to establish a name for himself. Once he had free passes on the Southern Pacific with unlimited travel, he took full advantage. He once said, "I caught the first train and have never stopped riding since."[2] His true education was in the "smoker" on transcontinental trains where he discussed the issues of the day with some of the most prominent businessmen of his generation. He frequently traveled to New York City, with stops in Chicago and Boston, becoming one of the first bicoastal capitalists. He had no desire to be known in Los Angeles as just a shopkeeper from the desert outpost of Needles. When his Brea Cañon oil fields began pumping black gold, he was pursued to sit on the boards of Los Angeles's banks, utility companies, and its chamber of commerce.

Murphy's propensity for anonymity made researching his life particularly challenging. I visited a total of thirty-seven repositories: institutional archives, university special collections, historical societies' archives, and libraries. In all of these locations, I found Dan Murphy's name mentioned in only thirteen. The most fruitful resources were the Needles Regional Museum, San Bernardino Library, and the Kansas Historical Society in Topeka, which holds the three-thousand-box archive collection of the Atchison, Topeka & Santa Fe Railway records. The entry of the Atchison, Topeka & Santa Fe Railway into California forever changed the history of the Southwest.[3] For me, a road trip along the Santa Fe line was enlightening, as I traveled through three states visiting archives of universities and historical societies on the way. My destination was Hanover, Kansas, where the Murphy family established their home, just about the time Dan turned twelve.

The richest source of research material was the Santa Fe collection in Topeka, which took several days of concerted effort to find what I needed. Those records brought to light not only Murphy's contracts with the Santa Fe, but also his influential, yet-unsung longtime colleague and friend Godfrey Holterhoff. This archive revealed the overlooked pivotal role Holterhoff played in bringing the AT&SF into Los Angeles. Back in California, at the archive at the Huntington Library, I was finally able to access its original card catalog, where I found a single document. Discovering that letter was suddenly a eureka moment. This handwritten letter from Dan Murphy changed the entire direction of the book, not because of what it said, but the letterhead it carried—that of the prestigious Union Club in New York City.

My access to the Murphy family papers was pure serendipity. My first stop on the long road of discovering Murphy was in Downtown Los Angeles, to meet with the Dan Murphy Foundation, which has assets in excess of $240 million. I asked if the foundation would be interested in a biography of its founder. Months later, a formal rejection letter from the president of the foundation arrived stating: "Mr. Murphy never sought publicity during his lifetime, and it is out of respect for his preference for privacy that this decision is made." Interested and now even more determined, I felt I had to write this book. Little did I know that "a preference for privacy" was a gross understatement and how challenging unearthing this enigma would be.

Word of my request reached one of the foundation's five board members, the sole living relative of the Murphy family (the cousin of Dan's daughter Bernardine's husband). She had inherited the Murphy papers and allowed me unlimited access to the collection. As extensive as that archive is, the items were dated starting only in 1904 through the 1970s. The material was usually in the form of letters between the women of the Murphy household. Murphy's business records, I was told, were extensive and maintained by the foundation until the early 2000s, at which time they were destroyed. However, there were several astonishing finds among the family's collection, including a large baseball-sized piece of quartz that was hollow on the inside and laced with crystalized natural gold, apparently a souvenir from Murphy's mining days. The other remarkable find was his vest-pocket ring binder containing alphabetical index tabs with a page for each of his investments, listing the year and the amount, all hand-entered by his faithful secretary Howard Bagley.

Those personal papers helped me to unravel some of the myths about the Murphy family, some that had been propagated as history, even in primary sources. Until the digital age, newspapers such as the *Los Angeles Times* relied on their morgues—archives of articles clipped from the printed pages of the newspapers—for "facts" from the past. Thus came a curious story in 1982, under the headline "Legend of Adoption," relating that, in the early 1900s, the Murphys visited an Italian orphanage in hopes of adopting a boy, when a girl of seven or eight tugged at Mrs. Murphy's dress. The Murphys took it as a sign from God, as the story read, and little Bernardine went home with them to California. In 1996, another *LA Times* writer retold the same adoption tale, in an article about the relatively unknown Murphy family. It wasn't until I studied the family papers that the real story came to light. Without access to the personal archive, I would never have been able to tell the true story in these pages. That experience gave me insight into the broader meaning of "alternative facts," and how untruths can come to be accepted as fact, whether by mistake or by design.

It took years of research and study to see the genuine Dan Murphy emerge out of his documented past. If it were not for the personal papers and Chronicling America, the Library of Congress's website of digitized newspapers, this book would have taken me even longer to research and write. In the beginning, I spent untold hours searching "Dan Murphy," a very common name. This combined with many years as a board member of the Los Angeles City Historical Society, West Adams Heritage Association, Windsor Square–Hancock Park Historical Society and years of researching and nominating historic homes to the Los Angeles Cultural Heritage Commission equipped me for this task.

But in all those years of research, words spoken or written by Dan Murphy were few and very far between. I found one article in the *Washington Post* that added some insight about his personality in his later years, but added little to my goal of telling his life story. His responses to the reporter were purely philosophical. Murphy was no stranger to Washington, D.C. Since 1900, he had been to the capital on several occasions because of a lawsuit involving his Needles National Bank, a case that almost made its way to the US Supreme Court. On one of his many trips to the nation's capital, he was approached by a *Washington Post* reporter while sitting in his hotel's lobby. Murphy must have been relaxed and caught off guard by the journalist, since he never gave interviews.[4] Rather than talk about the legal case, Dan pivoted the direction of the interview and ended up giving advice to young career-seekers. He recommended Oklahoma and Arizona as states with promising futures and, thus, good job possibilities: "These are the places where the young men ought to go. Hanging around the East here will do them no good." He couldn't help spouting platitudes, such as "Nerve is worth its weight in gold and sometimes more." Not much meat for a biographer.

Despite a dearth of quotes from Murphy himself, from all of this research, the full breadth of his life came into view. It spanned an incredible distance from gathering buffalo bones as a child to help feed his pioneer family on the Plains of Kansas, to arriving at the adobe village of Los Angeles, to observing the completion of Boulder Dam, a project he originally envisioned. His affection for Mojave Natives and his later generosity to three popes, stretched across all boundaries and all lands he encountered. Time and again throughout Murphy's life, contemporaries remarked that he was a "great guy." No doubt his easy-going personality served him well. He avoided controversy and had few enemies, which only exacerbated his obscurity. The local newspaper affectionately referred to him as "Our Dan." A year after Murphy's demise, the internationally respected magazine, *Petroleum World*, published its thirtieth-year-anniversary issue featuring oil industry pioneers. The special issue carried a unique multi-paged tribute to Murphy's record-setting oil field and concluded that "… there's one man who made his pile, and no one has a word against him."[5]

—JFR, Fall 2020

1

Hanover

Sliding off his horse, Dan Murphy took two paces and fell to his knees onto a white rock outcropping near the crest of the hill. A sharp pain shot through his thighs. Bending low, he shaded his eyes from the midday sun and stared at the glinting yellow lines in the rock. Dan had seen plenty of gold-streaked quartz. This was the real thing. His companion, Ed Jones, jumped down from his horse shouting, "I told you so. This is the place!"

Dan had been crisscrossing the Arizona desert ranges for months, hanging out at diggings and pitching camp with whatever mining outfit would have him. His offers of help, such as hauling rock for no pay, usually brought a grudging grunt of approval from the miners who didn't want to share their haul.

At five feet ten inches, the friendly twenty-eight-year-old appeared beefy enough to do mining work. Or, maybe it was his mule loaded with supplies and brand new store-bought tools that convinced them to let him join them? By the end of the day, his open-hearted spirit won them over.

Over a period of two years, Murphy traveled hundreds of miles of remote desert mountain trails throughout the Arizona Territory and New Mexico. He visited mining camps like Chloride, Goldfield, Silver City, and Tombstone. At Kingman, in the Arizona Territory, he befriended the local barkeep, Ed Jones, with whom Murphy had ridden north out of Kingman to this site where the gold was found. After a few swings with a pickaxe, Jones and Murphy determined that, at least on the surface, the quartz vein was worth their time.

Murphy set out to pursue financial backing through Dennis Sullivan, one of the "foremost mining men in Colorado."[1] Murphy's sister lived in Leadville, a roaring Colorado mining town, and she probably introduced the two men when Dan visited. On January 3, 1887, Edward Jones, Dennis C. Sullivan, and Dan Murphy named their claim

"Josephine" and recorded it at the Mohave County office in Kingman, Arizona Territory.[2] Their 1500-by-600-foot discovery turned out to be a gold and silver bonanza. Within days, Murphy was supervising a dozen or more men hauling crystalline gold and pure silver from veins that were, at times, four- to six-inches wide.[3]

Living in tents on a scrub-covered hilltop at an elevation of more than 6,000 feet, they found water and firewood to be nonexistent. Nor was there much edible wildlife, save for rattlesnakes and gophers. With this amount of wealth waiting to be mined in such a remote and unprotected area, speed and secrecy were most important. The ore-bearing rocks were loaded into sacks and carried by mule across more than twenty-five miles of desolate terrain to Kingman where the recently completed Atlantic & Pacific Railroad passed through with regular stops. From Kingman, they took the ore to a smelter where it was pulverized and heated in a retort. The resulting bullion that melted from the slag was cast into gold ingots. That ore may have been smelted near San Francisco in early 1887, but it was not until August 1887 that a smelter opened in El Paso, Texas, which was equal to the distance from Kingman to San Francisco. The scarcity of smelters in the area was a major problem for years to come. Transportation and processing of the ore were frequently a make or break situation for a miner. Murphy periodically traveled by train to the Federal Mint in San Francisco where he exchanged the ingots for gold and silver coins. Suddenly, he was rich! Born the son of an immigrant Irishman, Murphy had banished the poverty of his childhood.[4]

If it sounds like we are heading into a riveting novel about the heyday of California mining, we are not. This is a true story, the biography of Dan Murphy, a man who hid behind his simple name, and used its commonality to separate himself from some of the less respectable Daniel Murphys of his time. Murphy experienced the twilight of the closing of the American West. He had traveled by rail from the Great Plains of Kansas, intent on finding the Wild West. He found it, and much, much more.

Dan Murphy was only five years old when his family fled west from Pennsylvania after the battle of Gettysburg in 1863.[5] He was just old enough to remember those difficult early years when the family moved on to Illinois. The lush green prairie of the Midwest came as a great relief to the Murphys. His father, Thomas, was especially thankful that he no longer had to toil underground in dank coal mines. Their new central Illinois village, Tolono, was a farming community and a vital crossroads for two major railroads: the Illinois Central Railroad linked Chicago and

New Orleans with the Great Western Railroad line, which connected the western United States to the eastern seaboard.[6] In 1861, after having given his farewell address in Springfield, Illinois, Abraham Lincoln had stopped at the Tolono intersection, bound for Washington, D.C., to assume his presidency.[7]

It was love at first sight when Dan witnessed his first steam locomotive. Tolono was a hotbed of train activity as Civil War trains passed through the village to return injured soldiers from southern battlefields. Cattle by the thousands were shipped in from the Chisholm Trail and the Western Plains. Native Americans, heading east as part of a Wild West show, were dressed in colorful costumes and accompanied by their promoters. The massive wheezing steam engines, cowboys, and exotic passengers from faraway places made a lasting impression on the young boy. It filled his imagination with the wonders of the Far West. The Murphys lived in Tolono for six years: Dan's formative years, ages six to twelve. His days and nights were suffused with the melancholy wail of steam locomotive whistles—a sound that would accompany him throughout his life.

Lured by homesteading advertisements offering 160 acre-parcels on the Midwestern plains that could be had for nothing, Thomas and his wife Anna yearned to own land, so they set off by covered wagon for the northern Kansas village of Hanover.[8] The town had recently been founded by German immigrants and was nestled in a green valley, alongside the flowing Little Blue River. A picturesque spot, just next to a bend in the stream, called out to Thomas. On May 20, 1870, he filed his claim at the Hanover post office and set about building his dream.

G.H. Hollenberg, Hanover's founder, wrote that "the beautiful, high rolling ground overlooking the grand valley of the Little Blue" was "an inspiring site for a growing and important town."[9] In 1869, he sited the town near the legendary Oregon-California wagon trail, which then followed the Little Blue River north to Fort Kearny and continued west to the Platte River. With thousands of wagons passing on the Oregon Trail, this provided a source of income for the town's residents, who sold them fresh produce and grains. Six miles to the north, Cheyenne and Arapaho warriors had killed and scalped ten settlers in a raid, and several other pioneers had been murdered similarly in the immediate area. The Murphys had hoped the Indians were under control by the time they arrived in 1870. Troops at Fort Kearny and at Fort Hays to the west limited the threat. Nevertheless, local talk and gossip of danger added to the anxiety of their already difficult circumstances.

Fortunately, Hanover thrived like many pioneer towns along the Oregon Trail. The Holliday Stage Line tore into town twice daily amid swirling dust clouds. With snorting horses and flying lather, the stage made its scheduled stop at the Hanover House Hotel. The stagecoaches, one going east, the second going west, ran from Atchison, Kansas, to Sacramento, California. Hanover was a quick stop with time only for mailbag exchanges and passenger boarding. Next door was a general store. In the middle of the store stood a "salt bank" guarded by a big black dog. Salt was a valuable commodity to pioneers without refrigeration and was often stolen by passersby. Shops of all kinds were present: a blacksmith, a meat market, a wagon shop, a drug store, and a lumberyard. Hanover's sawmill was run by a water wheel and made use of the trees lining the banks of the Little Blue. Although some people in Hanover were bilingual, most spoke only German. In the typical German tradition, Hanover had its own brewery. Ice for the brewery and saloons was cut during the winter months from the frozen Little Blue and stored under straw in an ice-house to keep it from melting. Little did young Dan know, at the time, that he would have a significant nationwide influence on this very industry.[10]

The low banks of the Little Blue were verdant with cottonwood, elm, and hickory trees. Its waters moved swiftly through the gently rolling hills. Limestone outcroppings were abundantly visible along its path, ledges of limestone that could be easily hewn into blocks, a ready source of building material. The Murphys also cut this stone into six-foot posts to which they attached a newly invented metal web called "barbed wire." Although costly for a pioneer family, fencing was a necessity to protect their fragile gardens from roaming buffalo and stray cattle. Vast herds of grazing buffalo appeared as a moving black blanket over these plains. Tree growth had been suppressed over time by the pounding hooves of generations of migrating herds. This scarcity of lumber forced most pioneers in the area to live in dugouts, half-underground dwellings carved into a hillside or berm. The Murphys were blessed with their own source of lumber from the abundant growth along the Little Blue, so they built a log cabin to call home.

The expanding Murphy family was almost complete with seven children. With their cabin built, the immediate challenge for Dan's parents was to provide shelter and food. Being the eldest son, Dan spent his youth working on the family farm. His sisters Hannah and Anna also worked the fields, while their mother attended the three younger children and the baby. These three oldest siblings sweated and toiled, breaking rock-hard soil and planting cabbage, carrots, beets, beans, peas, and corn. This daily drudgery of endless chores convinced Dan that there must be a better way to live.

In addition to the hard labor, Hanover was an undoubtedly tough place for the newly arrived Murphy clan. Life for Dan, who was just reaching puberty, was about as awful as it could be. He was a poverty-stricken minority who spoke only English, whereas the other teens spoke German. The Murphys were looked down upon by the staunch German populace who saw them as "poor shanty Irish." In the beginning, the Murphys kept to themselves. Dan, however, was sent to school in the tiny hamlet. The schoolmaster tested Murphy at the fourth-grade level to determine class placement, but the teenager failed the exam, probably due to the language barrier. He was placed in the lower level with younger children, a humiliation Murphy carried for life. As time passed, the Murphys learned to speak German. Dan became fluent, which served him well throughout his adulthood. It was not until 1890, long after his school days, that English was used in Hanover schools.[11]

The Murphy family became a familiar sight at Hanover's Saint John the Baptist Catholic Church. At the time, there was no Catholic school available, so it fell upon the deeply devout Anna to teach her children about their faith. Having been raised in Ireland where she spoke Gaelic, she had a Celtic reverence for the soul in all things. She taught her children the seven virtues: humility, kindness, patience, abstinence, chastity, generosity, and diligence. Every Sunday and holiday, the family made the half-mile trek across town to "Gospel Hill" where the imposing gray limestone church loomed over Hanover. Anna's teachings made a lasting impact. All of the Murphy children would in later life devote significant time and money to the support of various Catholic institutions. Dan's sisters would become heads of local and state auxiliary groups. Catholicism was the common denominator that brought the Murphy clan into kinship with the Hanover locals, despite their cultural and language differences. The jovial Irish band of Murphys brought some levity to the serious German folk as they all became more integrated into the community. Dan began to accelerate in school, even taking a genuine liking to and appreciation of the strict and disciplined Germans, and his mother's lessons stayed with him. He had memorized the seven virtues which became his way of life, and the dominant characteristics of his personality—especially humility.[12]

Nevertheless, with all their staunch training the children were frightened and scandalized by the murders and gun-fighting outlaws who continued to rage in the adjacent county with its raucous boomtown of Hays. When Hays was founded in 1867, it was "the end of the tracks" for the Union Pacific Railway, truly at the edge of the frontier. The US Army built a fort there to protect the railroad workers and settlers from Indian defiance. Saloons, brothels, and outlaws filled this wild frontier town. There were more than thirty killings in and around Hays City in the late 1860s. Street shootouts and cold-blooded murders were common in Hays, and the town's notoriety far outstripped the lawless reputation that Dodge City gained a few years later. During these legendary years Wild Bill Hickok, George Custer, Calamity Jane, and Buffalo Bill Cody were all building their reputations. Just southwest of the Murphy homestead was the town of Ellsworth, Kansas. The Chisholm Trail, famous for its Texas-to-Kansas cattle drives, ended there. The legendary sheriff Wyatt Earp established his fearless law enforcement there and tamed the rowdy cowboys that celebrated their end-of-the-trail with drunkenness and gunfire.[13]

In 1872, the Murphy clan had a memorable year. That spring, Anna gave birth to her eighth child—Margaret.

A few months later, in the summer of 1872, the St. Joseph & Western Railroad reached Hanover. Suddenly it was a railroad town, complete with a train station and roundhouse for servicing steam locomotives. The homesteaders delighted in the arrival of the train, as it gave them an immediate outlet for their produce, freeing them from their dependence upon the passing wagon trains. The reach of the railroad went far beyond the wagon train businesses they had previously depended on. Still, Thomas Murphy's family of ten struggled to survive from sale of their garden produce and income from harvesting trees on their homestead.

The arrival of the St. Joseph & Western Railroad into Hanover also brought professional buffalo hunters and skinners to the region. This began a massive slaughter of bison, both nearby and in the western ranges as the trains continued toward California. Steam locomotives startled the herds, causing stampedes. Often the trains would slow to match the pace of the panicked animals, so hunting parties onboard could shoot them from their open train car windows just for sport. The more greedy and indiscriminate huntsmen became known as "hide hunters." They used the cruel tactic of "the stand" in which hunters, careful to remain downwind of the herd, crawled up to within two hundred yards of the buffaloes and killed as many animals as they wished. Amazingly, the crack of a rifle did not cause the buffalo to run, even as bodies dropped around them. If the mammals turned curiously to look back, they presented themselves broadside to the hunters as an easy target. A single hunter could down a hundred animals in an hour or two, changing rifles every few minutes to avoid the barrel being deformed from the heat. It's estimated that four to five thousand hunters were on the plains during the annual migration. It was the high cost of ammunition, rather than the wanton annihilation of the buffalo, that put an end to the senseless killing. Within a few years, the millions of bison that had roamed these prairies for eons were reduced to a few hundred thousand. Their carcasses were left to rot on the Plains, resulting in thousands of square miles of prairie being littered with bones.[14]

After the Civil War, Philip Sheridan and William Tecumseh Sherman, two infamous Union Army generals, turned their attention to the Native American issue. Sheridan advocated the deliberate extermination of the buffalo, which gave rise to the abhorrent hide hunters. Sherman addressed the Texas Legislature in 1874 regarding these hunters:

> These men have done in the last two years and will do in the next year, more to settle the vexed Indian question than the entire regular army has done in the last thirty years... let them kill, skin, and sell until the buffaloes are exterminated. Instead of stopping the hunters they ought to give them a ... vote of thanks ... and present to each one a medal of bronze, with a dead buffalo on one side and a discouraged Indian on the other.[15]

The height of this slaughter in Kansas was from 1870–1873 and came just as Dan was reaching his teens. Dan was enamored with the local Indians and was incensed at the mindless waste of not only the Native Americans' food source but also their culture, which was imbued with the sacredness of the buffalo. Their most important social and religious customs which had developed over millennia ceased to have meaning and they lost their very identity.[16]

After the fall harvest and through the winter months, Dan and his sisters were required to gather buffalo bones as a source of income to help with the family finances. Dan took his sisters out on the open plains to collect as many buffalo bones as possible. The girls would gather the bones into a pile, and Dan would come around with the horse and wagon to pick them up. Once the wagon was full he took them to the railroad tracks where they were loaded onto boxcars and sent east to be pulverized for fertilizer. This was a vital business for all buffalo land residents. In 1872, near the depot at Hutchinson, Kansas, a stack of bones "stretched three hundred feet east to west, piled as high as a railroad car, and easily filled twenty boxcars." More than one million pounds of bones were shipped on the Santa Fe railroad during this period.[17]

The winter of 1873–1874 was unusually harsh, with several snowstorms sweeping over the plains. It was only the Murphys' third winter in Hanover. The Little Blue froze over in November, and snowbanks lingered into March. The following summer, a drought threatened to decimate their corn and wheat crops. By late July, hot winds "like the breath of a furnace" blew over the plains with several days registering 103 to 109 degrees in the shade.[18]

A common sight in Kansas during the 1870s: buffalo bones stacked along the railroad tracks. The bones were shipped east where they were ground into bone meal, to be used as fertilizer.

On August 15, 1874, dark silvery clouds appeared in the west, as if a storm was approaching. Sixteen-year-old Dan witnessed the apocalyptic event. Clouds began to roil and swirl in slow motion. In the silence before the storm, a low crackling sound like that of a prairie fire could be heard. Suddenly bugs began falling from the sky. In an instant, the roar and whirl of millions of flying insects turned the sky black, blocking the midday sun. It was the onset of the epic 1874 Rocky Mountain locust invasion. The insects covered the ground like a crawling carpet.

An eyewitness reported:

> They alighted, and in a few seconds, every green thing in sight was literally covered and hidden with a seething, crawling mass several inches in depth. The beautiful field of corn melted down as if each leaf were a spray of hoar frost in the rays of the noonday sun.[19]

Another account:

> Crops were eaten to the ground, as well as the wool from live sheep and clothing off people's backs. Paper,

tree bark and even wooden tool handles were devoured. Hoppers were reported to have been several inches deep on the ground and locomotives could not get traction because the insects made the rails too slippery.[20]

A young girl who lived through the horror stated:

> I was wearing a dress of white with a green stripe. The grasshoppers settled on me and ate up every bit of the green stripe in that dress before anything could be done about it.[21]

The voraciousness of the feeding insects horrified observers. Farm animals, especially chickens and turkeys, devoured locusts in a feeding frenzy. Gorging on the insects tainted their meat and eggs beyond human consumption. The onslaught lasted for several hours before it subsided and left dying bugs behind. A dark greenish oil exuded from the decaying carcasses and polluted the streams and ponds. Farmers struggled to protect their wells and drinking water from contamination. The stench and reek of the rotting grasshoppers left a lasting impression on anyone who survived.

Pioneers who lived on the edge of the frontier experienced hard times but did not expect to endure plagues of biblical proportions. After the disaster, only one in ten families had enough food for the coming winter. Kansas lost one-third of its population as homesteaders, having ventured everything they owned, returned east before facing starvation during another harsh winter. Nothing documents exactly how the Murphys survived this calamity. However, it is a well-established fact that the effects on survivors of a natural disaster persist for a lifetime. Although minor swarms of locusts appeared the following summer, none were as severe as 1874. The Murphys and the other homesteaders endured these hardships and deprivation, but they persevered.

These were also thrilling times for a teenage boy. Indians and buffalo still roamed the high plains. With their reservation a few miles away, some Otoe Indians lived peacefully in Hanover, and young Dan Murphy had a special liking for them. His father told him that, during the famine in Ireland, American Indians had collected money for the starving Irish. In the mid-1800s, a potato blight spread through Ireland. The island was struggling with poverty under English rule. Its population had become dependent on the potato as an inexpensive source of food. With the onset of the blight, this essential crop began rotting in the fields. Year after year of crop failure resulted in what is called the Irish Potato Famine. Between 1846 and 1851, one million people died of starvation.[22] One of the most remarkable acts of charity at the height of the famine occurred in 1847 when the Choctaw Indians took up a collection out of compassion for the Irish, raising $170 as a donation. The Choctaw had experienced starvation and decimation of their people. In 1831, half of their tribe had perished when they were forced off their reservation and marched five hundred miles to Oklahoma to a new reservation. That fateful march became known as the Trail of Tears. The favor was returned 173 years later when the Irish raised nearly a million dollars for Native American reservations during the 2020 Covid-19 pandemic.[23]

Dan sought odd jobs around Hanover, lending a hand to anyone in need of a day's labor. Although he was needed at home, the possibility of cash pay persuaded his father to allow him to go into town. With the train's arrival in Hanover, Murphy adopted railroading as his new and compelling passion. Railroad men were admired and respected by every young boy and grown man. Anticipating the train's daily arrival, Dan washed his face, combed his hair, and perked his ears for the distant wail of a whistle. When he heard it, he dashed for the depot where he tucked in his shirt to be ready on the platform as the locomotive slowed to a stop, puffing through the billowing clouds of steam. His heart swelled with pride as the engineer waved his gauntleted hand to recognize the boy's smiling face. Breathless, he respectfully bowed to the conductor descending from the coach. With calm courtesy, Dan greeted each passenger, offered a hand with their bags and answered their questions. He made a point of introducing himself to every conductor, brakeman, and engineer. He cheerfully engaged each one in conversation. Young Murphy soon became a familiar sight at the Hanover stop.

The pennies he gained from an occasional tip helped the family. After the locust invasion, money was in short supply and there were few sources for obtaining it. In those days, small-town train stations were operated by one person. The work entailed ticketing passengers, loading and unloading freight, handling mailbags, and preparing bills of lading for goods and livestock. Murphy was vying for a job, any job, with the railroad—especially one that paid regularly. That had been his dream ever since seeing his first train in Tolono, Illinois.

By the time Dan reached the employable age of fifteen, his railroading acquaintances paid off. He landed a job at the home office of the St. Joseph & Denver City Railroad in St. Joseph, Missouri, one hundred miles east of Hanover. Although it was a difficult and painful decision to let their first-born son leave the homestead, Thomas Murphy knew it was time. He had left Ireland at fifteen himself, and realized that there was little hope that the family would move beyond a subsistence living with so many mouths to feed. Dan should venture out and earn whatever he could, his father reasoned.

St. Joe had gained fame as the river-crossing point for the Oregon Trail. Mississippi paddlewheel steamboats came and went with regularity, giving the town a cosmopolitan feel. It was the last outpost for covered wagons to restock as they headed for California. In the 1870s it was a bustling city, with several railroads and numerous passenger trains passing through its depot. Dan Murphy hired onto the railroad, likely as a freight agent clerk. The railroaders working the line and farmers shipping their goods by rail from Hanover knew him. It was this familiarity with the railroad's customers that gave him an advantage landing this job. Not long after he was hired, the railroad was extended 227 miles beyond Hanover to Fort Kearny, where it continued to Hastings, Nebraska.[24]

Once Dan Murphy donned the railroad's navy blue wool uniform, with its double rows of shiny buttons, he realized his calling. He loved the life of the mammoth steaming locomotives, and the changing landscapes and railroad towns. But more than anything, he cherished the camaraderie of the other railroad men. He charmed them with his Irish humor, and they admired his gentle demeanor.

Promotions came rapidly for young Murphy thanks to his dedication and resourcefulness. At nineteen, he was promoted to conductor of the St. Joe-to-Hastings line. It was an extraordinary job for someone so young. He possessed the dignity and cheerful disposition required for the position, and after all, it was only a frontier train on the plains. However, as conductor, Dan had to have skill and diplomacy. At times his job required telling a woman passenger that her son, who was of obvious shaving age, could not travel at a child's half-price fare. He also had to quiet down gamblers and admonish male passengers not to shoot their pistols at passing telegraph poles. One such incident appeared in the *Atchison Patriot* on October 13, 1877:

> A party of huntsmen flagged the engineer to stop. Conductor Murphy rang his bell to go on, whereupon the party began to throw stones and mud at the train, and the trainmen replied with coal. One of the party got very much excited over the fun and discharged his gun at the train, and the result was, Jimmy Griffin, representative of McPike & Allen (druggist from Atchison), who was on board, got thirty-two birdshot in his leg.[25]

Although Griffin survived his gunshot wound, Murphy had been dead set against buffalo hunting from childhood, so there was no way he would stop the train to give those hunters a ride back to town.

Railroads were the country's largest employers, and the US economy rested on this single industry.[26] However, easy money and speculation in railroad stocks and bonds precipitated a banking crisis. On September 18, 1873, the bankruptcy of Jay Cooke and Company, the largest bank and brokerage in New York, had triggered the Panic of 1873.[27] Within days, more than thirty other banks failed. The stock market closed for ten days as the first nationwide depression began. Tens of thousands of businesses went bankrupt, and hundreds of thousands of workers lost their jobs. The frantic building of railroads and the accompanying speculation "demonstrated that the center of gravity for the world's credit had shifted west—from Central Europe toward the United States."[28]

The month before the Panic of 1873, the St. Joseph & Denver City Railroad entered into foreclosure. Murphy saw first-hand how railroad executives were stunned by the news. His superiors were alarmed at their prospects for the future. Rumors based on fear flew through the offices. Desperate telegrams poured in from distant stations all along the line.

Most of the railroad's upper-echelon employees fled, as the entire company descended into years of haggling. During the contentious battle for control, many railroad employees were terminated. Layoffs began with the highest-paid and more senior employees, but soon enough even the lowest level workers were considered extraneous. Construction came to a halt as shipments and passenger traffic dwindled.

Dan survived these dreadful times, probably due to his youth and low salary combined with his accommodating and diligent work ethic. In 1877, convinced he was working at a dead-end job for a dead-end railway, he decided to leave just as the rail line emerged from bankruptcy under its new name, the St. Joseph & Western Railroad. He had been listening to the businessmen on his route talking about how the West was disappearing and the only little-known territory remaining was the largely unexplored Southwest. He overheard disgruntled businessmen from the East carping over the importance of "getting in on the ground floor," as they fled to the West to find financial opportunity. "Get there before the newspapers do" and "Borrowing money is how smart men go broke" were the mantras of the day. Young Murphy took all of this to heart. These simple phrases would become his constant affirmations and would govern the rest of his life.

Murphy's inventive father had completed several real estate deals involving the purchase of acreage from farmers wishing to cash out some of their lands. On one of these purchases, Thomas Murphy discovered a coal deposit. The *Leavenworth Weekly Times* said: "Mr. Murphy has spent

Hanover

Dan Murphy, around the time he left for California. Circa 1878.

seventeen years of his life in the coal mines of Pennsylvania, and is not at all likely to be mistaken on coal."[29] Thomas never lost his interest in mining and realized the value of these coal deposits. He promptly sold the coal-bearing parcel for a sizable profit. These funds, combined with his son's regular financial contribution, brought security to the family for the first time.

Nearing his twentieth birthday, young Murphy took the opportunity to strike out on his own and search for his fortune in the Southwest. The Comstock Lode rush in Nevada and the 1849 California rushes were long past. He didn't have "the fever" yet, but he had heard plenty of tales about the opportunities in mining in the Southwest. There were rumors of immense untapped mineral deposits. The territory was unknown and unexplored.

This was a place for Dan Murphy to "get in on the ground floor."

2

ATLANTIC & PACIFIC

Dan Murphy loved railroads from his earliest days. When the tracks of the Central Pacific Railroad successfully connected to those of the Union Pacific Railroad, creating the first transcontinental rail line in 1869, little Dan was just eleven years old. That was old enough to know that the Golden Spike being driven in tracks that joined the people on the opposite coasts of the United States was good news, after years of a Civil War that had divided the nation. But even work on the rails and his love of history gave him no idea of the world he was entering when he stepped off the train in Los Angeles in 1877.

He had so much to learn about the railroads whose tracks were being laid all over California. It seemed only natural to him that there was a railroad that stopped in Los Angeles, after all, its population was less than ten thousand people, much bigger than his hometown in Kansas. He had no idea what battles had ensued; he probably didn't know that railroads had been operating in Los Angeles for less than a decade. Indeed, he had so much to learn; so much background to absorb.

That first transcontinental railroad had been the hope of many business moguls and influential politicians for years. In 1854, a young civil engineer named Theodore Judah—a man with a passion for and experience in railroading—came to California from New York and was immediately sought out by the Sacramento Valley Railroad Company (SVRR), a fledgling railroad. The SVRR appointed Judah to find a route to the gold fields from Sacramento. But filled with the kind of dreams that brought men to California, Judah had much bigger plans. He wanted to create a transcontinental railroad. He just needed a route—*and* the money—to build a track as rugged and vast as the country.

Successful at building the local line for the SVRR, Judah turned his attention to his bigger dream—first, the route across California's Sierra Nevada mountain range. Washington, D.C., already had turned down his first route, which would have crossed at a central region of the state.

Discouraged, he returned to California and continued his search for a more northerly route. As fate would have it he made the discovery for a challenging but doable alignment. In his excitement, he announced his triumph publicly, and was promptly fired from the SVRR.

Judah immediately went searching for financial backers for what would be called the Central Pacific Railroad. Turned down by every financial source in San Francisco, he returned to Sacramento to continue his efforts. There he found four shopkeepers who had made significant fortunes by selling provisions to miners working the nearby gold mines. The four men were interested not only in enhancing business in Sacramento, but they also hoped to cash in on the recently discovered silver lodes in Nevada, just over the mountains. These four men would become the legendary "Big Four." Leland Stanford was a lawyer who ran a grocery store. He had taken mine shares in payment for a store bill. When the bonanza "came in," he made a small fortune. Since then he turned to state politics. Collis Huntington and Mark Hopkins were partners in a hardware store. Huntington was the financial mastermind, and Hopkins, a meticulous bookkeeper. Lastly was the man who would make it all happen—Charles Crocker. A merchant and financial backer of the enterprise, Crocker was the only one who had actually been a miner. But like the others, he knew nothing about railroading, especially about constructing a railroad. They would depend upon Judah for that. So now Judah had the route and the money. It was time to make it happen.

Just as Judah had piqued their interest in a transcontinental line, Stanford was nominated to be governor of California. Nine days later, on June 28, 1861, the four men formed the Central Pacific Railroad with Stanford as president and Huntington as vice-president, and of course, Judah as chief civil engineer (Judah died of yellow fever in 1863; he never experienced the fulfillment of his dream). After the government contracts were secured, the Central Pacific Railroad built east while a second railroad, the Union Pacific Railroad, built west across the plains from the Missouri River. Each railroad would be paid by the government through bonds which were awarded for each mile they completed. Therefore, it was a race to see which company could lay the most track in the shortest amount of time. To keep it fair, the government paid premiums for mountainous terrain. So the Central Pacific, whose men were blasting through the granite of the Sierra Nevada mountains, were compensated for their extra effort. These bonds were loans to be repaid with interest at regular intervals to the federal government. Making these interest payments would become extremely burdensome.

In 1862, just before construction began, Huntington had moved to New York to be near the financial centers there, and within close proximity of Washington, D.C., where the decisions were made regarding the transcontinental line.

Hopkins was the financier for the operation, and Crocker was in charge of construction. A second company was formed to handle the monies used for construction, named "Charles Crocker and Company." Although they weren't always in agreement—and often were at odds—with Huntington in New York City, Stanford and Hopkins at the home office in Sacramento, and Crocker physically overseeing the construction, the Big Four succeeded in creating the biggest commercial entity in the West and made a national dream into a reality.[1]

Following Judah's plan to lay tracks over the Sierra Nevadas, Crocker was faced with his biggest problem: too few workers. The first thirty miles of track had taken over a year, and they were still in the foothills. He was forced to bring laborers by ship from the East around the tip of South America to San Francisco. Of the thousands of workers he imported, only two out of five reported for work—the others had taken off for the silver strike at the Comstock Lode in Nevada. Crocker made the shrewd decision to employ the many Chinese laborers who were already in California, ready to work. He also recruited thousands more men from China. Despite their diminutive size, the men laboriously cut through the granite of the Sierra Nevada range, displaying incredible courage, bravery, and loyalty as they did it.[2]

The transcontinental line was completed in 1869, when the two railroad tracks joined in Utah. T.C. Durant of the Union Pacific and Leland Stanford, the only member of the Big Four, were present for an event to drive the Golden Spike, a solid gold marker signifying the union of the east-to-west tracks. Although the celebration was originally scheduled for May 8, on his way to Promontory Point, Durant was held hostage in his railcar by four hundred disgruntled laborers demanding their pay. After they threatened his life, he telegraphed for the money. The next day, $80,000 arrived, so the event could proceed.[3] On May 10, 1869, after hours of arguing which of them would drive the spike, the men agreed that Stanford would have the honor. The engraved spike was placed in a pre-drilled hole, Stanford swung the silver mallet, and missed, striking only the rail. No matter; the wire went out and church bells and gunfire echoed across the nation.[4]

As marvelous as the new transcontinental line was, it was plagued by winter snows and avalanches that rendered it undependable for five months of winter. Although the Big Four had profited from the construction, they realized this alone would not make their Central Pacific Railroad commercially viable. Huntington, frustrated by the expensive maintenance and unreliability of the frequently snowbound route across the mountains, insisted that they needed a two-phase plan. First, they would have to control all of the railroads within California, and second, they needed to construct their own transcontinental railroad that would be accessible year 'round. Huntington speculated that a rail line along the nation's southern border would achieve this grand goal. But Crocker did not want to build outside of the state, and Crocker feared that he would face the rest of his career behind a desk. Both were anxious to be bought out.[5] There was not enough money available to pay off Crocker, and furthermore, they were all greatly in debt. Therefore, Crocker and the other two were resigned to moving forward with Huntington's master plan for the Sunset Route, a line from California to New Orleans along the nation's southern border.[6]

As the Southern Pacific set about its long range plan, it did, in fact, buy up most of the short line railroads that existed in California and in the process absorbed the Central Pacific. All of these rail lines together formed the new Southern Pacific Railroad in 1865. By linking them, the Southern Pacific suddenly extended south from San Francisco through California's interior valley, and then southeast to the Mexican border across the desert to Yuma, where the Colorado River enters Mexico and continues south to the Gulf of California.

However, cutting across the desert in a southeasterly direction would bypass the vital population centers of Los Angeles and San Bernardino. It also bypassed San Diego, which was just 150 miles west of Yuma and had one of the best natural harbors on the West Coast. The SP had no interest in San Diego or its harbor, because it would only dilute their profits from the Bay Area harbors where the SP was heavily invested in the shipping industry.

From the Southern Pacific's point of view, Los Angeles was considered little more than an adobe pueblo. But a long and heated battle ensued when news of the route surfaced. LA businessmen and citizens began to negotiate furiously with the railroad, offering sizable monetary incentives from the city's tax base to convince the Southern Pacific to lay tracks into their city. Los Angeles prevailed at enormous cost—to both the citizens and the Southern Pacific—to bend the route into Los Angeles, which required digging a 6,975-foot long tunnel through the mountains into the San Fernando Valley. It was the longest tunnel in the West.[7A] In 1876, the first Southern Pacific train entered Los Angeles from San Francisco—and just one year later, Dan Murphy would arrive in Los Angeles by train on this same route.

As soon as the agreement to reroute into Los Angeles commenced, Southern Pacific began laying track toward its original destination: Yuma, about 270 miles southeast of Los Angeles. Just like the northern transcontinental route, Congress did not want one railroad to own the entire line. Therefore, the Texas & Pacific Railroad (T&P) was to build part of the road through Texas to the Colorado River, including a bridge across the river at Yuma into California, where it would be joined by the Southern Pacific Railroad. Huntington feared that the T&P would enter California and keep on going, thereby breaking the Big Four's monopoly in the state. He intended to block that possibility by arriving at the river first. He did. And he kept going by building a bridge across the Colorado River, which was in clear violation of Congressional law. A Southern Pacific train steamed into Yuma on September 30, 1877. Huntington, who lived in New York City, went to Washington, D.C., to visit President Rutherford B. Hayes, noting afterward "He was a little cross at first and said we had defied the government, etc., but I soon got him out of that belief."[7B] One of many examples of Huntington living up to his legacy as "the great persuader." The SP continued building across the Arizona territory, and the Yuma Line carried the construction materials.[8] It was on this Yuma Line train that Murphy would land his first job in California.

The "Yuma Crossing" was an ancient passage across the river. Primitive Indian trails converged here at a narrow channel where a granite outcropping restricted the width of the mighty Colorado River to a crossable distance. Early explorers found the surrounding area populated with thriving communities of Quechan and Cocopah tribes which were collectively named "Yumas" by the Spanish. In 1851, at a high point on the western bank of the river, the US Army had established Fort Yuma. The Gila Trail, a snow-free year-round Southwestern pack trail for immigrants and traders also used this crossing. The trail began in Santa Fe, New Mexico, and led to the Gila River, over eight hundred miles south along the Rio Grande, where it swerved westward to Yuma. The Butterfield stage route also crossed the Colorado here, which included crossing the river on a rope ferry.[9] This 1,200-mile stage route connected San Diego and San Antonio, Texas, along a fairly flat trail.

During its long history, Fort Yuma saw only one skirmish with the Yumas. However, the real challenge for this isolated desert outpost was maintaining a reliable supply line for the troops at the fort. The Army found that supplies could be shipped by sea to the mouth of the Colorado River and then hauled by twenty-mule team wagons to the post, nearly eighty miles away. As early as 1854, the first steam-powered paddlewheel boat was shipped from San Francisco around the Baja Peninsula to the river delta where it was assembled for use on the river. By the time Murphy arrived, six steamships and five barges were plying the waters of the lower Colorado River. Miners hauled ore by mule or wagon to the river where the ore was taken by paddlewheel steamer to Yuma and then transferred to railcars for transport to Los Angeles.[10]

Ever since the US Army Corps of Topographical Engineers had identified several possible routes west during its 1853–1854 survey, Eastern financial investors wanted a dependable year-round route to California. The best path was across the Arizona Plateau. It was just a matter of which railroad company had the fortitude and money to cross the vast Southwestern wastelands. In 1879, two took on the challenge—the Atlantic and Pacific (A&P) and the Atchison, Topeka & Santa Fe Railway (AT&SF or Santa Fe) agreed to work together to develop what would become known as the 35th Parallel Route.

The A&P charter carried an enormous land grant nearly equal in size to the land awarded to the Central Pacific during the construction of the first transcontinental route. Half interest in this land grant transferred to the Santa Fe Railroad when the two lines merged. Prior to the merger, the Santa Fe was mainly limited to the Kansas Plains, but now they had access to the A&P land grant which ran along the 35th Parallel Route. The A&P's intention was to build along the 35th Parallel Route from southwestern Kansas to the Pacific Ocean. It was essential that the rail line have access to a port.

Meanwhile, like the civic leaders in Los Angeles, the powers that be in San Diego were embittered that the SP had bypassed their city and its ocean port, despite the fact that the railroad had long-promised a link to Yuma that would connect San Diego to the new southern transcontinental route. San Diego decided to be proactive and start its own railroad company. On October 12, 1880, San Diego chartered the California Southern Railroad (CSRR) to construct a hundred-mile long rail line from San Diego north to San Bernardino, the other town that had been bypassed by the SP in Huntington's haste to reach Yuma. This CSRR line would be linked with the 35th Parallel Route of the A&P.

Now supported by the Santa Fe, the A&P was faced with incredible engineering challenges The immense semi-arid Colorado plateau extends southwest of the Rocky Mountains into Northern Arizona. This limestone and red sandstone plateau average 5,000 feet in elevation. It terminates at an escarpment two hundred miles in length, known as the Mogollon Rim. Crossing this plateau and descending its rim was beyond challenging.

About 300 miles west of Albuquerque is a vast and frightful declivity nearly 250 ft. deep and only 540 ft. wide, called Canyon Diablo. Sheer limestone canyon walls plunge down to the narrow riverbed. Surveyors were sent months in advance to the rim of the canyon to prepare specifications for a bridge to span the canyon. The bridge, in a feat of prefabricated engineering, was built in New York and transported in sections

Atlantic & Pacific Railroad built the Canyon Diablo bridge, 1882–1890. The eastern side of the canyon was the site of Hell Street, touted to be "meaner than Tombstone."

by flatcar to Canyon Diablo. Behind schedule, it was discovered when it arrived it was too short to cross the canyon. A two-month delay ensued, as construction was halted at the canyon while the labor force waited for a new bridge.[11] Immediately one of the West's most deadly wild towns sprung up, reputed to "be meaner than Tombstone and Dodge City combined." Its single street, dubbed Hell Street consisted of fourteen saloons, ten gambling houses, four brothels, and two dance halls." These lurid establishments were open twenty-four hours a day to the 2,000 workers, drifters, gamblers, and outlaws.[12]

Westward, beyond Canyon Diablo, the Atlantic & Pacific engineers tackled the steep descent from the Colorado Plateau. The solution was to bridge two gorges. Once, the first gorge had been bridged, the tracks entered a 328-foot hand-dug tunnel. Upon exiting the tunnel, the tracks were cantilevered over a sheer cliff into a sharp curve. This was a dangerous and hair raising passage.[13]

As the Atlantic & Pacific advanced west and progressively overcame these challenges and Collis Huntington heard of its plan, he panicked and swung into action to block the competitors from entering California. He contacted Crocker, instructing him to drop everything, turn his attention away from the Yuma-to-Texas route, and focus on the 35th Parallel. He ordered Crocker to build a line as fast as possible to the Colorado River. The closest point along the SP San Francisco-to-Los Angeles route that crossed the 35th Parallel was a remote desert stop called Mojave. This hastily built "Mojave Line" would preclude the A&P from entering California on their own tracks forcing them to pay to use SP's trackage. As surveyed, this route would cross the Colorado River and enter California at a place called "The Needles."[14]

In 1882, Crocker penned a letter to Huntington in New York City:

> Dear Sir:
> I returned last evening from my trip south [Yuma Line into Texas]. I telegraphed you from San Antonio, and also wrote you, but not on the matter of the A&P.
> I met Mr. Nutt [president of A&P] and went over his road with him, staying overnight at the front, & returning the next day. I talked with him very fully, and am satisfied that he is only anxious to delay meeting, so that he can get to the river before we do . . . I tried to make him see that it would be to his interest to build slow and cheap. He said that the slower they build, the more it would cost. I believe that is true. All of their steel is bought and paid for and is piled along the road . . . I do not believe they will delay a single day . . . Now I believe it is our policy to go along with the construction there as fast as we well can, for several reasons. One is the values of the mines that are now being opened up in the Calico and Providence Mtns . . . I understand from Nutt that it is agreed that they shall build the bridge across the river. I regret this, but suppose it cannot be helped. If they get over [to] this side of the river, I am afraid that their inclination will always be to "lead out," whereas with the barrier of the bridge between them & us, they would hesitate about building a second bridge.[15]
> Yours Truly,
> Chas. Crocker[16]

So build they did. Crocker's engineers identified where the 35th Parallel crossed the SP mainline trackage from San Francisco to LA: at a desolate water stop named Mojave, after the desert that surrounded it. Mojave was nearly three hundred miles due east of The Needles on the

Colorado River. Supplies were delivered both to Mojave and to Yuma for ferrying by paddlewheel steamboats two hundred miles north from Yuma to The Needles. By the time the A&P made it across the Arizona desert to the Colorado River, they found the SP happily building a division point and a large roundhouse at The Needles. Within a few years, the railroad would simplify the name to "Needles."

The Western Development Company. and its successor the Pacific Improvement Company [PIC], played an indispensable role in this materialization. It is one of the least understood and most overlooked aspects of western history. Why, because California's railroad history has been distorted by the rancorous politics of its day. For over one hundred years historians have relied on "The Octopus" myth of the SP. This politically charged myth held that the aggressive Collis Huntington, as the evil head of the SP, overshadowed the entire state. The source of the "octopus" term is from a newspaper illustration labeled "The Curse of California" depicting the railroad's monopoly as a giant octopus with tentacles controlling every enterprise in the state. Even the California state historian, Kevin Starr, known for his five-volume *History of California: Americans and the California Dream*, followed the same superficial belief when he wrote: "The SP offered the most obvious instance of what was grossly wrong with California: a very few of the super-rich virtually owned the state—its land, its economy, its government—and were running it as a private preserve."[17]

In reality, this was far from the truth. The Big Four ran the Central and Southern Pacific Railroads, which were the largest enterprises west of the Mississippi. But in the 1800s, California was an undeveloped backcountry part of America that by mid-century was overrun by fortune-seeking Forty-Niners. Most of these adventurers gave up on mining and returned to their families back east. Those miners who stayed and the pioneers who followed, turned to agriculture and ranching to eke out a living. But they didn't just wander off into the wastelands and decide to grow walnuts, almonds, and citrus to build towns and establish water supplies as they went along. No, it didn't just happen: Pacific Improvement Company (PIC) strategically planned and developed the infrastructure so people could make a life in this region called California; the SP needed people who needed railroads. Wholly owned and operated by the Big Four, the PIC had one prime objective: to increase rail traffic and commerce, while simultaneously benefiting the state and its citizenry.

Nineteenth-century railroads like the Southern Pacific founded holding companies to handle town site surveys, fostering business and community developments including water developments which were forbidden by railroad charters. The PIC policies and programs included: providing scientific agriculture; promoting small family-owned farms; development of water supplies for the advancement of towns; promoting national parks; water conservation and even publicizing the phenomenal characteristics of California. Contemporary historians knew that "the company (PIC) was a major force shaping agricultural, industrial, commercial, and urban growth and modernization." Dan Murphy was one of these PIC contractors. He participated in these projects for both the SP and later Santa Fe's similar development company.[18]

The Pacific Improvement Company's purpose was:

> among other things ... carrying on construction, manufacturing, mining, mercantile, banking, and commercial business and all their branches, and also for the purpose of constructing, leasing, and operating all kinds of public and private improvements. That is to say, its powers were made as extensive as could well be imagined.[19]

Most California history concentrates on the Big Four and completely overlooks the numerous lower level executives who brought about these improvements. The impact the PIC had in the West was profound. Its enormous influence established much of California's cultural heritage as it had control over: "shipping, mining, publishing, urban and rural land development, resort hotels, electric streetcars, and water systems and other public utilities throughout the railroad's territory."[20]

The Southern Pacific tracks were often railways to nowhere. They were laid in a wilderness bereft of talented workers. There were no established businesses with the appropriate expertise, financing, or available material to carry out the necessary improvements. It fell upon the directors of the PIC to establish a reliable supply of water and construct depots, roundhouses, railyards, appurtenant buildings, sheds, way stations, water tanks, and coal chutes. Over time, the improvement company developed towns, by surveying lands, selling lots, and financing associated businesses. Contractors paid by the PIC knew little or nothing of its operations. "The contract of these men was with Stanford, Huntington, Hopkins, and Crocker. They neither knew nor cared whether they received orders from the associates in their capacity as directors or its stockholders. The various corporations interested in the building of the Southern Pacific were, after 1870, only different manifestations of the activity of one group of men."[21]

Charles Crocker was the "on-location" director of railroad construction and the president of the PIC. He straddled both sides of these operations and had a huge impact on the development of towns, big and small, throughout the state, wherever the railroad tracks led. The very personal interest Crocker took in Murphy would change Dan's life forever.

The Southern Pacific Coast Route between San Francisco and Los Angeles ran through mostly privately owned old Mexican ranches. With no land grants along the coast, the company was forced to purchase the right-of-way. "In order to increase traffic along the line and to convert this relatively isolated and low-value land into profitable investments, the improvement company undertook projects that left a lasting imprint on California's seacoast. In 1880, the PIC, with Crocker leading the charge, built Hotel Del Monte, first and perhaps most famous of the great western resort hotels."[22]

It was constructed on 126 acres of forested land, with ancient breathtaking wind-warped cypress trees blanketing the peninsula. Along the coast's rocky bluffs, cloaked in succulents, they stand unperturbed by the pounding ocean waves. Sprays of water shoot into the air as wave's pound it's granite shores. When Charles Crocker first saw these spectacular Pacific vistas outlined by the windswept cypress trees he declared that he would build a resort hotel on the spot that would outclass any European establishment. He outfitted it with the most luxurious furnishings and a first-class dining room. This section of coast with its wind-tossed shoreline is arguably California's quintessential coastline. Wrapped on three sides by the Pacific, it remains an elite playground for the world's super-rich. Known today for its magnificent Seventeen Mile Drive, the area is also home to world-class golf courses which host US Open Golf Championships, and the annual Concours d'Elegance classic automobile show.[23]

Of the many perks Murphy would receive with Crocker as his mentor, one of the most significant must have been Crocker's invitation to visit the Hotel Del Monte resort, the first opportunity for the boy from Kansas to see how the other half lived. From his earliest days in Needles, Murphy made numerous trips each year to the Del Monte. Since the resort was a development of the PIC, the Southern Pacific built a rail line, the Monterey Express, which made a direct 3 1/2 hour trip from San Francisco. It was an easy train ride for Murphy coming from Needles direct to San Francisco, requiring only one transfer to the Monterey Express.[24]

When Crocker and Murphy worked on the Yuma Line, Crocker had become fascinated by the exotic Saguaro cactus, yucca, and all manner of desert plants. He embellished the Del Monte grounds with several formal gardens including one he called the Arizona Garden. It became the fa-

Hotel Del Monte. Circa 1880. Image courtesy Dudley Knox Library. Naval Postgraduate School, Monterey, California.

vorite of the guests, and Murphy was anxious to see it. As a special guest of Crocker, he was encouraged to take advantage of the many pastimes available to guests. Murphy became a regular guest and was a charter member of the Rod & Gun Club at the resort. The PIC lands included a 7000-acre forest that surrounded the resort. These woodlands were open to hotel guests for hunting. Murphy, being an excellent shot with a rifle or pistol, brought down a specimen deer on one of his hunting jaunts from the hotel. The Rod and Gun Club had the head mounted and hung in the rustic clubroom in the grand old hotel. He enjoyed hobnobbing with glamorous guests and dining in the hotel's first-class restaurant. The environment, the accommodations and the excellent fare were all a stark contrast to Needles, so it was a perfect getaway for Murphy. Once the AT&SF took over the Mojave Division it was not long before Murphy knew every trainman between Albuquerque and Los Angeles. Pebble Beach and the resort were SP property and avoided by Santa Fe people and Los Angelenos in general. The Hotel Del Monte remained Murphy's favorite spot throughout his life, one of the lasting gifts from Charles Crocker.

3

Night Train

Stepping off the train in El Pueblo de la Reyna de Los Angeles, Dan Murphy was excited, but his fervor quickly turned to culture shock.[1] The one-story adobe buildings appeared as if they were centuries old, a far cry from the bustling Mississippi River town of St. Joseph or the elegant bayside city of San Francisco, which he had just passed through on his way south. Mexicans and Chinese far outnumbered the Yankee cowboys and the few businessmen in three-piece suits. The din of languages was bewildering. He rarely heard any German, his second language.

But the sight was beautiful in its unique way, with red bougainvillea bushes gracefully draping over fences, garden walls, and lean-to hovels. Stately sycamore trees, towering palms, and gnarled olive trees combined to make this the most exotic place Murphy had ever seen. Jasmine and orange blossoms scented the air. The strange town was sprinkled over gently rolling hills with a few scattered brick buildings. The business district consisted of a newly constructed block of two- and three-story buildings. A baroque bell tower topped the new church, which was built of gleaming white limestone. On his first walk around, Murphy learned it was the Cathedral of Saint Vibiana. Engraved on its cornerstone was "D.O.M. 1875," the Latin timestamp for *Deo Optimo Maximo*, "to the best and greatest God." Decades later, Murphy's friends would tease him that it stood for "Donation Of Murphy." Many decades later, it would be Murphy's money that would replace it.[2]

In 1878, Murphy was far from making any donations and was, himself, in immediate need of money. Armed with recommendations from the St. Joseph & Denver City Railroad, he applied for work at the local Southern Pacific office. Railroad jobs were highly sought after. Murphy's previous experience put him at the head of the line. However, being single and hardly twenty years old, he was offered the dangerous job of brakeman. In the previous ten year period, it was reported the dangers of railroading were "one out of every twenty trainmen died or was disabled." For brakemen, who did the most dangerous job, the statistics were even worse: one in seven were killed or disabled. Westinghouse Air Brakes for trains had been available since 1869, but they were expensive and rarely installed, that is, until 1893 when federal legislation demanded their use.[3]

To Murphy—an invincible youth, impoverished in a strange land where he knew no one—being a brakeman spelled adventure. He accepted the job. He was assigned to the Yuma Line, a sixteen-hour nightly run across the Sonoran Desert to Yuma—Arizona Territory. After an eight-hour layover in Yuma, the train would return to Los Angeles.

Inspired by the businessmen on the trains back in Kansas, Murphy saw a job on the Yuma Line of the Southern Pacific as a stroke of luck. He now would have his opportunity to investigate the fabled mineral-rich region. His purpose for moving to the West Coast had been to discover what opportunities were waiting for him in the relatively unexplored Arizona Territory. On his very first trip to Yuma, he saw numerous miners loading their sacks of ore onto the flatbed cars of his train. He knew he had made the right choice when he heard the miners bragging about their "diggings."

Murphy was fortunate to work with Frank Monaghan, a likable engineer on the Yuma Line, his first big job in Southern California. Monaghan taught him a lot about being a brakeman, and the two established an easy friendship. Little did Murphy realize that Monaghan would become his steadfast business partner, and more importantly, a friend for life. With plenty of hours to get to know each other on the round trips to San Francisco from Los Angeles, Murphy learned a lot about his colleague.

Before the Los Angeles & San Pedro Railroad (LA&SP) became part of Southern Pacific (SP), the lanky, twenty-eight-year-old Frank Monaghan had for several years been the engineer on the LA&SP's twenty-one mile Wilmington Line, which ran several times a day between Los Angeles to the seaport south at San Pedro.[4]

Although he had been born in New York City in 1850 to Irish-immigrant parents who named him Francis Monaghan, he always went by Frank. Restless for adventure, when he was nearly fifteen, he took a job on a sailing ship bound for San Francisco, and made his way around Cape Horn. Rounding the Horn in a three-masted sailing ship is a perilous experience even today, since that's where the Atlantic, Pacific, and Antarctic Oceans all crash into one another. Ferdinand Magellan had made the same trip in 1519, but Monaghan's passage was not much more

Frank Monaghan. Date unknown.

comfortable than that. The only significant difference was that, thanks to Magellan, the route was charted, so ship captains knew passage was possible—but in all other regards, the trip was treacherous.

Ten-story waves and gale-force winds plagued the voyage, just as it had for others who attempted it. Legend held that some eight hundred ships and more than ten thousand sailors had been lost attempting the route. On this venturesome and tempestuous trip, young Monaghan proved himself to the captain and crew to be a courageous and popular little voyager. Upon the ship's arrival at San Francisco, the captain took such a liking to him that he recommended him to his shipping company as a "willing worker and a bright lad;" he even referred to him as a "little hero."[5]

After the ship reached San Francisco, Monaghan found work with Central Pacific Railroad (CPRR, which would later become the SP). Within a few years, CPRR sent him to Los Angeles to be conductor of the Wilmington Line of LA&SP.

In 1875, Frank married twenty-one-year-old Mary Eudora Guthrie, whom he always called Dora, and they had two girls and a boy. Dora and Frank set up a household near her parents in Santa Ana. Her father, Col. Robert Burns Guthrie, a Confederate soldier and significant landowner in the area, had brought his family from Texas by wagon train through New Mexico and the Arizona Territory to Southern California, where they started a farm in 1875, the same year Frank and Dora wed. That was also the year that Valencia oranges were introduced in the area.[6] The father and son-in-law planted citrus trees in their fields and soon had acres of productive orange groves. Guthrie became an influential citrus grower, instrumental in resolving packing and marketing problems in the trade—indeed, he helped put the "Orange" into Orange County, which was not officially established until 1889. Until his death in 1909, Guthrie was the president of the Orange County Fruit Growers Association.[7]

Monaghan had already been railroading for nearly fifteen years by the time he was thirty, and at $3.50 a day, he was making what was considered good money. Working the Wilmington Line, he was able to return home every night. But tragedy struck on the faraway Yuma Line, changing the course of Monaghan's life.

The Yuma Line was primarily a supply train. It hauled flatcars heavily laden with rails, ties, and construction materials to "the Front," the head of the track where roadbed grading and rails are actively being laid. It was a constantly changing site filled with great turmoil, as numerous four-horse teams traversed with wagons of fill for grading the roadbed, amid the cacophony of ringing sledgehammers driving spikes to secure rails to the ties. This construction work was in its third year when a runaway train killed the conductor on duty. Monaghan was suddenly reassigned from his pleasant job near his family to be the new conductor on the nightly Yuma run.

After he was transferred to the Yuma Line, Monaghan only saw his family weekly. With his growing family and increased responsibilities, he could foresee his destiny. To him, it was a far cry from his teenage adventures sailing around the Horn, and the get-rich fantasies that his Forty-Niner friends in San Francisco had planted in his head. Still yearning for a gold strike, he was once again afflicted with "gold fever." The only positive of this new assignment was that he was closer to the mining world. And there was that new hire, the kid named Murphy. Murphy, was Monaghan's brakeman on the line. Their train left the downtown Los Angeles station every other day at 2:25 pm and arrived, if all went well, at Yuma at 7 am the following day.[8]

Monaghan had become an experienced conductor on heavy freight-hauling trains when he worked at the San Pedro port. He had undoubtedly heard about what happened to the former conductor on this line. The accident had happened in the middle of the night as the train ascended a southeast grade. The engineer became aware that he was missing several loaded cars that had uncoupled, something that could only happen if a brakeman didn't properly secure the coupling pin. Realizing the problem, the engineer reversed the locomotive to go back to find them. In the darkness, he misjudged the speed of the missing cars that were rolling freely down the grade. The two sections of the train collided in a colossal smashup, killing the conductor. When Monaghan retold the story, Murphy undoubtedly focused on the fact that the conductor had lost his life because the brakeman had not done his job properly.[9]

Here on this nocturnal ghost train, the romance of Murphy's life began to unfold. The journey through the desert at night was fraught with danger as the track ahead of the steam locomotive was lit by a single carbide lamp. Drifting sands that covered the tracks were a constant threat in the darkness, so the engineer kept a keen eye on the tracks. Once a drift was spotted, the engineer pulled the whistle to signal a full stop. Murphy and the other brakeman leaped from car to car, atop the roofs, to set the brakes on each car. In the dark, the men maneuvered the swaying cars which were dusted with blowing sand. The unlucky ones met with instant death by falling between the moving cars. The brakemen would turn a large horizontal wheel using a brakeman's club (similar to an axe handle) to set the brake blocks against the wheels of the car. The engineer's whistle indicated how many car brakes to set. Once stopped, the brakemen jumped from the train to shovel sand from the tracks. With the rails cleared, the brakemen signaled the engineer with their lanterns. Soon the locomotive steamed back to life and resumed forward motion. As the passenger car rolled past, the brakemen grabbed the car's hand-bar and stepped onto the platform while swinging the other leg up, all in one graceful movement—"the brakeman swing."

Steam locomotives use a tremendous amount of water and fuel. In the early days, wood fired the engine boilers. But in the West, wood was scarce, so low-grade bituminous coal from Gallup, New Mexico, was the alternative. Water tanks placed strategically along the line are used to "water up" the tenders. Scarcely twenty to forty miles could be covered before a water stop was required. Again, the brakemen traversed the top of the cars setting the brakes. On clear straightaways, 40–60 mph was the norm, but with the many coal and water stops, they averaged only 15 mph.

As busy as Monaghan and Murphy were on these endlessly long night crossings, the two Irishmen had ample time to become well-acquainted. As their train smoked its way across the starlit desert, Monaghan wove a dream of veins of gold and silver buried in the passing hills. He pointed to rock ledges that begged to be explored. Since his youth, he was absolutely certain that the hills were filled with ore. Beginning with his arrival at the Golden Gate in 1865, Monaghan had listened to countless hours of tales told to him by the very miners who remained in California after the rush of 1849. Monaghan had a passion for making a big strike. Born and educated in New York, he projected self-confidence and intelligence that Murphy found intriguing.

Murphy and Monaghan bonded as a team. This fast friendship "led to over 38 unbroken years." Murphy referred to Monaghan with "affectionate regard and esteem of a true, loyal, and faithful partner."[10]

One bright afternoon, as the two men reported to the Los Angeles terminal for their 2:25 pm departure, Monaghan was alerted that a private car had arrived from San Francisco that morning, and it would be added to their Yuma-bound train. Business cars carrying railroad management were common, but the opulence of this one far exceeded anything Monaghan or Murphy had ever seen. Their inquiries to the station manager were met with a shrug. Just prior to departure, they learned the luxury car carried Mark Hopkins, one of the railroad's Big Four. On this trip, eager for Yuma's warm desert air, the sixty-five-year-old executive was escaping the cold damp weather of San Francisco that caused his rheumatism to flare up. He had been plagued by rheumatism for many years that severely affected his knees and ankles, hobbling him, and causing him to need two canes to walk. He was accompanied by his physician.

Hopkins never left the car before it joined the Yuma train. As the train slowly backed into the siding, it was Murphy's job as brakeman to "drop the pin," coupling the boss's car to the train. Its dark velvet green curtains edged with gold bullion trim were drawn tight. They traveled through the night to the Colorado River when the shiny, black-enameled car with brass lanterns and fittings was quietly rolled to a siding near the Yuma Depot. After a few days in the comfort of the desert climate, Hopkins felt greatly improved. He felt so much better, in fact, that his doctor returned to Sacramento, leaving Hopkins in Yuma. But the following day, on March 29, 1878, Mark Hopkins was found dead in his car having peacefully passed away in the night. He was the first of the Big Four owners to die. He left no will. His wife Mary inherited his estate, estimated at $20 to $40 million.[11]

Construction east of Yuma continued unabated. Crocker was in charge of overseeing the project which had now progressed through the Arizona Territory. It was not long before Crocker's private car and its accompanying livestock car, carrying his personal horse, made regular trips on the Yuma Line to supervise the construction.

From more than a mile away, a tremendous roar and racket split the desert silence as dust rose on the thermal wind. An apocalyptic vision appeared as scores of horses, wagons, and two- to four thousand Chinese men labored in pandemonium under the scorching sun. This is the Front. This is where the roadbed and rails are being laid. Wagons loaded with rock and sand were being hauled by lathering horses to the graders bent over their shovels leveling the roadbed. More horses were dragging rails and wooden ties to the gangs of track layers. The ear-splitting ring of sledgehammers striking steel rails mixed with the cries of the teamsters driving their teams into the turmoil.

Crocker, a huge 200+ pound brute of a man, would dash from his

Charles Crocker of the Big Four. Date unknown.

private train car as soon as the supply train arrived at the railhead. He would mount his chestnut mare and gallop along the line to the Front. In this milieu he would shout orders at workers. Never pleased with the speed of the work, Crocker sought to drive workers to their limit. Pacing up and down the line, he loomed over the crew, cussing up a storm and forcing more and faster work.

Monaghan and Murphy were at once fascinated and appalled by him. By comparison they were gentle doves to this loud and boisterous man. But it was this very man that they wanted to emulate in his path to success. On their long nights crossing the desert they were entertained with endless tales of good fortune from the miners aboard their trains. They also observed the richness of the ore that they loaded at Yuma.

Murphy caught Monaghan's gold fever and they hatched a plan to imitate the Big Four by opening a mining supply store in the gold district. They knew how the Big Four railroad executives had started out as retail merchants during the 1849 gold rush. They also had heard many times how the miners had gone broke while the owners of the stores supplying them profited significantly. This was exactly their plan. In order to explore the mineral riches in the area they had hoped to establish a hardware and grocery store in the mining region.

Over the months of construction, Murphy and Monaghan became well-acquainted with the boisterous Charlie Crocker. They were both loyal Southern Pacific trainmen, which made Crocker their boss, albeit several levels above them. They worked for him, albeit indirectly. Even though they had opposite personal temperaments, Murphy admired Charlie Crocker's business prowess and had studied his path to power. Dan and Frank wanted to emulate Crocker's success by becoming shopkeepers selling supplies to miners, just as he had done in Sacramento before his railroading career. Frank always believed that if they could create a money-making base like a store near the gold fields they could then go out prospecting, Dan observed Crocker closely and learned firsthand one of his keys to success. Once Crocker had determined that a man had the intellect and determination to carry out an assignment, he would give the man full latitude to make decisions and the authority to complete the task as he saw fit. Over time, Crocker became Dan's mentor and influenced how Murphy would handle his numerous employees later in life. One of the most important lessons Murphy learned from Crocker, and one he would use to great success was to allow his men to make their own decisions in the management of his companies. Both men were excellent judges of character and this tact allowed them to oversee numerous diverse industries.[12]

Hopkins's death in 1878 had a profound effect on the Southern Pacific and surprisingly, upon Murphy and Monaghan's future. The extension of the Southern Pacific beyond Yuma and outside its mandated territory of California had caused great consternation among the four owners. Construction costs of $72,000 per mile was an astronomical amount of money for a cash-strapped company. Revenues were diminished due to the disappointing northern transcontinental route that was seasonal and required sharing of the profits with the Union Pacific. The owners knew that the railroad would not be profitable until the vacant districts their tracks passed over were developed and populated. Until that time they had a railroad to nowhere, such was the lack of development of California at the time. Collis Huntington, on the other hand, believed in short-term gains over long-term investments. He insisted that their money concerns would vanish if the SP owned its own transcontinental line and no longer had to share its profits on a frequently snowed-in rail line. The railway which they were constructing across Arizona and Texas would solve both problems. Hopkins's untimely death brought these issues to a head. Mrs. Hopkins wanted her share of the profits which were held by the Western Development Company, a subsidiary of the SP. The remaining Big Four—Stanford, Huntington, and Crocker—each held one-fourth of its stock, and Hopkins's widow was demanding her 25%.[13]

Murphy had been working on the Yuma Line for nearly five years. On one of his seemingly endless round trips, in 1882, Murphy was called to Crocker's private train car. With its gleaming wood fittings, velvet window drapery, and crystal barware, his luxury coach was a vivid contrast to the desolate landscape outside. Over the years, Crocker's executive car had traveled their Yuma Line numerous times and frequently remained on a short track, called a siding, in Yuma, while its occupant would be at the front. But this trip was different, Murphy had never been invited inside the opulent car. Unbeknownst to him, he was stepping into more than just a luxury coach. He was entering a world that would propel this hardworking son of an immigrant into a place far beyond his imagination.

There sat Charles Crocker in his tight-fitting three-piece suit, the epitome of a Gilded Age tycoon. Like Murphy, Crocker was raised as a poor farm boy. Growing up in upstate New York, he had little education, but he believed he could do any job that came his way. He was a fair-faced man, five foot ten inches tall, with a "tremendous appetite" that caused him to be more than portly.[14] But he was also described as a first-class businessman, fearless, decisive, unshakable, quick to make decisions, and willing to admit when he was wrong. "He loved work for work's sake ... a man of remarkable energy, of strong physique and power of will. He knew how to manage men in gangs ... he knew the value of money."[15]

Crocker offered Murphy a seat opposite his ornate desk. Leaning in, he told Murphy that he had a proposition for him, with the caveat that it was to be held in the strictest confidence. Bewildered, Murphy listened intently. Crocker proceeded to tell him that he had just received word from Huntington that the company had a change of strategy. He confided to Murphy that they were to be redirected 220 miles upriver to The Needles, where the railroad was to establish a division point. The SP would lay track from the closest point on its main line, which was the water stop called Mojave, east along the 35th Parallel across the desert to The Needles. Murphy was savvy enough to know that a division point included a roundhouse and a full workforce with the ability to repair or rebuild entire locomotives. Crocker informed him that the track-laying crew would number as many as two thousand Chinese laborers. Machinery and equipment were already ordered for the construction of the roundhouse at The Needles.

At first Murphy probably thought Crocker was telling him all this because it would affect their workload on the Yuma train. However, Crocker visibly changed his demeanor and told Murphy he wanted him and Monaghan to run a commissary car for the Chinese track-laying crew.

A commissary car is not to be confused with a dining/meal car. With thousands of Chinese workers who needed to be fed, the railroad had huge dining tents and numerous Chinese cooks who prepared their traditional foods. Monaghan and Murphy's commissary sold sweets, candy, tobacco, and replacement clothing such as the typical indigo-dyed cotton shirts and pants, as well as hats both conical and western-style felt.

The commissary carried premium items, much in demand at premium prices. It was clear to Murphy that Crocker was offering a very lucrative opportunity. He was likewise astonished at Crocker's proposition, since he knew nothing about the merchandising business.

Continuing, Crocker explained that Pacific Improvement Company (PIC) would lease boxcars at the going rate to Murphy and Monaghan, and they would bear the cost of provisioning the car. They would be paid a commission for their work, and they could pocket the profits from the merchandise they sold. The catch was that they both would have to give up their jobs with the Southern Pacific to become private contractors for PIC, of which Crocker was the president.

Pausing, like the seasoned negotiator that he was, Crocker awaited Murphy's response. Murphy was no doubt stunned and dubious. Then came the hook. If they were successful at running the commissary car, Crocker would put Murphy in charge of developing the townsite for the railroad men working at this new division point. Railroad surveyors had laid out The Needles, so the PIC would supply all the labor and materials for its construction. Monaghan and Murphy were to schedule, develop, and requisition everything needed to build the town. They would be paid a general contractor's commission based on the costs of construction, while the Chinese did the actual labor.

Monaghan and Murphy were reluctant to give up their railroad jobs and their seniority at Southern Pacific. The unwritten rule was simple: once you left the railway, you were not welcome to return. The loss of financial security would be a hard sell for Frank to make to his wife Dora.

Murphy was able to convince Monaghan that the lure of being stationed so close to the gold fields dovetailed perfectly with their desire to open a store for selling supplies to miners. This literally was a golden opportunity. Merchandising to Forty-Niners was how the Big Four had made their wealth, and this same path was now available to Murphy and Monaghan.

Financing the commissary car was a challenge. Murphy had saved little money from his brakeman's salary of $2.38/day, as the majority of his pay had been sent home to Kansas to help support his parents and siblings. The *Los Angeles Herald* reported on June 16, 1882, that Monaghan was offering lots in Los Angeles at $350.[16] He was selling at a loss, since he had speculated on them only a year before, but he needed capital to finance the commissary car. For equity in this arrangement, Frank did most of the supply runs, thereby enabling him frequent visits home, while Murphy took care of the Chinese workers from the commissary car.

In the months leading up to the launch of their business, Murphy took a room at the Cosmopolitan Hotel in the heart of the downtown business district in Los Angeles, at 47 Main St. There, he invited prospective vendors to lunch to explain the new venture. The fashionable Cosmopolitan was at the time the premier "power lunch" spot in town, under the management of Hammel & Denker, with Andrew Denker as the proprietor.[17]

In addition to the sizable outlay of money to numerous vendors to get the commissary car underway, a leasing fee had to be paid to SP for rental of the car. Murphy headed to the SP's downtown Los Angeles offices to finalize the execution of the lease. Sixty carloads of track laying materials were stationed at the Mojave stop awaiting the commencement of the desert operation. Murphy and Monaghan, anxious yet optimistic, were prepared. Their fully stocked commissary car was cued and timed to the imminent arrival of the first seven hundred Chinese workers.[18]

4

Mojave Line

Scorching winds blew incessantly, day after day, across the barren and desolate flats of the Mojave Desert. The project began with more than seven hundred Chinese laborers, but the number of workers soon expanded to two thousand as Huntington pushed for greater track-laying speed. Vultures and red-tailed hawks circled in the cloudless skies above, effortlessly gliding on the thermal currents. Joshua trees and cholla cacti appeared to move as heat shimmered across the desert landscape. It was so intensely hot that the buzzing in their ears led to the conviction that the heat could be heard.

All along the graded rail bed, hundreds of workers hauled 550-pound steel rails and redwood ties. Each rail was carried by five men, set into place, secured with three strikes per spike, and ten spikes per rail. As they pounded down the rails, the clanking and ringing of sledgehammers was punctuated by braying mules and whining horses that reared and shied at the racket of the whole scene. Hardly a human voice rose above the clamor. Men with waist-length pigtails and conical hats were bent low over their work, systematically advancing the road. Every man and beast was stretched to their limits as the burning glare of the sun bore down upon them.

Murphy and Monaghan were not exempt. From dawn to dusk, the pair worked together, hauling sacks, barrels, and wooden boxes from the supply train to their commissary car. Dried fish, oysters, clothing, tea, medicinal herbs, liquor, and crystallized ginger were the staples. The commissary was on a pay-as-you-go basis. With cash nonexistent, Murphy and Monaghan kept ledgers of the transactions. One would retrieve the goods while the other recorded the transaction. The Irish, the other minority laboring on the line, mainly bought whiskey. Supply trains arrived every other day. Murphy and Monaghan took turns on a weekly basis, returning to Los Angeles on the supply train to replenish stock.[1]

As the workers continued laying track eastward from Mojave to the Colorado River, the spring of 1883 slipped away and the workforce swelled to more than 3,500. Temperatures soared to 110° and higher. Metal hand tools could not be left in the open as they became so hot they caused third-degree burns when picked up with bare hands.[2]

Meanwhile, at the eastern front, the Atlantic & Pacific Railroad was rapidly advancing across the Arizona Territory and on to the Colorado River. On May 9, 1883, F.W. Smith, the superintendent of the A&P western division, reported to its president, Henry Nutt:

> [For the last six months] two out of three trains from Winslow west have been water trains, hauled one hundred and thirty miles on an average. This has been enormously expensive, but could not be avoided. As of this writing, May 9th [1883, we are] within twenty-four miles of the bridge across the Colorado River. We hope to connect with the Southern Pacific on the west bank of the river about June 10th.[3]

With nearly fifty steam locomotives between Albuquerque and the front at Winslow, the A&P appeared to be ready to storm California. However, the river was at peak flood stage due to the snowmelt coming from the Rockies and bridge-building across the mighty river would prove challenging.

The first Southern Pacific train pulled into Needles from the west in early June 1883. The Chinese and Irish crew had completed more than two hundred miles of track in near-record time. The generally poor quality of the work, due to speed demanded by Huntington, would not come to light for several years. Nevertheless, Murphy and Monaghan unloaded their remaining goods from the commissary car and stacked them on the lonely desolate riverbank. Curious natives from the Mojave village across the river gathered around watching.

The pair struggled to put up a canvas tent to keep their goods out of the sun. They were sweltering—since a tent in the blazing desert sun quickly became a furnace. The Mojave came to their aid. They began dragging saplings, reeds, and brush up from the river banks to build a shelter like the wickiup homes they lived in across the river. Over the tent, they wove vertical and horizontal supports of saplings into a loose frame, then used reeds and brush to fill in the gaps. The structure of natural materials blocked the sun's rays from hitting the tent, yet provided ventilation and a cool environment inside. Murphy and Monaghan proudly named their wickiup store Monaghan & Murphy General Merchandise. Monaghan's name was first because he had the largest stake in its financing.

A *Los Angeles Herald* reporter wrote:

> These young gentlemen have spread out an imposing tent which is surrounded (except in the front) and topped by a brush 'Wickiup' which adds greatly to the coolness of the establishment. They are doing a rushing business, as they know the railroad boys and keep a stock of articles both for the inner and outer man.[4]

The supplies they brought to the front were primarily for the Chinese who vastly outnumbered the European workers. They stocked liquor for the "railroad boys;" it was forbidden to sell alcohol to the Native Americans. Murphy was protective of the indigenous Mojave and well aware of the laws forbidding the sale of alcohol to them. From the first day at the site, Murphy and Monaghan were working with the Mojave and were struck by their friendliness and goodwill. Murphy's father's kind words and compassion toward the Native people in Kansas had a lasting effect on Dan, and he looked forward to knowing more about the locals and even to learning their language.

A flurry of activity was going on around their wickiup store. Foundations for a 250-foot long depot were well underway. Its construction was unique: long decks ran along both sides of the building. These long platforms along the sides of the depot could each accommodate six to eight train cars. The enormous new depot would include a hotel for passengers and a dining room for travelers. The fourteen-stall roundhouse was already much further along and was nearing completion. A 50,000-gallon water tank was in place and operational. It supplied both drinking water and water for the steam engine tenders.

Since the intent of the Southern Pacific building in Needles in the first place was to keep the A&P out of California, the depot was designed to make this power play perfectly clear. Huntington mandated that all A&P trains not only halt at the depot but also that all passengers and freight were required to transfer from the A&P trains across the depot platform to the waiting SP trains on the opposite side. The arrangement precluded any further travel of A&P equipment into California, regardless of the inconvenience to the passengers or the expense of transferring the freight.

According to an article in the *Los Angeles Herald*:

> There is a small army of men at work on various buildings and work is going ahead at a lively rate. The location of these improvements is upon a sandy beach, some

half a mile from the river and the town will no doubt be at this point. As yet, no private buildings are erected; several parties are ready to build as soon as the town is bid off.[5]

The delay in this matter appears to be due to doubts as to whether the railroad company or the government owned the land. The railroad was remiss in issuing a clear title to its land grant holdings. The construction of permanent buildings was delayed due to this uncertainty. The issue of land ownership would haunt Needles well into modern times.

The Southern Pacific's roundhouse and depot were well underway at Needles on the west bank of the Colorado River. However the challenging task of bridging the swift and powerful Colorado was the job of the Atlantic & Pacific construction crew as stipulated in the potentially lucrative government contract. Huntington had feared that the A&P would race across the river and continue into California, the same way he had illegally done at Yuma by building into the Arizona Territory. This was not the intent of the A&P executives but all based upon Huntington's personal paranoia.

The Needles had been named by Lt. A.W. Whipple in 1853, while he was on the Government Survey along the 35th Parallel. It referred to the pinnacle formation in the mountains, southwest of the locality. The Native Americans called the same formation "Moh-cah-vah."[6]

With the arrival of the Southern Pacific at The Needles:

> The tent town on the California side… quickly became the largest port on the River above Yuma. Within a month the town also boasted a Chinese wash-house, a newsstand, a restaurant, a couple of general stores and nine or ten saloons, dispensing whiskey at two bits a drink. For three months after they [the competing railroad—Atlantic & Pacific] reached the river, the crews struggled to bridge the Colorado just below Needles, it was an ill-suited time and place for building a bridge.[7]

The river was at flood stage. The channel was 1600 feet wide at that point with no solid banks on either side. The swift current uprooted pilings almost as fast as they could be driven. A wide gap midstream resisted all efforts before it was finally conquered, with the aid of the Mojave (steamboat) and a pile driver mounted on Barge No.3. Even then, the bridge was criticized as a 'flimsy-looking structure' and an obstruction to navigation since it lacked a draw.[8]

The June 10 deadline flew past, as flood-level waters continued washing away the hard-earned pilings throughout the month. As summer temperatures soared, the workmen began quitting in droves "due to the general cussedness of it all," as one newspaper put it in 1883.[9] Word reached the Mojave crews toiling in the desert about a strange disease afflicting the bridge-building gang at the Colorado River. On July 30, two men died and fourteen more workers were taken by train to the Sacramento railroad hospital. "The Disease at Needles" was widely reported to have struck two healthy men who would "fall, dizzy in a fit" with cramps and chills. They died within an hour and a half. Fear and speculation rose among the laborers, believing it was some miasma rising from the river or poor quality water. The bridge-building gang was toiling in the direct sun, high above the river that reflected its searing glare. The reported temperature on that late July day was 115 degrees. They were in the habit of drinking ice water, supplied by the railroad, in the dry, blazing heat. It was weeks later that the two deaths were determined to be due to heatstroke coupled with drinking ice water under such extreme conditions. The Chinese laying track in the open desert drank only tepid tea, despite the heat. There are no reports of the Chinese falling ill.[10]

As soon as the tracks were laid to the river, trains began arriving from the west loaded with lumber and building materials which were all supplied by the PIC. Thousands of Chinese laborers, having achieved the goal of laying track from Mojave to the Colorado River, were transferred back to the Front of the southern transcontinental line east of Yuma. A few hundred stayed at the river to work for Murphy and Monaghan constructing dormitories, homes, shops, a post office, three saloons, and two Chinese restaurants. The remaining laborers were experienced in building construction, having built houses and dormitories at other locations on the statewide rail system, as well as auxiliary structures—station houses, tool sheds, storehouses, and watering stations at regular intervals along the Mojave route. Railroad surveyors had already laid out the streets and water mains for the town-site. A large open plaza area had been set aside in front of the depot. Across the plaza, a strip of stores was planned to face the plaza and to be in full view of the depot.

The first order of business for Murphy and Monaghan was to construct dormitories for the nearly two hundred railway workers who were bachelors and twenty to thirty houses for the married men and management personnel. In fact, the heat was a common topic among Needles residents, and it always was spoken of with disdain, as if it weren't a fitting place for a tolerable life: "Needles might do for men and dogs, but was too hot for women and children."[11] Arthur L. Humphrey, foreman at The Needles division, wrote in his autobiography regarding this period:

There was not a house or shack of any description. [The railroad workers were required to] eat, sleep, and live in the outfit cars provided by the railroad for this purpose. The nights were so hot that the entire population slept on top of the cars. I distinctly remember the thermometer registering 115 degrees Fahrenheit at two o'clock in the morning ... The Southern Pacific usually established yards, shops, and local railroad offices, while the holding company [PIC] surveyed, laid out the streets and lots, constructed buildings, and made other improvements, particularly installing a water supply.[12]

As a foreman for the Southern Pacific Humphrey was in charge of constructing the railroad-related buildings while Murphy and Monaghan, PIC contractors, were responsible for overseeing the construction of housing and commercial property.[13]

The Needles was strictly seen as a division point with a roundhouse for servicing the steam locomotives coming in from long desert runs. By the time they reached The Needles, most locomotives required significant maintenance. Regardless of their condition, all steam locomotives arriving from the East or the West were taken into the roundhouse for inspection. The fourteen stall roundhouse at The Needles was enormous, even in its day, and was able to perform the most demanding of repairs such as drive wheel replacements, boiler repairs, re-balancing and all manner of work to maintain the locomotives. The diversity of locomotives from various manufacturers frequently required the machine shop to fabricate replacement parts.

Humphrey was the first Southern Pacific rail man to be assigned work at The Needles. He came from the Central Pacific Railroad shops in Sacramento where steam locomotives were built and repaired. At the time, "the Sacramento Shops were maintaining 480 locomotives of forty-eight different types and from fifteen different engine manufacturers." Because of his experience with this variety of equipment, he was chosen to be the Divisional Foreman at The Needles. His first responsibilities were to oversee the construction of the depot, machine shops, water tank, coal docks and all necessary buildings for the division point terminal. The 242-mile long Division between Mojave and The Needles was crucial to the successful operation on the line. Humphrey was twenty-two at the time, making him two years younger than Murphy. The two young men became lifelong friends and no doubt supported each other on this demanding and involved work in this desolate desert outpost. Humphrey had been raised in the Midwest receiving little formal education. He had traveled through the Pacific Northwest working as a miner before hiring on at the Sacramento locomotive shops. Young Humphrey carried out his duties brilliantly on this desert assignment. After years of railroad work with the SP and later with the Burlington Northern Railroad, he left the railroads for the Westinghouse Air Brake Company and later became its corporate president.[14]

    With so many skilled and ready workers construction sped along rapidly and soon the village of Needles rose from the desert sands. Lots along the commercial strip across from the plaza and depot were bid off to interested parties. Typical frontier storefronts sprang up facing the plaza with the Monaghan & Murphy General Merchandise & Mining Supplies store being the largest of all the establishments. Business was steady from the very first day. Counters lined both sides of the cavernous store with pails, wooden tubs, saddles, harnesses, chains, rope, and spades hung from the overhead rafters. Barrels stood all around the center of the room filled with crackers, sugar, dried peas, beans, molasses, and coffee. White and brown sugar, as well as flour, was sold in 100-pound sacks, and five-gallon cans of kerosene could be picked up from the shed out back. Dried peaches, apples, prunes, and raisins were sold in twenty-five-pound boxes. The smell of salami, cheese, coffee, apples, and harness leather scented the air, but none was headier than the fragrance of freshly ground coffee. A large coffee grinder stood at the rear of the store with a two-foot diameter wheel for grinding. It was usually operated by one of the young boys who begged to grind the day's coffee just for the fun of it. A steady stream of locals came to stock up on supplies. When the passenger trains came to a halt alongside the depots' long covered platforms, riders poured from the coaches. The crowd inundated the store to shop. It was a welcomed diversion as many had spent several days traveling from the East aboard the rocking passenger cars.

    Murphy slowly enhanced his offerings to appeal to the wealthy and fashionable women from the westbound Pullman cars. He stocked merchandise from noted suppliers like John B. Stetson—fancy cowboy hats and boots, Marshall Field's of Chicago—lace handkerchiefs, linens, small table decorations, Crane & Company—elegant stationery and fancy parasols. If all went well, westbound trains arrived each day at 7:30 am and departed at 9 am, allowing time for breakfast at the depot restaurant and a stroll to the Monaghan & Murphy store for a little shopping. Eastbound trains arrived at 9:40 pm and departed at 10:10 pm when the store was closed. Usually, several men hopped off the train and dashed to a saloon for a quick shot. With the advent of regularly scheduled trains, the railroad shortened the name of the division point from The Needles to simply "Needles."[15]

Throughout these early days, the Monaghan & Murphy General Store remained profitable not only because of the miners but also because of the pricey business they transacted with the train passengers. Initially, the business was booming. But as soon as the rail line and bridge were completed, the thousands of Chinese workers were relocated to other SP railroad jobs and this left a vacuum in the tiny village. The remaining population, all railroad men, was less than a five hundred. This workforce remained steady but lived primarily in dormitories and ate at their dining hall and therefore was not a significant source of income for the Monaghan & Murphy store. The store's steady business came from the few families that occupied the married men's houses and the trickle of miners who trailed in from the surrounding mining districts. Passenger train customers far exceeded the partner's expectations, even though there was only one westbound train per day. Frank soon became anxious to go prospecting. A newspaper article from August 16, 1883, reported that "he sold some of these claims for $13,000, and he has more left of the same sort." He must have collected these mining claims when he was still conductor on the Yuma Line. By selling at a profit he had the capital to go prospecting and purchase mines he thought would be even more profitable.[16]

Frank Monaghan's desire to stock all kinds of mining tools and supplies was paying off. This resulted in Monaghan & Murphy's being the largest and best-stocked supply store for hundreds of miles. Miners traveled from as far away as western Texas and New Mexico to their store. Some miners and settlers took the newly built rail line through these states to Yuma where they caught one of the many barges to take them up the river to Needles. Other miners trailed in for days and sometimes weeks to reach Monaghan & Murphy's. Too frequently, they packed on their mules' sorely used or broken pieces of machinery. Stamp mills, which were used to crush the rock to extract the ore, were from a variety of countries and manufacturers. New parts were not an option, and the cash-strapped miners hoped to either get the part fixed or remanufactured in Needles. Sheared camshafts, broken winch handles and worn out iron stamp mill shoes were common, but each one was often unique. Monaghan tried his best to come up with fixes for the broken machinery. However, frequently their only recourse was to send the part to Los Angeles or San Francisco. This delay took weeks and was unacceptable for the haggard miners.

Murphy and Monaghan put the word out at the railroad shops and roundhouse for a mechanic. They reasoned that a machine shop, although not bringing in more customers, would be an excellent service to their clients and get the miners up and running sooner, thereby limiting

Monaghan & Murphy General Merchandise Store. "The handsome warrior" employed at Monaghan & Murphy's is standing in the center of the doorway. He was previously on the war path with Geronimo. Circa 1886.

their losses. From the fourteen-bay roundhouse in town, they soon hired a master machinist, Silas J. Lewis, nicknamed "St. Louis." He was a veteran of the AT&SF workforce. They helped set him up a machine shop, financed the equipment, and gave him free rein in running the adjunct business. It was named Needles Machine Works, which "succeeded in building up a large business, handling all the machine work from the neighboring mining camps …"[17]

Lewis was the same age as Murphy. His father had moved to Pennsylvania where he owned oil property and operated several wells. Silas, as well as several members of the family, had been employed by Standard Oil Company. He later moved to Topeka, Kansas, to work for the Santa Fe railroad where he became the foreman of the water service between Mojave, California, and Williams in the Arizona Territory. This company serviced nearly four hundred miles of track. Silas remained at Needles with the Monaghan & Murphy Company for many decades in various endeavors. In 1903, when the Monaghan & Murphy Company owned an interest in the Colorado Steam Navigation Company that ran barges on the river, they named one the *Silas J. Lewis* after him. Lewis was later put in charge of the Water and Ice Company that iced refrigerated cars on Santa Fe trains.[18]

Because Murphy and Monaghan took turns at the store, Frank was able to return to Los Angeles regularly and to be with his wife and family in Santa Ana. As a Pacific Improvement Company (PIC) contractor, he could board any train coming or going to Los Angeles. He also took the train east into the Arizona Territory to do his prospecting. Murphy, on the other hand, took less frequent but lengthier trips east. Several times a year, he would jump on the train to Chicago. The congenial Murphy preferred to renew his supply contracts directly with each company. In this way, he met new and influential businessmen. Frequently, a chance meeting with a fellow traveler in the trains' club cars lead to profitable investments. Additionally, he could keep abreast of the latest developments and trends. Murphy appears to have deliberately avoided Los Angeles business dealings. Since his arrival in California, the only business he had in Los Angeles were when he negotiated for the supplies for their commissary car. He did not have a very high opinion of underdeveloped Los Angeles. Its population had hardly reached 12,000 in the early 1880s. His first job as a teenager had been in St. Joseph, Missouri which at the time had a population three times the size of Los Angeles and was a bustling Mississippi River shipping port. He relished his anonymity in Los Angeles and saw no reason to make known the extent of his business by purchasing his stock there. Besides, Dan loved traveling by train and it cost him almost nothing since he had free passes from the railroad. He

One of many complimentary annual passes of Dan Murphy. All of his passes were marked "All Stations," enabling Murphy to travel for free and adopt a bi-coastal lifestyle.

purchased his stock directly from Chicago sources and got a better price and greater selection than what was available in Los Angeles. As will be seen, he extended his reach to New York City by making regular trips to his suppliers and business contacts on the East Coast. Dan Murphy could rightfully be called one of the first "bi-coastal" businessmen. No other merchant or capitalist is known to have taken such immediate advantage of the transcontinental line.

Days at the general store consisted of waiting on the regulars and engaging the miners/prospectors in lengthy conversations. These discussions were part of Monaghan's plan to cater to the miners. Within a few years, according to the Los Angeles Pioneer Society, "The Monaghan & Murphy name grew to become a household name throughout the region."[19]

Being the only source of supplies and the only machine shop in the desert helped their notoriety. Moreover, just as Monaghan had predicted, they soon were knowledgeable about who was successful and how much each mining camp was bringing in.

5

Murphy and the Mojave

Across the river from the Monaghan & Murphy General Store, the Mojave village was home to around one thousand Native Americans. Dan Murphy had taken an immediate liking to the Mojave people from the moment he arrived in Needles in 1883. He was fascinated by these stately indigenous people. Perhaps it was his strong empathy for the poor and oppressed, a sensitivity that his Irish-Catholic mother had instilled in him. That empathy certainly extended to all Native Americans, especially the few who lived in the Murphy family's hometown of Hanover, where he had witnessed the devastation of their culture. Throughout his life, he looked for ways to right this wrong.

The Mojave Nation had been living and farming the eastern banks of the Colorado River for millennia. Like the ancient Egyptians they depended upon the annual flooding of the river for the fertile silt it left behind. Traditionally the Mojave only planted what was needed for the year. If there was no flood or their crops failed due to disease, widespread famine and death would inevitably follow. Because of the harsh desert environment, game was scarce. Mojave depended somewhat on fish, but in the swift moving waters they were difficult to catch. In general, the Native people lived a primitive and precarious subsistence lifestyle.

Consequently, after he observed such oppressive conditions faced by the Mojave in Needles, Murphy took it upon himself to help them by teaching them how to help themselves. First, as the PIC representative on location, he would not tolerate any exploitation of the Mojave. And, instead of financial handouts, which were not his style, he found productive ways for the Mojave to earn money. As the town matured, he strove to procure fair employment for the Native people, thereby building their self-esteem.

Murphy always hired at least one statuesque member of the Mojave Nation as a full-time employee at the store. One of these indigenous people was named Smokestack, a man who was hard to miss since he stood nearly seven feet tall. Smokestack showed up daily at the store to do odd jobs and errands. He was a man of few words who struck an imposing visage around the store. One of his duties, which he took seriously, was to assist shoppers with their purchases, to the delight of train customers and locals alike. Women in their bustled Victorian dresses followed in awe as the statuesque Smokestack carried their packages across the plaza to a waiting train.[1]

In 1540, Melchor Díaz, the first Spanish explorer to cross the Colorado, documented the settlement along the river. Almost two centuries later, in 1857, the US Army established Fort Mohave, a few miles north of Needles, on the east side of the river. Steamboats plied the two hundred miles of river between Fort Mohave and Fort Yuma, bringing supplies that had been shipped there by sea. Since the mid-1800s, the Mojave and surrounding tribes had peacefully existed with the immigrant Europeans. Mojave men had been working on the steamboats for more than twenty years by the time the railroad arrived. In his 1858 report, Lieutenant Joseph C. Ives, of the US Army Corps of Topographical Engineers, wrote that Mojave men

> have noble figures, and [the] stature of some is gigantic. Having no clothing but a strip of cotton, their fine proportions are displayed to the greatest advantage. Most of them have intelligent countenances and an agreeable expression.[2]

The Mojave possessed great dignity, according to Lieutenant Ives, who recorded how the tribe transported one of its chiefs to their first meeting, using "… a truly regal method of crossing [the river]. A raft was provided, and four of his tribe, one swimming at each corner, conveyed him over the water. He stood erect in the center, and the water, for an acre or two around, was alive with his swimming followers."[3]

The first year Murphy and Monaghan were in Needles, they had taken a boat trip up the Colorado River with Mojave guides. Murphy documented this 1883 trip with his own camera. They had been concerned about the Natives' dependence on the annual flooding of their fields. These flood cycles effectively mimicked the ancient flooding of the River Nile. They traveled up the Colorado River to see if the water could be regulated for Mojave agriculture. In a narrow area of the river known as Black Canyon, they found the ideal site for creating a dam. Even though their plans were modest, they could not interest the railroad in their proposed project. Twenty years later, Murphy directed US Geological Sur-

Above: A Mojave guide on the upper Colorado River, heading to Black Canyon. Photo taken by Dan Murphy on an exploratory river trip in 1883.

Below: Black Canyon is a natural narrows in the Colorado River, the future site of Boulder Dam. Circa 1883.

veyors J.B. Lippincott and J. Ahere to Black Canyon and showed them the area as a potential dam site. But in typical government bureaucratic fashion, the surveyors continued to search several less desirable locations from 1902 to 1903. Still, more than a half-century later, the US government built a dam at the very location that Murphy had pointed out and changed the entire Southwest; it was named Boulder Dam.

An early and spectacular demonstration of Murphy's benevolence toward the Mojave was when the railroad bridge across the Colorado River washed out. Every spring, the Colorado River reached its flood stage as the snows in the distant Rocky Mountains melted and flowed down through the Grand Canyon. From there the floodwaters reached Eldorado Canyon and turned south toward Needles. The spring of 1884 was the first true test of the new railroad bridge. Over the winter months, there had been a precipitous drop in Needles' population as bridge construction came to an end and the workforce was reassigned. Only a handful of industrious Chinese had remained, with one starting a restaurant and another a laundry.

Murphy was concerned for the bridge's integrity. At daybreak, he saddled up his horse and rode down to see for himself. It was worse than he dared to imagine. With the river steadily rising, actual waves were heaving down the Colorado's main channel. Whirlpools formed and then dissolved as they chewed away at the river's banks. Murphy heard boulders rumbling in the torrent and the sharp crack of logs splitting in two. Huge limbs, brush, and debris lodged against the bridge, causing rapids to form around its supports. Murphy saw a few rail men standing helplessly on the bridge and staring down on the muddy red torrent. The center bridge supports, those most burdened with uprooted trees and logs, gave way by midmorning as pilings, trusses, ties, and rails crashed into the raging river. This released the dam of driftwood which violently crashed into more pilings bringing down the remainder of the bridge.

This was not the first time the bridge had washed out. The year before during the spring flood, it had collapsed when it was only twenty feet from completion. To keep the trains running, passengers were ferried on barges across the river.

In '84, the work began immediately at a new bridge site further downstream where the river banks and its channel provided a more secure location. This time, a draw was placed in the center of the bridge to enable the passage of steamboats headed upriver toward Eldorado Canyon and Fort Mohave. The new site on the west bank of the river required a significant amount of grading. Murphy saw an opportunity for the Mojave to profit from its construction. He obtained an ample supply of brand-new long-handled shovels from the railroad. He called together a sizable group of Mojave men and with great fanfare gave each a shovel and marched them down to the construction site. With shovel in hand and a brief demonstration, Murphy showed them how to build a graded road, creating a ramp for the approach to the bridge. His focused personal interest in each of the Native laborers gave these workers an obvious pride of accomplishment. Some were surprised to receive pay for their day's work—they were just happy to be part of the bridge and rail-building operation.[4]

With keen insight into the indigenous mind, Murphy paid each one with a bright and shiny silver dollar. They treasured the heavy coins and always shunned paper money. Full-time railroad graders were required to turn in their tools at the end of the workday. However, the Mojave crews considered the shovels to be their badges of honor. They carried them everywhere, even proudly displaying them outside their wickiups.[5]

By the time the grading crew had completed its work, Murphy had become the unofficial chief of the Mojave. The Native Americans now looked to him for more work. There was no electric light or natural gas available at the time, so everyone cooked and heated with wood-burning stoves. Therefore, as the legend goes: "Dan Murphy persuaded the Indians that he owned all the driftwood on the river, a bit of counsel said to have resulted in their dutifully bringing it to the Monaghan & Murphy fuel yard for subsequent sale."[6]

Perhaps Murphy himself told the story in this amusing way simply to play down his compassionate approach to the local people. But more likely, the townspeople—who had been pilfering the gathered firewood—were ashamed of their own greed and wanted to divert attention from Murphy's good deeds by belittling his efforts. Until Murphy paid these locals, Native Americans had not been compensated for their work; the Mojave continued to make income from the wood for more than fifty years. It was Murphy's determination to help the people who had been there long before the white man.

Since his arrival in Needles, Murphy had been learning to speak the Mojave language. He kept a notebook in his pocket at all times to record the meanings of Mojave words and to spell them phonetically. He was unique in this. Murphy was the only person in town who attempted direct communication with the native people, without resorting to hand signals and guttural sounds. He soon became a trusted friend of the Mojave, which was viewed skeptically by the townspeople who continually made him the brunt of their mockery.[7]

Needles was always a company town—nearly everyone worked for the railroad. In fact, the only people who were not on the payroll were the men who had started businesses for the railroad workers, Monaghan and Murphy, among them. The agreement between Dan, Frank, and Charles Crocker was that as PIC contractors they were to lay out the streets, with the aid of SP surveyors, Chinese labor, and materials provided by the company. Once utilities were in place and a strip of businesses was established in the center of town, Monaghan and Murphy shifted their attention to making a profit from their Monaghan & Murphy General Merchandise store.

But that wasn't always easy. Having been charged by Crocker to build the town, they were also responsible for running it. Needles was a railroad town, so the civic rules of conduct followed those of the SP: brawling, drunkenness, and gunplay were strictly forbidden. "The first justice of the peace (1884–1887) was Frank Monaghan, who made a model judge, and who was then known as all the law and order west of the Colorado River." It is recorded in the *History of San Bernardino County* that Judge Monaghan adjourned court for fifteen minutes while he took a heckling troublemaker outside for "a sound drubbing": he beat the heck out of him.[8]

The same book records that "Dan Murphy was the first constable and deputy sheriff. He was a terror to evil-doers, but kind-hearted, charitable, and just to all." At the time, there was no jail in the town, and if a spare boxcar was not available, Murphy "used the safe and effective method of handcuffing his prisoner to a telegraph pole with plenty of cool water at hand and a comfortable bed to sleep on, which the kind-hearted officer always provided the prisoners."[9]

In 1885, there were some altercations between the townspeople and the Mojave Indians about firewood. The Mojave people traditionally gathered driftwood and stacked it on the river banks near their village for their cooking needs. Unscrupulous citizens, who were unwilling to go to the effort to collect their own firewood, would pilfer these stockpiles.

In his capacity as town sheriff, Murphy wanted to put a stop to the thievery and solve the problem without pointing fingers at the townsmen, and inciting more trouble for the Mojave people. So he convinced Monaghan that their store should get into the firewood business. First, they paid Mojave men to construct a fenced-in "fuel yard" near the store and had them stock it with driftwood. When the townspeople came to the store to buy groceries they paid a small charge for the firewood. The money from the wood sales was turned over to the Indians in silver dollars. Gathering firewood was primarily a woman's job since it had to do with cooking.

Therefore, for the first time, Mojave women had a steady occupation and income. But, the setup was not ideal. The river was nearly a mile from the store at the town center and the river banks were steep and wet.

Needles Plaza. Circa 1884.

Murphy observed how the stooped and muddy women carried the heavy loads of driftwood on their backs to the woodlot. Again, Murphy was moved by the dirty and laborious work the women were doing. So he devised another plan.

Since many of the Mojave men worked for the Atlantic & Pacific as section hands and helpers, they were skilled track layers. Using his influence on Pacific Improvement Company—and on Humphrey, the roundhouse foreman—Murphy obtained a few spare rails, ties, spikes, and wheels from the scrap pile. He gathered his grading crew and had them excavate a gentle slope up from the river into town. The men expertly spiked down a rail line on this bank. Murphy persuaded a couple of railroad machinists, probably for a handful of cigars or a bottle of whiskey, to construct a cart on their off-hours, using the spare wheels. With the cart on the rails, the women filled it with wood and the men did the "man's job" of pushing the loaded cart up the embankment into the town. Thus began "Murphy's Push-Cart Line." Curiously the Push-Cart Line still appears on historic railyard maps.[10] This became a sarcastic joke amongst Murphy's railroad buddies, to his own amusement and that of others.

The Mojave wickiup village was a mile distant from town across the river on the east bank of the river. The west bank of the river was quite steep and muddy. The Mojave people were delighted with their cart on rails for hauling wood, but they still struggled on foot to climb the slippery embankment. It was particularly arduous for the women who had their infants tied to their hip. These impoverished families owned neither horse nor mule. Murphy, at his expense, ordered dozens of two-wheeled hand carts shipped by rail to his store. He then distributed these carts, free of charge, to each extended family. The carts made hauling their goods back and forth much easier.[11]

It was due to his cheerful thoughtfulness and desire to please that the term "Our Dan" was adopted. He was usually referred to this way by Dr. Booth, the editor of the local newspaper which had the whimsical name of *Booth's Bazoo*. Murphy's patient and kind manners were well-known to the Indians, and the Atlantic & Pacific management. They assigned Murphy the responsibility of being the monthly paymaster for the Indian men who worked as laborers on the railroad.[12]

Every month a strange scene happened on Front Street, the dirt road in the center of Needles. On one side stood the grand two-story depot. Across the street was a row of single-story commercial buildings including a post office, a bank, a Chinese restaurant, two saloons, and the Monaghan & Murphy General Merchandise store. A sizable dusty plaza with a few mesquite trees lay between the depot and the stores. On this

Monaghan & Murphy letterhead stationery depicts "The Needles," a natural mountain peak formation in the Chemehuevi Mountain range, southeast of the town that became known as Needles.

day, a hot desert wind blew through Front Street kicking up dirt devils. A steam locomotive panted alongside the reddish-brown depot as Mojave families gathered in the plaza. Some women carried their babies, and most were pushing their two-wheeled carts. The men stood silently with their long-handled shovels held over one shoulder, the well-worn blades pointing upward, glinting in the sun. The calm broke when several cowpokes and inebriated miners noisily pushed out of the saloon onto the boardwalk to witness the monthly event. It was well over 100 degrees. A shrill steam whistle sounded from the roundhouse announcing it was noontime.

The crowd of Mojave men, women, and children formed an orderly line as all eyes turned toward the Monaghan & Murphy store. A jovial young man in a three-piece suit stepped outside, hands raised in greeting. It was Murphy, and it was payday. The people were lined up in the plaza outside the store, waiting to receive their pay in silver dollars. The locals mockingly called the monthly line-up "Dan's Pushcart Railroad." It was a double insult, not only to Murphy and his workers, but also a deliberate jeering remark about the Mojave people's firewood business. Murphy, as he had throughout his life, cheerfully diverted attention from himself by making light of his dealings.[13]

By 1887, Monaghan & Murphy General Store had been in business for four very successful years. Word spread about their store throughout the mining areas in the Arizona Territory and as far south as North Texas. In this vast region, theirs was the only store of its kind. They carried an extensive array of mining equipment and supplies including explosives, which they kept in a bunker behind the store. But most importantly, they had a fine reputation for fair dealing and would extend credit when needed.

The storekeepers were working partners in the mercantile business, but their mining claims were strictly individual investments, probably due to the high risk. Monaghan had purchased some mine claims even before they left the Southern Pacific to build Needles. As planned, customers kept Monaghan and Murphy well informed about where claims were being struck and where the most promising areas were.

Murphy and Monaghan were perfectly situated in Needles. They could alternate pursuing their independent mining dreams on weeklong prospecting trips in the mountains and desert, while the other manned the store. If one of them found a mineral-rich vein, he could file the claim in Kingman, the county seat, which was only a few hours away from Needles by train.

Monaghan had an active mine named Black Metal that was in operation to the south, along the river on the California side. Soon, Murphy struck his own deal with another prospective miner, Ed Jones, a barkeeper in Kingman who had a lead on a claim about sixty miles northeast of Needles.

Once Murphy and Jones agreed the site looked promising, they needed to act fast. To turn it into a working mine, they needed a crew of at least a dozen men, who would need to be outfitted and continuously supervised during the dig. That meant Murphy and Jones needed more money than either man had, so Murphy started thinking strategically about how to finance the operation.[14]

He remembered a man he had met while on his way to see his parents in Kansas, when he stopped in Colorado to visit his sister Mary. She had introduced him to a successful Denver banker named Dennis Sullivan, who invested in mining. Murphy immediately telegraphed him regarding an investment, and Sullivan responded with cash. Details of the agreement are unknown, but no doubt Sullivan would be paid a larger share of the profit for putting up the money. All three men were listed as owners on the claim, which they named "Josephine."[15]

When Josephine started "coming in," Murphy made numerous trips to the San Francisco Mint, loaded down with gold ingots to exchange for coins. Because he had frequently traveled to San Francisco for business, he was already a familiar sight onboard, well-known to most of the rail

Dan Murphy. Circa 1884.

employees. And since most of his trips had involved stopovers at the Hotel Del Monte in Monterey, he always had carried the same large black satchel. Few of the train people even noticed that now his bag was always bulging. The vein at the Josephine played out within a few very successful months. After they had removed all the ore that was profitable, the three partners—Jones, Sullivan, and Murphy—sold the claim, and each went their separate ways, much richer men for their efforts.

One day during the eventful year of 1887, the very year that Murphy struck gold at the Josephine mine, he was back from the diggings, attending to business in Needles. An angry mob of shouting townspeople gathered in front of the store. They were dragging a half-drunk, protesting Mojave man. That morning, a Fort Mohave soldier named Gorman was found "on the edge of town with his head crushed in." The crowd accused the tribesman of killing him, since a club was the only weapon Indians used. The mob wanted to lynch him. Murphy was appalled at the hatred the townspeople displayed toward the indigenous people.

Roused by the clamor, Sheriff Murphy stepped onto the boardwalk in front of the store. "His appearance had a quieting effect on the leading advocates of violence, for he represented the Law and all its majesty, and Needles prided itself on being a law-abiding town."

As calmly as possible, under the circumstances, Murphy spoke to the gathered crowd, both Mojaves and the local mob. There would be no lynching, he told them, and asked the tribesmen to summon Chief Askeet, their leader, in hopes he could help get to the truth.[16]

Seated, Askeet and his son. Standing, from left: Dan Bunnell, a locomotive engineer; W.S. Hancock, master mechanic; Dan Murphy, merchant; and Deputy Sheriff J.H. West, justice of the peace. 1887.

Askeet was an old man and wore a scraggly white beard, an oddity among the Mojave men. For many years, he had been a firm friend of the "White People." After Askeet arrived to question the suspect, as Murphy asked him to do, the Mojave chief made the straightforward announcement, "This man did not kill the soldier." He asked Murphy to release the young man, promising to bring in the guilty party. Murphy agreed and dispersed the crowd.[17]

Askeet returned with two young Mojave men who confessed to repeatedly giving the soldier Gorman money after he had promised to buy them liquor. "The soldier came back time and again with no whiskey, but some kind of excuse and a request for more money." Finally, they watched him as he entered the saloon. They peeked in the window, as natives were not allowed in the saloon. They saw him gambling away their money. "So when he came once more and approached them, they promptly knocked him on the head—simple retributive justice according to their aboriginal philosophy."[18]

When Askeet presented the two men, "The feeling of that old Indian when he delivered up his son to the white man's justice may be imagined but not described."[19] Murphy was devastated by the irredeemable situation of his friend, Askeet, his son, and himself. True to his oath as a deputy sheriff, he brought the two boys to the county courthouse in San Bernardino. This county seat was more than two hundred miles away. The young men received a light sentence: two years each in San Quentin prison.

"But the son of Askeet never completed his sentence. He died in prison, among strangers, doubtless pining for his old home on the banks of the Colorado." No further details exist about the boy's death. But it obviously was a crushing loss to his father, not to mention the tribe's disillusionment toward justice. For Murphy, it was yet another sign of the tragic impasse between his race and these trusting indigenous people.[20]

In the spring of 1893, while sitting in a Gilded Age watering hole—the bar at San Francisco's Palace Hotel—Murphy told a journalist about an experience he had just a few weeks before, yet another example of the trust the Native people had placed in him. His story was more than a dream, although at first Murphy said he thought it must be.

In the middle of a very ordinary night, Murphy awoke to see faint yellow lights dancing around his bedroom. Not sure if he was dreaming or seeing an apparition, he suddenly became aware of a presence very nearby—a living, breathing presence. Paralyzed with terror, he realized this was no dream.

Sitting bolt upright, he was shocked to see several Mojave Indians standing around his bed, staring silently down at him. A tall Mojave man

Murphy picked up the hobby of photography—an expensive pursuit in the late 1800s—after purchasing a high-quality Eastman camera on one of his trips to New York City. Aware that Mojave people had an aversion to being photographed, Murphy clandestinely took a photo of Captain Joe's cremation. He could not resist. Circa 1893.

holding a candle lantern leaned in, "Come, Chief dead." The group of Indians spoke not another word. Their intense stares and silence showed their certain expectation for Murphy to follow them. Shocked but relatively composed, Murphy convinced them to wait until daybreak.

The chief who had died, whom the townspeople called "Captain Joe," was an old friend of Murphy. Many years before, Captain Joe had come into the store calmly and confidently announcing that he was growing old and losing his strength. He told Murphy that he had decided to prepare for death and that his wish was for Murphy to be sure that his funeral would be conducted by traditional Mojave customs. He went on to say that he had already told his family and tribe that his friend Murphy would be in charge. Murphy agreed, putting Captain Joe's request out of his mind until the group of Mojave men showed up at his bedside.

At dawn, the same delegation stood waiting outside his door. For the next three days, hundreds of Mojave people arrived on the banks of Colorado, about two miles from town. The tribe gathered bundles of mesquite and created an enormous heap of firewood for a funeral pyre.

All of Captain Joe's personal belongings were taken from his wickiup and thrown on top of the pile. Lastly, they placed his body on top and lit the fire. The Indians formed a great circle around the blaze and began wailing and dancing. The whole affair continued for hours until the cremation was complete. After the fire burned itself out, the Mojave mourners covered the ashes with a mound of dirt, and the feast began.

In quick order, they slaughtered Captain Joe's nine horses, six cows, and seven sheep. The meat was roasted over an open pit while steaming pots hung over open fires to cook various parts of the feast. All the while, the widow of the chief was not allowed to eat. She sat alone with her face painted black with axle grease from one of the railroad cars. She wailed and moaned for a period of three days, while the gathered assembly feasted.[21]

A few early travelers to the remote Southwest wrote of these cremation ceremonies. Lieutenant Whipple, one of the early government surveyors, recorded the ritual in his 1850s journal. The burning of all the possessions of the deceased, including their livestock, precluded any form of inheritance and kept the people at a consistent income level and free of social classes.

6

Godfrey Holterhoff

In 1884, a second wave of dreamers poured into California in numbers that far surpassed the number of gold-crazed Forty-Niners who had come West. The region had just been promoted as the "Golden West" in a popular guidebook that proclaimed it "a pastoral paradise" where fields, orchards, and vineyards yielded bountiful harvests and the scenery was of matchless grandeur and beauty. Above all, it gushed, the state offered "one of the most genial and salubrious climates in the world."[1]

The onslaught began when Collis Huntington blinked. He was in desperate need of money to pay the interest on government bonds the railroad had been granted. Unfortunately, the payments were due just a year after the Southern Pacific (SP) and the Atlantic & Pacific (A&P) met in Needles, thereby completing the third transcontinental railroad route.

Huntington had effectively stopped the A&P at Needles and brazenly required all its passengers and freight be transferred to an awaiting SP train to continue west. The A&P threatened to lay its own tracks, paralleling the SP tracks from Needles to San Francisco. But the SP was financially overextended by the extraordinarily expensive construction of its route from Yuma to New Orleans: the Sunset Route and the SP's hasty construction of the Mojave Line to keep the A&P out of California had cost the SP dearly.[2]

Huntington's financial straits precipitated a showdown between the Southern Pacific and the Atlantic & Pacific. The A&P offered the SP a deal—a reciprocal lease with the A&P taking the Needles-Mojave tracks and SP taking the A&P Sonora Railway. The Sonora was a rail line the A&P had built from Arizona into Mexico. The two railroads agreed to these terms and the SP's Pacific Improvement Company (PIC) sold the Mojave Line including the Needles Division, to Santa Fe, the financial backers of the A&P. Once the A&P owned the Mojave Line, it had broken the Big Four's monopoly on the railroads in California.[3]

Both railroads had their own improvement companies; the SP had the

AT&SF #446 "Official Special" 4-6-0 built by Baldwin in 1894. At Needles, February 26, 1902.

PIC and the A&P had its Pacific Land Improvement Company (PLIC).

What was the effect of the ownership transfer on the crew at Needles? Murphy, Monaghan, and Humphrey, the divisional foreman, all remained at their posts in Needles, but now they reported to different bosses—the Atlantic & Pacific, headquarted in Chicago. The nearest A&P divisional roundhouse and offices were in Albuquerque, and no doubt many of the roundhouse workers transferred out. Monaghan and Murphy smoothly transitioned from one company to another. Now they were contractors for the PLIC in Los Angeles, and their main contact for contracts was Godfrey Holterhoff.

Holterhoff had heard of Dan Murphy and that he was a valued friend of Charles Crocker. Murphy became Holterhoff's eyes and ears in Needles regarding the smooth operation of this important division. Murphy frequently had lunch with Holterhoff in LA by taking the morning train west and returning into the Needles Division on the eastbound, which arrived at Needles in the evening.

Work at the Division Point at Needles had settled into a routine: trains coming and going like clockwork from San Francisco and Los

Angeles. Trains arriving from either direction were in extreme need of repair after a scorching desert crossing. Needles's well-equipped roundhouse was able to handle any repairs required. Arthur Humphrey, as well as numerous other competent workers, had been trained at SP's Sacramento yards, where he became a master mechanic of steam engines, regardless of the original manufacturer. Every type of engine from across the nation would eventually show up at Needles. Most of the locomotive power used 2-8-0s, 4-4-0s, and 4-8-0s built by Baldwin, Brooks, Manchester, Pittsburgh, Rhode Island, and Rogers, steam locomotive manufacturers that were based throughout the United States. If the various parts were not available from the original source, Humphrey's team was able to machine manufacture parts on site in Needles.

The Mojave Line, now owned by the A&P, still ended at Mojave in the middle of the desert, 242 miles west of Needles. From there the SP controlled the ninety miles of track into Los Angeles and the more than three hundred miles of track laid north to San Francisco. To use either track, A&P was forced to pay expensive leasing rates to the SP. The A&P, chafed under these leases and needed an ocean port for shipping if its transcontinental line was ever to become profitable. San Diego's rail line, the California Southern Railroad (CSRR), had completed a 100-mile route north to San Bernardino. To complete the link to the ocean port in San Diego, the CSRR just needed to lay seventy miles of track north from San Bernardino to the end of its line at Mojave. The challenge was that the San Bernardino mountain range lay between the two points. But within months of gaining control over the Mojave Line, disaster struck.[4]

During the summer of 1883, when A&P was completing the bridge over the Colorado River, a volcano erupted in the South Pacific. It was the most cataclysmic volcanic explosion in modern times. It occurred at the Pacific island of Krakatoa in Indonesia, and no one could have predicted its environmental impact. An unprecedented amount of ash was propelled fifty miles into the atmosphere, affecting the global climate. As ash spread around the earth, fire-red sunsets made headlines all across Europe. Cities on every continent reported mysterious midday darkness. In the following months, record rainfalls were recorded around the world. Enormous levels of snow blanketed the Rocky Mountains the following winter, and Los Angeles recorded thirty-eight inches of rain, a longstanding record for the region.[5] Floodwaters washed out the trestles and rail line at Temecula Canyon, which connected CSRR's rail line between San Diego and San Bernardino. "Ties and bridge timbers were found floating out in the Pacific Ocean," ruining the CSRR.[6] In retrospect, it is no wonder that the bridges over the Colorado at Needles had washed out that same season.

The CSRR seemed beyond salvation, but rather than allow it to slip away into bankruptcy and lose all hope of a Pacific Ocean port, Atchison, Topeka & Santa Fe Railway (AT&SF) financed the rebuilding of the washed-out route. After the repairs were made, the line was reconnected between San Diego and San Bernardino. Once it reached San Bernardino, CSRR began grading Cajon Pass north from San Bernardino through the mountains toward Mojave, a distance of seventy miles.[7] With the completion of this strategic link, AT&SF had its long-desired route to the port of San Diego. On November 9, 1885, with much fanfare, the first train from Chicago steamed into San Diego.

The financial power behind A&P's extension across Arizona was the AT&SF. In AT&SF's move to gain access to the coast, CSRR had become its subsidiary. Although AT&SF had gained access to a port.

Los Angeles-bound A&P trains continued to pay the SP's high trackage fees from San Bernardino into Los Angeles. Godfrey Holterhoff, a young executive with the CSRR, brought an end to leasing any SP trackage. What had eluded AT&SF all these years was handed to them by Holterhoff. When the behemoth railroad decided to save the CSRR from oblivion by making it a subsidiary, Holterhoff, CSRR's longest-term employee, saw the writing on the wall. His little railroad was about to be swallowed by the great transcontinental AT&SF.

Several short line railroads existed that provided rail transport into the cities of Los Angeles and San Bernardino. There were eight short lines, the largest being the Los Angeles and San Gabriel Valley Railroad. But to Holterhoff, right-of-way was of most interest. To the amazement of everyone in the home office, Holterhoff brokered the purchase of these small railroads and patched them together to create access into downtown Los Angeles. Now, because of his strategic thinking, AT&SF had its most coveted prize—a line directly into Los Angeles and to its existing port.[8] The executive board of the Santa Fe in Boston had been negotiating and politicking with the Southern Pacific for years over the exorbitant trackage fees SP charged, all for naught. It took a local innovative young man like twenty-five-year-old Holterhoff to see the possibility of doing an end-run around the SP.

In June 1885, AT&SF bought out the CSRR, and the man who had negotiated the biggest deal in recent history–Godfrey Holterhoff—was rewarded with the position of assistant treasurer of the newly incorporated Western Division of the Atchison, Topeka & Santa Fe Railway. This mighty and influential man became close friends with Dan Murphy, and that friendship would last for decades.[9]

Godfrey Holterhoff Jr., western assistant treasurer of the Atchison, Topeka & Santa Fe Railway Company. Holterhoff was not only the highest ranking AT&SF employee on the West Coast, he was also one of most respected executives in the entire company.

Godfrey Holterhoff was born and raised in Cincinnati, Ohio, where he graduated from Woodward High School in 1877. After working as an accountant for a local tobacco company, he moved to San Diego, hopeful like so many who left the Midwest for California that its curative air would solve his respiratory problems.[10] The fair-skinned nineteen-year-old arrived in 1879, and a year later, his health restored, landed a job as a secretary for the newly formed California Southern Railroad.[11] That same year he traveled by train to Tucson in the Arizona Territory. He was an ornithology enthusiast and a member of the Nuttall Ornithological Club of Cambridge, Massachusetts. There he wrote an article from this trip to Joseph Grinnell, *A Bibliography of California Ornithology*. Arizona, "A Collector's Notes on the Breeding of a Few Nesting Birds" that was published in the *American Naturalist*. Over the next four years, he had eight articles published in ornithological periodicals.[12]

His promotions at the railroad had come rapidly as he ascended from secretary to cashier to the paymaster, and then treasurer. When Atchison, Topeka, and Santa Fe Railway (AT&SF) came to the aid of the devastated CSRR, Holterhoff moved to Los Angeles and put his passion for bird-watching on hold. He applied his eagle eye to the business world. By modern standards, he'd be called a Type-A personality: organized, ambitious, and a stickler for details. Within five years of his arrival in California, his title got more complex: "Assistant Treasurer of the Atchison, Topeka, and Santa Fe Railway Company—Coast Lines" which frequently was called the "Western Division." It belied his status within the company. Although his title was "assistant treasurer," he was actually almost as powerful as any board member at the Boston headquarters. Holterhoff was forever honored by AT&SF as the person who brokered the company's entrance into Los Angeles.[13] Furthermore, he was on a first-name basis with Aldace F. Walker, chairman of the board. Holterhoff, known as a high-strung detail manager, casually wrote to Chairman Walker regarding one of the more significant contracts that Santa Fe executed. This important document was the title transfer of the California Southern Railroad to the Santa Fe. He wrote to Walker in 1898 (twelve years after the event):

> In recently looking up certain matters ... I find that the first mortgage of [CSRR] to the Boston Safe Deposit & Trust Co. of date Jan. 1, 1886, appears not to have been recorded in San Bernardino County ... I think it highly essential that it should be, and shall be pleased to see the recording thereof if it is forwarded to me.[14]

"Highly essential" was an understatement, and his note probably caused an uproar in Boston. The implication was that the powers-that-be in the East were not taking care of business as well as he was in the Western Division. In those early heady and frantic days of railroading in California, important legal and financial matters were frequently drawn up in haste. Holterhoff's attention to detail and his habit of correcting similar oversights, continued to embellish his value and reputation.

"Code books" were the 1800s answer to modern-day computer security encryption. When the first overland telegram was transmitted in 1861, secure communication became a serious issue and has been ever since. Communication of critical transactions, investments, and the plans of any railroad were of interest to investors of every stripe. Security of the mail, telegrams, and, after the 1870s, the telephone, were major concerns. Therefore telegrams were transcribed by the railroad using secret code books. The AT&SF had an elaborate system of coding the communications between Chicago, Boston headquarters, and far-flung outposts. For example, the Santa Fe comptroller in New York sent the following telegram to E.P. Ripley, president of the Santa Fe in Chicago: "Crescendo grabbing today; present slattern, slickens, slimness, sluggish, sluttish, jobes, smilingness, snakey, smith, steel. Declared a common dividend of two percent ...." And then he translated: "Directors meeting today; present are Berwind, Duval, Fowler, Haven, Jones, Jobes, Morawets, Ripley, Smith, Steel. Declared a common dividend of two percent ...." They obviously had chosen their codewords with tongue-in-cheek, since they referred to their board meetings as "crescendo grabbing" and gave each other humorous names—Ripley dubbed himself "snakey." And Godfrey Holterhoff was codenamed "slothful," the antithesis of his true nature.[15]

Since Holterhoff was the local go-to guy for the Santa Fe's Western Division, he was a noted powerbroker in the region, and his opinion carried significant weight with the Boston board of directors. Although division managers came and went, it was Holterhoff who held the highest seniority in the AT&SF Western Division and the utmost trust of the company's executive branch. As soon as the SP turned over the Mojave Line to the A&P, Murphy became an essential ally of Holterhoff for the development of this critical juncture in a transcontinental route. Very nearly the same age, both were career railroad men and bachelors. They became fast friends. Holterhoff was also an executive officer of the Pacific Land Improvement Company (PLIC) and therefore the source of contracts for Murphy. They relied on each other and performed favors for each other. It was Holterhoff who had authorized the rails and supplies for Murphy's "Push Car Railroad" and requisitioned the carts Murphy distributed to the Indians. As time passed, Holterhoff would pave the way for some of Murphy's most spectacular investments.

Holterhoff's achievement of establishing the Santa Fe's own right-of-way into downtown Los Angeles was a boon to the Monaghan & Murphy General Merchandise store in Needles. Regularly scheduled trains from Chicago to Los Angeles were now booked to capacity and additional coaches were added. A ticket, in 1885, from Chicago to California cost $125. Once the Santa Fe had direct access to Los Angeles, a historic rate war began, the likes of which has never been seen before or since. Rates dropped to $95.[16]

The climax came on March 6, 1885, when both Southern Pacific and Santa Fe engaged in a ticket price war for trips between Kansas City and Los Angeles. That morning, the Southern Pacific matched the Santa Fe at $12. Then Santa Fe dropped its price to $10, and SP followed suit. Santa Fe cut its fare again, this time to $8 and SP matched it. With price-cutting happening faster than a speeding train, Southern Pacific—through some misunderstanding—undercut itself, first slashing the price to $6, and then suddenly, to $4. Finally, shortly after noon, the Southern Pacific announced a rate of $1.[17]

Santa Fe officials claimed they sold no tickets for less than $8, but intentionally set a trap into which the Southern Pacific neatly fell.[18]

This $1 rate lasted only a few hours, but a one-way ticket stayed at around $25 for nearly a year.[19] An avalanche of passengers headed for Los Angeles to take advantage of this incredibly low fare. In the single year of 1887, known as the "Great Boom," Los Angeles's population exploded from 12,000 to 80,000. Real estate prices soared.[20] In Los Angeles, a 22-acre lot that cost $12,000 in 1883 sold for $40,000 in 1887. Farmland priced at $100 an acre in 1886 brought $1,500 an acre the next year.[21]

Prior to the boom, the western city limit of Los Angeles was at Alvarado Street. From there to the ocean at Santa Monica, there was nothing but a few bean fields. The Santa Fe went into full swing. The PLIC, in the spring of 1887 laid out thirteen new town sites. That fall there were twenty-five new townsites between Los Angeles and San Bernardino. Curiously, Murphy and his partner Frank Monaghan could have easily cashed in on this real estate frenzy, but neither of them was interested in "get rich quick" schemes. Besides, they had their hands full in Needles with the increased rail traffic. Many of the towns that sprung up in these heady years went bankrupt. Some moved buildings and all. "Pomona woke up one morning to find La Verne coming across the city limits in half a dozen wagons and it wasn't two hours until the La Verne addition to Pomona was set up and open for business with hotel, barbershop, four bungalows, and a real estate office."[22]

7

SCREAMS IN THE DARK

On one dark, moonless, February night in 1887, the Atlantic & Pacific Express slid across the faceless desert terrain lit only by the light of its single headlamp. Under a full head of steam, the Express was on time and only four miles west of Needles.

Originating in San Francisco, the train had added additional Pullman sleepers from Los Angeles at its last depot stop in Mojave. It was customary to have Indians catch a ride on the open platforms at the front and rear of the cars when the train stopped at one of the many watering tanks along the way. Indians had crowded all the car platforms on this fateful evening.

At slightly after 9 pm, the engineer was barely able to perceive smoke at the limits of the headlight. But then, almost instantly, it was clear, horrendously clear, that there was a fire ahead. The trestle was on fire.

The engineer quickly threw the engine into reverse, and the seven-car Express screamed into the darkness, hurling toward the burning trestle. "... the locomotive, mail car, express car, baggage car, and a Pullman parlor car were precipitated into the abyss below." The locomotive boiler burst with a deafening explosion that was heard four miles away at Needles roundhouse. The mailcar followed by the baggage car "...came crashing down upon the engine, while on top of them all fell a Pullman sleeper, filled with passengers preparing to retire for the night." The engine and three cars completely filled the chasm, thereby preventing the remainder of the train from adding to the pileup. The engineer, mail clerk, and baggage man were killed instantly. Passengers from the surviving cars pulled people "from the Pullman car, resting on top of the debris, the passengers were extracted before the flames had completely enveloped it."[1]

Arthur Humphrey immediately dispatched a locomotive from the Needles roundhouse with Murphy to help the injured. The nearest physician was more than three hundred miles away and would not arrive until the next day. Humphrey, Murphy, and his sister, Margaret, were left to their own resources to care for the mangled and wailing victims. They removed limbs from several victims, amputations that were necessary, since Native American culture demanded that any tribesman who had a seriously injured limb could not rest until the crushed member was removed and out of sight,

> We arrived in time to rescue several of the passengers from burning but some did burn, and many others were so seriously injured that they died later. This, together with the poor, mutilated, pain-crazed Indians made the scene one of horror never to be forgotten. Indian mothers, whose children had been crushed or burned, were frantic in their efforts to rescue them ... [At Needles] an improvised hospital was provided in the waiting room of the station for the White injured and another on the floor of the roundhouse for the Indians.[2]

Murphy had stocked first-aid supplies at the store for just such occurrences.

> Murphy was a big fellow, kind-hearted, and sympathetic. The scene was too shocking for the ordinary person. Outside of Murphy and his brave sister, who was the only woman in the town, we had no further help from the time we unloaded the injured until the next morning. Murphy, his sister, and myself were busily engaged in going from one (victim) to another, bandaging the best we could the mutilated limbs, straightening broken ones so as to relieve the pain, and helping to remove those who had died, so as to lessen the horror for the living.[3]

Three years earlier, a railroad commissioners inspection report of the roadway across the desert noted an astonishing "661 bridges all built on pile foundations." The bridges were of redwood or red cedar, which had baked tinder-dry from years in the blistering desert heat. The locomotives at the time ran on soft low-grade coal from Gallup, New Mexico. The burning coal gave off excessive cinders and sparks which escaped from both the smokestack and the ash pan beneath the locomotive's firebox. Smoldering and burnt bridges caused by these burning embers were a constant danger.[4]

The newspaper reported that "only" $200,000 was recovered from the strongboxes in the wreckage of the mail car and the remainder was lost. The reporter did not know how much was lost, because no one knew how much money actually was on that train. Often these trains

Westbound Santa Fe passenger train with the inscription "Leaving Needles 8 AM 1/22/1902."

hauled large sums of gold coins from the San Francisco Mint to the mining camps, but the most valuable bags were undoubtedly those carried by miners, who were on their way to the mint, but trying to keep a low profile to avoid robbers. During his regular runs to the Hotel Del Monte, exchanging railroad payroll for silver dollars, and hauling gold bars or coins, Murphy frequently rode this same train. Several accidents, due to burned bridges, occurred that year (1887), and the thought of another such accident undoubtedly troubled Murphy on his frequent trips from one coastal city or another, so he never let his satchel out of his sight.[5]

Murphy's fortuitous Josephine gold strike in January of 1887 was in a desolate area north of Kingman, in the Arizona Territory, at more than five thousand feet elevation. Murphy had hired a crew of a dozen miners to work the claim. Mining was expensive and backbreaking work. It was usually accompanied by extreme hardship, cave-ins, groundwater flooding, mechanical breakdowns, and sometimes, even death. Conditions on this barren mountaintop were miserable. The men worked amid bitterly cold winds and intermittent snow. All work came to a halt on April 16, 1887, when eight inches of snow fell in the region.[6]

Murphy kept his mouth closed and maintained his typical casual demeanor about his share of the strike at the mine. It is unclear exactly how much even Monaghan knew. Undoubtedly aware of it, he joked at Murphy's good fortune, but they both submitted to the unwritten code of miners—do not broadcast your take. The ore came out of unmistakably rich veins. However, until the ore was reduced and smelted, no one, let alone the men who pick-axed it from the earth, fully knew its value. When mine owners finally shared knowledge of its full value, it was the cause of many deadly gunfights. After a reporter from the *Mohave County Miner* had come snooping around the Josephine diggings, he spotted the ledge they were working on and reported in an article June 4, 1887.

> I must say that the ore they have on the dump and in sacks (ready for shipment), and what you see in the ledger shows... it will be one of the bonanzas of Wallapai District yet.... I do not know of a district in the Territory that has a better showing [visible gold] than the old Wallapai.[7]

Word was out, but Murphy bypassed inquiries about his newfound wealth as though it were insignificant. He joked that reporters are notorious for their exaggerations. Steeped in humility from birth and an instinctively private man, he eluded all pretense.

The Josephine mine bonanza was absorbed into Murphy's operating capital. Discovery of a gold vein was indeed a windfall, but the cost of extracting the bullion was considerable. Mules carried tons of ore to the nearest stamp mill, where the ore was immediately crushed into fine dust. The gold was then extracted using mercury. Mercury forms an amalgamation with gold. When this amalgamation is heated, the mercury evaporates into a toxic vapor, leaving only the molten gold, which can then be cast into ingots.

The entire mining process had taken less than six months before the vein was exhausted. Murphy's other two partners, Sullivan and Jones, had to be paid their share of the profits. The Denver banker, Sullivan, who had provided the initial financing, took the more substantial proportion. The actual amount that Murphy pulled from this mine was never known, but it evidently provided him with sufficient capital to cover expenses and pursue future investments.

Murphy had scarcely wrapped up operations at Josephine when temperatures soared to a brutally hot 120 degrees on July 2, 1887; the weather remained blistering hot throughout the month. Then, on August 7, flames burst out of Monaghan and Murphy's store. The roaring fire quickly engulfed the entire wood-frame building, despite the efforts of a bucket brigade that quickly formed. With its intense heat, the blaze spread to the post office and the Murphy-Briggs Saloon. Townspeople watched helplessly as the inferno destroyed the entire row of wooden structures. In a matter of minutes, the frontier town had burned to the ground. "Five buildings were consumed, together with all the stock of Messrs. Monaghan and Murphy...."[8]

As shocking and devastating as this fire was, only a single entry in the *Mohave County Miner* documented the catastrophe. Hastily built with shared wood-framed walls, boomtown business districts were commonly victims of fire. For Monaghan and Murphy, the loss of store stock alone would have been immense, but the PLIC came to their aid to help them rebuild. They were fortunate, too, that the population was booming due to the completion of the Santa Fe route, so the general store had been doing an equally booming business. Both men had been lucky as miners: Murphy's Josephine mine and Monaghan's Black Metal mine were bona fide strikes, even though neither was notable enough to make history. Because of his success at the productive Black Metal Mine, Frank had been buying up real estate in Los Angeles. So the partners were ready to rebuild, and they both had enough funds to make it happen. Both were determined to start from scratch—again.

This time they added a second floor and built a bank next door. Down the street, buildings reconstructed were Murphy-Briggs Saloon, a Chinese restaurant, and two other saloons.

As bad as times were at Needles, westbound trains passing through were loaded with passengers taking advantage of the low-priced tickets. Needles's sharp new stores enticed the passengers off the parlor cars to pursue some shopping. Monaghan & Murphy, the largest emporium, offered the best selections. Business was good. And on the homefront, Murphy's sister, Mary had moved from their parents' home in Kansas to the roaring mining town of Leadville, Colorado. As a welcome ending to a trying year, Murphy planned to attend Mary's wedding there on Christmas Eve of 1887. He had no idea that attending her nuptials would set his life on an irreversible track.

8

LEADVILLE

In 1859, the discovery of gold a mile from the remote mountain camp at Leadville, Colorado, had yielded more than ten tons of the precious metal. Leadville's population soared to nearly 15,000, far surpassing that of Denver, but the rush was over in eight years. Then, in 1879, the Leadville Silver Boom started after some clever miners assayed the black sand discarded during the gold mining operations, and discovered it contained an oxidized form of silver. Despite Leadville's 10,000-foot-elevation, during its heyday in the 1880s, nearly every notable figure of the time—from Doc Holliday and Bat Masterson to Wyatt Earp—passed through this glittering boomtown, making the Colorado town the biggest and richest mining center in the country. With mines at times producing $15 million annually, Leadville single-handedly earned Colorado the nickname "Silver State." The first railroad climbed the mountain to Leadville in 1880, and due to the volume of ore extracted there, three railroads eventually serviced the area, including the Santa Fe.

A local reporter, R.G. Dill, observed:

> The streets in the evening filled with an army of miners, speculators, capitalists, gamblers, crowded from curb to curb. Pedestrians often choose the middle of the street rather than the sidewalk although it meant taking their chances at being run over by the dashing horsemen and coaches that whirled over the road at any hour, day or night.[1]

Another journalist, T. Ammons, wrote:

> All sorts of wicked persons, murderers, thieves, bronco-steerers, confidence men, good and bad members of the gambling fraternity, pickpockets, thugs, yeggs [safe crackers], and promoters of all sorts of swindling enterprises poured into Leadville from all over the world.[2]

Vast fortunes were made and lost in the Leadville mines. So much silver entered the market that the federal government stepped in to shore up the price with the Silver Purchase Act of 1890. The law created an imbalance between the values of gold vs. silver and had to be rescinded. This led to the collapse of the silver market, driving some investors to the Arizona Territory in search of gold. This was most likely the reason that Denver banker Dennis Sullivan had financed Murphy's Josephine mine in January 1887. Frequently Denver banks were opened with profits from mines in Leadville. The connection with Sullivan and Murphy was likely through Dan's sister Mary since Murphy made many trips to Denver, and stopped off to visit her whenever he could.

Just how Mary, a poor farm girl from Kansas, landed in Leadville is a mystery. Perhaps she was looking for a husband, and a mining town sounded like a good place to meet one. Bordering on the timberline, Leadville appeared as a muddy black smudge, surrounded by low-lying hills and scraggly stunted pines, not the easiest place for a young woman on her own to make a life, but Mary, not yet twenty-four, did. Fortunately, Murphy made many trips to Denver for his work, so he'd visit her. Likewise, each year, when he went to Kansas to visit their parents, Murphy would also make a stop in Denver and take a side trip to see his sister in Leadville.

On one of those trips, Mary announced she was marrying Winters Morrell, ten years her senior and the founder of the first and largest lumber mill in Leadville. His lucrative business had supplied nearly all the timber used to brace the tunnels and mining shafts throughout both booms. Morrell was prosperous and well-respected in this bawdy mining town; Murphy was no doubt pleased that Mary was marrying a prominent man.

As it turned out, Murphy and Morrell had much in common, since both men were from pioneering Kansas families, and both were merchants catering to miners. Murphy was three years younger than Morrell and enjoyed the company of his ruggedly handsome brother-in-law. Although the mines around Leadville had been in decline since 1881, Morrell continued to do a thriving lumber business in the town.

When Murphy arrived in Leadville for their wedding, on that bleak December day of 1887, snow covered the ground, and the bitter winds of winter had closed in on the mountain town. The wedding was scheduled for Christmas Eve.[3]

Mary, eager to find her brother a bride, invited the Sinnott family to her wedding reception. John and Delia Sinnott were residents of Leadville at the time, but their four single, adult daughters lived at the family home in San Jose, California.

The patriarch of his family, John Sinnott was a wealthy Leadville miner, who was wounded in a Leadville courtroom shootout in 1884. Circa 1870.

The Sinnott girls were an interesting quartet and their residence, The Alameda, was equally fascinating. It stood on the corner of Alameda Avenue and Naglee Street in San Jose, the onetime capital of California. The home was a large, two-story Victorian with a mansard roof and a spacious wraparound porch. The second-story featured a porch with an ornately decorated balustrade with turned posts. Its spacious corner yard was dotted with California palms and rose bushes.

Everything about the house wreaked of "rich." Indeed, as schoolgirls, the Sinnott siblings attended the Sisters of Notre Dame de Namur's College of Notre Dame, which was within walking distance of The Alameda and was an all-girls private school taught, as the name would imply, by the Sisters of Notre Dame de Namur. The school was listed in *Where to Educate, 1898-1899: A Guide to the Best Private Schools, Higher Institutions of Learning, Etc., in the United States*, accompanied by the following entry: "Careful attention is paid to manners, morals, and physical culture." Its nuns were steeped in French culture and infused their pupils with both religious and secular values. All the Sinnott girls—Delia, Kathryn, Antoinette, and Susan—received both primary and secondary education under their tutelage. Therefore, they were fluent in French. "Antoinette" was no random name. The values and the demeanor of the school would remain with her and her siblings for life. The two eldest daughters taught elementary school and occasionally visited Leadville on holidays and during the summer.

On Mary's wedding day, only Antoinette, now thirty-two, the Sinnotts' most reticent and meticulous daughter, accompanied her parents to the party.

Mary graciously introduced her brother Dan to Antoinette, but the two spoke only briefly. At the time, Antoinette had her artwork on display at a ceramics show in San Francisco. She recently had been singled out in a newspaper review of the show for her *jardinière*, which was "exquisitely decorated with representations of *La France, Marechal Niel*, and other roses." Painting dainty flowers on ceramic ware was a favorite pastime of hers. Her above-it-all attitude was hard to miss, but Murphy was courteous.

It was Antoinette's father, John Sinnott, a crusty sixty-three-year-old miner, who interested Murphy most. Sinnott had gotten his start in Barrington, Illinois, where he met his future wife, Delia Ela. In his younger days, he had run ox-trains loaded with supplies on the old Bow Trail across the Great Plains in the 1850s. For a while, he worked the Comstock silver mines in Nevada before settling in San Jose, where he and his brother ran a dry-goods store.[4] He was outspoken about his disdain for retailing; he had "the fever" and couldn't get over mining, even though it meant leaving his family in San Jose for seventeen years.

> I hated it. And as soon as I heard of the silver strike, I sold out and came up here, in '79 . The first year up here, I partnered up with the London Consolidated Mining, Milling, and Smelting Company. We capitalized it for $10 million at twenty dollars per share.[5]

London Consolidated was a group of mines which included the Paris, Hard to Beat, Mother, Grinsby, and others. Sinnott was the supervisor of those mines, which were all in a narrow, two-mile-long strip following a gold-quartz vein. Perhaps more intriguing, Sinnott had shot a man not too many years before, as he revealed in this article from the *Leadville Daily Herald*:

> … this young buck Irishman McKenzie and I had a claim we named, Saint Kevin, up in Sow Belly Gulch. We had a bond on it till I found out McKenzie took in some other men and left me out! So I sued him in District Court. Next time I saw him, he came at me swinging, hitting me in the face, and knocking me down. Now, mind you, he was not a big man, but he was about forty and me, sixty. Some bystanders had to pull him off me. So I went to the court and swore out a warrant for his arrest, on a charge of assault and battery. A few days later we were called to court. He showed up, but Judge

Kroll had to hunt down the attorney. Just about then, McKenzie came into the courtroom. There we were just me and him and Constable Milner. McKenzie said, "God damn your jaw—it isn't swelled up now." I told him he'd better not try anything now. He shouted back "God damn, I wish I had stamped your liver out" as he came at me. I stepped behind the table as the Constable went and stood between us saying, "We'll have no trouble here." He called me a blackmailer, and I called him a liar. He came at me again as the Constable tried to hold him back so I drew a forty-four caliber British Bulldog revolver, reached around the Constable, and fired the ball into his left thigh. I fired again, but the ball hit the back of a bench, and went through it, and fell on the floor. McKenzie said, "The old son of a bitch has shot me in the leg." I was locked up but soon released on $1500 bail. McKenzie went to the doctor and fixed up okay.[6]

Sinnott had a crew of men working the Dolly B and Famous mines, both of which had "good show," mining jargon that meant the mines were producing considerable amounts of ore. He had promising claims at lodes named for four of his children: the Delia Sinnott Lode, Susie Sinnott Lode, Katie Sinnott Lode, and Johnny Sinnott Lode. Sinnott's only son, Johnny, had died at an early age. No lode honored his eldest daughter Grace Mae, probably because she was already married to Charles Weber II, the well-to-do son of the then-legendary captain of the first wagon train of immigrants to enter California in 1841.[7] The elder Weber was also the owner of a vast Spanish land grant, which in the late twentieth century became the site of California's Silicon Valley, including San Jose, Santa Clara, and the land that houses all of Stanford University.[8]

The mining talk around Leadville and from John Sinnott at the wedding, sounded all too familiar to Murphy. These were the usual tales of boom and bust, with broken dreams, but ever so hopeful, always confident that the next bucket of ore would be a real bonanza.

Murphy was always ready with an earnest and uplifting story. Ever the booster of Arizona mines and wanting to convey his enthusiasm, he told the Leadville men about the rich mineral ores already pulled from the mines along the Colorado River. Murphy's latest project was to get a smelter built on the Colorado. Rail and steamship transport were already available to bring ore to the proposed smelter. Murphy believed that such a smelter would prove the Southwest to be the next Comstock or the next Leadville. A smelter's purpose was to extract base metals, such as silver, iron, copper, and others from their ore. They all knew that a smelter was a significant investment and that not just anybody could run a smelter, rather someone with "real smarts" and "know-how."

Although Murphy considered this wedding party and meeting the Sinnott family to be a pleasant affair, he had no idea the impact that this family and their affairs would have on his life.

Following the wedding, Murphy boarded the train in Leadville for Denver, continuing on to Hays, Kansas, on his annual visit to see his family who had moved to the former Wild West town with its gun-fighting past. They had sold their homestead in Hanover, making enough profit to afford a comfortable two-story Victorian home in the center of Hays, an easy one-block walk to Saint Joseph's church for daily mass. Although he was not yet thirty, Dan's life had changed dramatically since sixteen years before when he had headed to the Southwest.

Several of his sisters were still living at home, as was the youngest sibling, his brother Tom, who was only five when Dan left home. Having promised his parents that he would pay for Tom's education, Dan arranged for Tom to attend accounting school in Hutchinson, Kansas, and after graduation, there would be a job waiting for Tom with his brother in Needles.

Word had spread regarding Murphy's gold discovery. Charles Crocker, his mentor, contacted him to congratulate him about his newfound wealth. Monaghan and Murphy had successfully been following Crocker's example by selling supplies to miners. Surprisingly, to Crocker, they had also discovered successful mining claims.

Monaghan and Murphy had convinced themselves that their future success would be guaranteed by investing in mines, a business that had been only marginally profitable. Both men lured their brothers to follow them into the desert in search of their destiny. Murphy's brother Tom earned his diploma in accounting in Kansas and came directly to Needles. He was immediately helpful to the Monaghan & Murphy enterprise, revising its accounting system and freeing up some of the partners' time. Frank's brother Charlie, a single man from Los Angeles, came out to the desert to seek his fortune. Charlie Monaghan went in with his brother on the Black Metal mine.

Over the years, Murphy had built up an extensive collection of Indian baskets representing many Southwestern tribes. It's probable that he influenced Charlie and piqued his interest in Native American artifacts.

Charlie was not only busy mining, but also sold what he called "Indian Curiosities" —all manner of blankets, baskets, pottery, and relics from the neighboring tribes of the Chemehuevi and Mojave. Charlie sold these relics by mail order.[9]

With Charlie minding the Black Metal and Tom busily attending to business, Monaghan and Murphy were free to go prospecting. They traversed the vast and barren trails of the Southwest by horseback for months on end, weathering scorching sun by day and sleeping under the stars, warmed only by a campfire and bedroll. Murphy called these prospecting trips, going "On the Trail of Geronimo," for this was historically Apache territory.[10]

The partners were seeking prospectors willing to sell out. Many of the men they encountered were prone to giving up because many could ill afford the costs of shipping and processing their ore. If a miner was interested in selling, they inspected his diggings. The type of mineralization they were looking for required little more than a hunting knife to scrape at the decomposing white quartz and look for the telltale flecks of gold or the black streak of silver.

They took every precaution to avoid the old Western lore quip, "A mine is a hole in the ground with a liar at the top." Most gold seekers were "prospectors," not "miners." As popularly depicted, the prospector was a lone, bedraggled fellow with a stubborn mule trailing behind him. Miners, on the other hand, were usually paid working men who lived in a mining camp or nearby boomtown. As suppliers of mining equipment, Monaghan and Murphy fancied themselves as miners, however they employed miners to do the digging. This was certainly true of Murphy, at least.

Crocker was always proud of his protégés; in fact, he admired them. The pair had saved him and the SP by constructing the Division Point at Needles without a hitch. He suggested that Murphy go to New York City to meet some of his friends, and offered Murphy lodging at his private club in the city along with a few letters of introduction to several influential businessmen.

March 1888 found Murphy ensconced in the paneled and draped magnificence of the Union Club, New York City's most exclusive men's club of the Gilded Age. As exclusionary as it was at its founding in 1836, by the time Murphy arrived, its limited membership included: Cornelius Vanderbilt; the financier' J.P. Morgan; Henry Flagler, the founder of Standard Oil; George Westinghouse, inventor of railroad air brakes; and J.D. Rockefeller of Standard Oil.[11A] As a guest of Charles Crocker, it is unknown whom Murphy may have met during his three-week stay at the privileged residence. What is certain is that he was residing at the

Union Club as evidenced by a letter dated March 22, 1888[11B]. The letter was written by Murphy on Union Club stationery while snowbound in these elegant surroundings. Due to the weather conditions, it is probable that several of these tycoons were also snowbound inside the club. The *New York Herald* headline called it the "Great White Hurricane: 60 mph Winds that Left 50 feet of Snow in its Wake" and the article followed:

> So quick and ferocious was the storm that thousands were stranded. The Astor Hotel turned its corridors into sleeping rooms for the stranded; ladders were used to allow stranded elevated train passengers escape, at 50¢ a head. Three locomotives at Grand Central Station derailed trying to push, under "full pressure," out of their loading bays. An ice bridge formed over the East River and several thousand crossed on foot between New York and Brooklyn.[12]

It should be noted that later in life Murphy preferentially directed his affairs toward several of these gentlemen's companies, and he became the largest shareholder of Standard Oil of California stock. The following year local newspapers noted his frequent departures for the East and quipped that "Murphy was off to see Vanderbilt."

The summer following Murphy's return from New York's Union Club, his benefactor Charles Crocker died on August 14, 1888, at the Hotel Del Monte at Pebble Beach. He was sixty-six. With Crocker's death, Murphy lost his last close friend at the Southern Pacific Railroad.

On October 12, 1891, Murphy and Monaghan strolled into the Kingman County courthouse to record their ownership of five claims they had purchased: Independence, Balmaceda, Juniata, La Junta, and Minahaha mines. They were definitely bullish on mining: between October 1891 and July 1896, they purchased a total of nineteen claims.[13]

9

Great White City

It was the chance of a lifetime for Murphy when he attended the Chicago World's Fair in 1893. More informally called "The Great White City," its official name was the World's Columbian Exposition, in celebration of four centuries since Columbus's discovery of America. More than twenty-six million visitors swarmed to its six-hundred-acre fairgrounds. Attendees invariably said that nothing they had read or heard, had prepared them for what they saw.[1] Immense exhibition halls of gleaming white Neoclassical Beaux-Arts buildings were gracefully arranged along faux Venetian canals, and manicured lawns were lined with blooming baskets of flowers. The Administration Building, "the crown of the Exposition Palaces" with its Brunelleschi Dome was on the main court of the exposition grounds, flanked by imposing pavilions dedicated to such worlds as Manufacturing, Agriculture, Electricity, and Horticulture, to name a few. All these palatial buildings faced an immense canal, which doubled as a reflecting pool.[2]

This was no mere vacation for Murphy. He was attending the fair to see what new inventions and technological trends were on the horizon. In particular, he had been consumed in Needles with a desperate need for a smelting operation. He knew first hand from his store that the miners coming in from their diggings were on a knife's edge between success and failure due to the lack of a nearby smelter. Their ore was good, but not good enough to justify shipping the long distance to the nearest smelter. Furthermore, truly refined smelting was only available across the Atlantic in Wales, so he was determined to change that. In the process, he would single-handedly enable the surrounding mining region to turn a profit and alleviate its miserable conditions. In this frame of mind, he was especially looking forward to seeing the exhibits in the Mines and Mining Building. Its central nave was aptly named "Bullion Boulevard," with an incredible amount of gold and silver on display.

The entryway to California's lavish mineral exhibit had triple arches made of granite and white marble from quarries in Colton, California. This magnificent entry was designed to display the gems and precious metals found in the state. Rare mineral specimens collected by its State Mining Bureau and private collections formed an astonishing display: "The center of interest in the California section was the actual historical nugget (discovered) on a January morning in 1848, which had revolutionized commercial conditions of the world."[3] This discovery had set off the famed Gold Rush of '49.

Huge boulders of silver, copper, and lead made up several of the exhibits. Attendees marveled at how these enormous specimens were transported. Several states constructed towering displays of mineral ore. The *piece-de-resistance* was in Montana's exhibit, which featured a solid sterling silver statue of *Justice*, holding her iconic scales in one hand and a sword in the other. The female form stood on a globe, upheld by an eagle, with outstretched wings, and two huge bronze lions stood guard on either side. The whole sculpture, which included nearly a ton of silver, stood on a two-foot square block of pure gold. Both the silver and the gold were borrowed from mine operators for this sculpture, which was melted down after the fair.[4]

All of these glittering and impressive displays, however, did not feature any new or inventive ways to smelt ore. Outside the building, Murphy was confronted by a huge monument commemorating the German State. Appearing as if made of bluish limestone, it was composed of Portland cement: a broad stairway leading to a two-story pedestal with four square columns, whose capitals featured an eagle with spread wings surrounding the statue of "heroic Germania." The massive figure and surrounding colonnade looked entirely different than any cement he had seen in California. He recalled the cement works just outside of Los Angeles at Colton where his Yuma Line train stopped on every trip it made. He had never seen cement look like this.

Intrigued, he returned to the Mines and Mining Pavilion to find Germany's exhibit. There he found displays of machines and apparatus used in the production of cement. Numerous German chemists were on-hand to explain Portland cement's exceptional strength and answer questions about the exacting process. Murphy engaged one of the scientists in an in-depth conversation.

Portland cement takes its name from its resemblance, when cast into a block, to Portland stone, a natural building stone of England where the cement was first developed. Limestone and clay are burned at high temperatures and ground into a fine powder to create cement. The cement is mixed with sand and gravel which hardens when mixed with water, resulting in a water-resistant product.[5]

Great White City

This was exactly what Murphy was looking for. He had found a true expert in thermochemistry, the science required to refine limestone into cement (indeed, the word smelt is derived from the German word *schmelzen*). The chemist Murphy spoke to at the exhibit was well-aware of the process of smelting mineralized ore into an amalgam and using the addition of trace minerals to reduce the metal to its pure form. Precision in the process was key and that is why the Welsh smelting operations exceeded the competition.

That evening Murphy's head must have been swimming with ideas. He also understood the challenge it would be to realize his goal. He was thirty-five, and he felt his life changing. Both Monaghan and Murphy were feeling the strain of haggling over mining leases and undeserved lawsuits. Still musing over his experience with the German chemist, he recalled his youthful days with Frank on the Yuma railroad, the watering up stops at Colton near the cement plant and the looming mountain next to it. Suddenly inspiration struck. That mountain behind the cement plant was nearly pure limestone - the raw material—the ore—it doesn't have to be dug up - it sticks up out of the ground. It was a Eureka! moment for him. All his problems with risky claims that may or may not pay out, mediocre ore quality and no smelter, became clear to him in an instant—the Colton cement plant was upside down mining. The ore is in a mountain instead of below ground, with a dedicated smelter right beside it. This method was already being done by someone else, so Murphy was not "getting in on the ground floor," but now he knew the secret to perfect smelting—be it gold, silver, or cement.

Still whirling from his experience at the fair the day before, Murphy passed again through the gates anticipating what the new day would bring. He had seen attendees taking great delight in their concession-stand drinks. The crystal clear "artificial ice" used in the drinks was totally new. Murphy was interested and knew that the Southern Pacific was experimenting with using railroad cars cooled with ice to ship citrus to the East Coast. Furthermore, he knew that Santa Fe was lagging behind in this endeavor. Ideas were coming to him fast and furiously.

The Manufacturing Building was the largest pavilion at the fair, covering thirty-two acres. Inside the cavernous structure, displays of equipment of all sorts drew large crowds, but Murphy headed straight to the artificial ice exhibit. Refrigeration had only recently been invented, so the display of equipment used to make artificial ice intrigued him. Murphy wasn't alone in his fascination with artificial ice. The exhibition caused a national sensation. This world's fair was one of the first large-scale commercial users of crystal-clear ice—a five-story cold storage building was used to store ice and food for concessionaires at the fair.

Most people—the concessionaires and the public visiting the fair—had never seen artificial ice.[6]

Harvesting and storage of ice had not changed in the history of mankind. The term "artificial ice" differentiated the process from that of creating "natural ice." Natural ice, which is cloudy and often contains visible impurities, was cut by hand from frozen lakes in the Northeast and delivered to homes by wagon in most US cities. Artificial ice, which is crystal clear when frozen, uses distilled water (from condensed steam) so there are no visible impurities. To freeze water, compressors condense ammonia gas into a cold liquid. This liquid runs through coiled tubing surrounding cans filled with water, causing it to freeze. Immense steam engines drove these huge compressors.

Murphy was intent on bringing back to California at least one of the technologies he had seen at the fair. He was fascinated with how limestone is smelted into cement, but that interest would have to be put on the back burner. The Colton cement plant was not only owned by someone else, it would be a radical change from his current mining works. Applying what he had learned at the fair and in tune with the fair's motto "Science Finds, Industry Applies, Man Adapts" he found his answer. He would bring ice, water, and electricity to Needles. In one fell swoop he could accomplish this if he could purchase the existing equipment from the fair. Before returning to California, he would find the person responsible for the ice-making equipment.

After his inquiry at the refrigeration display a short, round, full-faced man in his late twenties approached Murphy, hand outstretched in a hearty welcome. Murphy found him more eager and fast-talking than he liked, but this enthusiastic character interested him. The man introduced himself as Phil Ball.

Three years before, Philip De Catesby Ball or PDC Ball, had been given control of his father's enormous Ball Ice Machine Company in St. Louis. "Ball Helps to Refrigerate the World" was its slogan. Ball was, indeed, one of the largest producers of refrigeration equipment in the country.[7] After a few words of praise from Murphy regarding the impressive display of compressors, pumps, and freezing pans, Murphy asked what he intended to do with the machinery at the close of the exhibition. Ball was visibly excited. Smelling a sale in the air and more over not wanting the trouble and expense of hauling the colossal equipment back to St. Louis, Ball offered Murphy a sweet deal if he took them right off the floor. Murphy anticipated that Ball would be more inclined to sell at a deep discount than transporting the equipment after the fair's closing. Using the fact that the equipment was so huge and weighing tons, he rightfully claimed that the job would be a daunting move for anyone. Of course, Ball knew this well since his company had moved the machinery by rail from St. Louis. He reassured Murphy that it could be done because a rail spur had been built onto the fair grounds for this very purpose. No doubt Murphy had done his homework and had already seen the rails.

What Ball did not know was that Murphy had the brawn of the Santa Fe Railway behind him. Murphy and Ball negotiated, with Murphy pointing out the great expense he had in transporting it to California. In short order, Ball lowered his price, and Murphy accepted with the caveat that he be given time to return to California to gain consensus from his clients.

On the trip back to California, the miles sped by, rails clicking. Murphy was undoubtedly filled with ideas inspired by what he had seen and heard. He dreamed of applying this newfound knowledge to his business and to his future. The Columbian Exhibition was lauded by the press for its display of the world's first Ferris Wheel and a promising novelty food—hamburger. But the fair was also known for its lavish use of electricity. Electricity was first introduced at the Philadelphia Exposition of 1876, but it was at Chicago's fair where it was used to turn night into day. As far as his personal businesses, the store and the mines, the store was fine but a smelting business would take time. But thinking more about the Santa Fe and Needles, he conjectured that they could both profit from the new technologies for which the fair was known: ice and electricity. By the third day of his journey, Murphy was writing down what he planned to propose to the PLIC upon his return.

His first order of business upon his return was to meet with Godfrey Holterhoff Jr, the executive for the Santa Fe's Pacific Land Improvement Company, to gain his approval and commitment for this grand plan. A new manager had been assigned to the railroad's Western Division, including the PLIC—Almon P. Maginnis, who had come to Los Angeles when the Santa Fe attained right-of-way into the city. His primary job was to oversee the development of property along the railway routes. A big bear of a Scotsman with a short-cropped brush of hair, Maginnis had been railroading with the Kansas Pacific for many years before joining the Santa Fe. Although he was nearly ten years older than both Holterhoff and Murphy, Holterhoff was the more senior executive at PLIC, and he held the power to authorize capital improvements. For that reason, Murphy scheduled a meeting with both Holterhoff and Maginnis.

They listened intently as Murphy presented his plan. He gave them a lyrical account of marvelous ice machines that amazed World's Fair crowds as they sipped drinks cooled by crystal-clear ice, the likes of which had never been seen before. He described the powerful water

GODFREY HOLTERHOFF, JR.,
Treasurer Santa Fe.

When Holterhoff was in his prime, he was an executive at the Pacific Land Improvement Company, a division of the Santa Fe Railway. From *As We See 'em*, a book of cartoons and caricatures of Los Angeles, circa 1900.

pumps used to keep the fair's lagoons filled with water pumped from Lake Michigan. He spoke of the awesome sight of electric lights that made the "White City" so dazzling at night.

Holterhoff and Maginnis, who had read newspaper accounts about the marvelous fair, were enthralled with Murphy's first-hand story. With the groundwork laid, Murphy skillfully explained how the railroad would benefit from a world-class, large-volume ice factory at Needles. This huge facility could ice rail cars and enable them to carry fresh produce and oranges all the way to the eastern seaboard. Shipping California produce and citrus was a new business that was just getting underway, but the Southern Pacific had a huge head start on the Santa Fe.

Murphy pointed out that Santa Fe's new larger steam locomotives required more water, which were putting a high demand on the water plant at the Needles Division Point. Murphy promised he could solve the problem with a pair of pumps capable of pumping a million gallons of water per hour. He also assured the Santa Fe team that if they acted quickly, he could purchase at a discount both the enormous water pumps and the actual ice machines used at the fair. And, if they were interested in such a facility, he could also electrify its depot, train yards, and the roundhouse with incandescent lights—just like the Great White City. This would enable Santa Fe to service locomotives around the clock. Excellent salesman that he was, Murphy also pointed out that the sight of electric lights as the nightly trains arrived in the desert outpost would make a huge impression on passengers and speak volumes about Santa Fe's modern approach to railroad technology, especially since Los Angeles, at the time, was still relying on a few arc lamps mounted on 150 foot towers to illuminate its entire downtown.

Murphy concluded his pitch by requesting twenty-four acres of land to be deeded to him for the construction of the facility *and* a seven-year contract between him and Santa Fe stating that he would supply the railroad and the town of Needles with ice, water, and electric power as needed at prices spelled out in the contract for the full seven years. Murphy was to construct and operate the facility. The materials and supplies were to be at PLIC discounted prices and—very important to Murphy—the shipping rates were to be one cent per ton per mile (that is, nearly free). This enabled Murphy to ship the mammoth pumps and refrigeration equipment from Chicago to Needles at a reasonable rate.[8]

Holterhoff and Maginnis quickly agreed. Holterhoff promised to process the land transfer with the directors in Boston. Murphy slipped in that the terms of lading for the supplies and equipment would be the same as those he had with the Southern Pacific's PIC. Maginnis nodded, not really sure what he was agreeing to. After hearty handshakes, Murphy left the office, and Maginnis was amazed at how perfectly Murphy had worked these facility upgrades for the benefit of the railroad. Privately, Maginnis savored the fact that upper management would be impressed by their forward-thinking. Maginnis would later personally profit on Murphy's ingenuity by copying Murphy's railcar icing plant at other locations along the rail line.

For Murphy, securing the terms of lading was a critical achievement, as was the land handed over free and clear. The ice machines were of mammoth proportions: the pressure wheel alone was nearly 20 feet tall by 8 inches deep, all of cast steel, and each of the pairs of million-gallon water pumps weighed more than fifty tons. Nevertheless, it was a lucrative deal for Murphy and a solid customer at fixed rates for at least seven years.[9]

On October 3, 1893, two executives of the Atlantic & Pacific Railroad—J.W. Reinhart, its president, and D.B. Robinson, first vice president—signed contract #338 between Dan Murphy and the railroad, which stated that the plant would provide all the ice, water, and electricity needed by the railroad and the town of Needles. The equipment would be hauled from Chicago to Needles at one cent per ton, while other building supplies such as lumber, pipes, and fittings would be secured at cost, from the suppliers to the Pacific Land Improvement Company.[10]

What a perfect deal. A&P discounts the cost of moving all the equipment nearly two thousand miles and provides free land for the plant. The price Murphy had negotiated with PDC Ball for all this machinery would definitely be paid off in less time than the seven-year contract. He now was committed to fulfilling that contract. The fair would not close until the end of the month. He had neither the equipment nor the proven ability to produce the required amount of ice. He was certainly applying his belief that "nerve is worth its weight in gold and sometimes more."[11]

Murphy was on the train back to Chicago the week the fair closed. It was a melancholy sight. The once glamorous and teeming fairgrounds were now abandoned. The vendors and small displays were gone. Heavy equipment was in the process of maneuvering the largest exhibits off the grounds. Even the once-lush beds of dramatic flowers and specimen trees were stripped clean, and the lagoons had been drained, leaving a murky, muddy canal.

Having wired PDC Ball that the deal was on, he headed straight for the Machinery Pavilion to complete the purchase. After some searching of the vast building, he found Ball. Murphy had already requisitioned Santa Fe flatbed cars for the move, and they were waiting on a siding, just outside the fairgrounds. Under Ball's supervision and with a team of laborers, they loaded the equipment onto the flatbed cars.

The sight of these gigantic engines traveling on west-bound trains attracted the attention of newspapers along the route. On November 4, 1893, the *Mohave County Miner* reported on the spectacle passing through town. It mentioned Murphy as "that enterprising merchant" responsible for the flatcars loaded with mammoth machinery.

Within months of the fair's closing, the biggest pavilions went up in flames—arson. The day after the fire, the colossal Columbia statue, symbol of the entire fair that once stood proudly at its center, now stood

A crew of indigenous Mojave workers was in charge of icing "reefers" with block ice.

alone amid a pile of charred timbers. Murphy had already removed the equipment, and now Needles and Murphy were proud to have their own piece of history. The *Albuquerque Weekly Citizen* reported:

> "Engine from the World's Fair"
> In February, one of the best ice plants in the West was set in motion. It has a capacity of 30 tons per day. $60,000 has been invested in the plant, principally by Monaghan and Murphy who operate the waterworks. The Washington pumps, with a capacity of 1,000,000 gallons, can supply the town with water when found necessary.[12]

On November 30, 1902, the *Los Angeles Herald* ran a piece titled "Metropolis of the Desert." The reporter had been given a tour of the new ice plant where many large metal pans of water were being frozen by a colossal refrigeration condenser. Smokestack, one of the tall Mojave Natives, who carried packages for Monaghan & Murphy customers, accompanied the tour. Smokestack was a minor celebrity amongst the Mojave. Many years before, he had been part of a Western Native American troop, representing the Mojave Nation, which toured several Eastern cities. Ever since, his people considered him to be famous. The reporter wrote that Smokestack looked at the water in the pans, walked over to the freezing room, looked at the big condenser, and then saw the great three-hundred-pound ice cakes as they came rolling out of the equipment. He put on his coat, started toward the door, and being a man of few words, expressed his concern to Superintendent Si Lewis. "Dan Murphy was a big man; he made ice in Needles; God no make ice in Needles." His superstition was so strong that he never entered the ice-house again. Apparently, Smokestack thought Murphy was breaking the laws of nature by making ice, or that some dark magic was at work. Either way, he wanted nothing to do with it. Fortunately for Murphy, not all Mojave Natives felt this way, since he hired them to do most of the labor to ice the trains.

The Needles ice plant ran on Mojave power. Murphy primarily employed Mojave men to load the huge blocks of ice into the refrigerated cars. This was yet another way he found to provide them with steady jobs. The previous foreman for the A&P, Si Lewis, ran the Needles Machine Works before he was appointed superintendent of the ice plant. He was given full responsibility for the plant which ran smoothly for many decades. Lewis was the best man for the job because he was a seasoned steam engine mechanic who meticulously maintained the ice plant's steam engine.

Refrigerated cars, called "reefers," were specially built boxcars that were heavily insulated with ice bunkers at each end. The ice bunkers were each filled with three or four three-hundred-pound blocks of ice. The ice blocks were loaded from a hatch door on the roof of the cars directly above each ice bunker. Within three months of the closing of the World's Fair, Murphy's ice plant was fully operational. It was "the most modern and economical (icing station) design known."[13]

Pre-chilled fruit was loaded into reefers in California and cooled by their ice-filled bunkers. The reefers were in need of re-icing in Needles after a hot two-hundred-plus mile trek across the desert. Icing stations were spaced strategically across the country to assure spoilage was kept to a minimum. The plant's 250-ton refrigeration machine was capable of producing thirty tons of ice per day. The icing station was a two-story building on a siding track off the main rail line in Needles. From the second story there was an eight hundred-foot long platform onto which blocks of ice slid down via chutes. Its entire length was equipped with electric flood lights enabling nighttime icing. The waiting train would be on the siding parallel to the station. Once stopped, the workers would throw a plank across the gap between the platform and the top of the train car, open the hatch, and then use long hooks to drag the blocks of ice and drop them into the car's bunkers. Teams of two Mojaves per car loaded ten cars in about five minutes. Then the train would index forward and the men would load the next ten cars. Speed and efficiency were required when working with ice and critical timetables. In 1900, the *AT&SF Journal* reported that fifty to one hundred cars/day were coming over the line from California. Seven thousand cars were iced that season.[14]

Murphy's ice plant was run by coal-powered steam engines. It ran continuously for twenty-two years providing ice, water, and electricity to the railroad and the town of Needles. Expert maintenance for these steam engines was available locally from the Santa Fe roundhouse. By 1915, steam was far too costly to maintain. Murphy switched to "oil engine power, such as was established by Mr. Diesel of Berlin, Germany."[15] Murphy had seen these engines in use at the 1915 Panama Exposition in San Francisco and bought them when the venue closed. More than twenty years later, Murphy still was taking advantage of World Expos for the latest technology and machinery.

Once the Atlantic & Pacific established a direct connection to Los Angeles in 1883, the train traffic in Needles increased tremendously. "Thirty-five conductors run in and out of Needles daily." In this railroad town, the shrill sound of steam locomotive whistles, screeching brakes, and the loud clanging of iron from the roundhouse was nonstop, day and night.[16]

This also meant that the population in Needles had increased to 2,500, mainly railroad men. "Just a twelve-hour ride from Los Angeles," Needles was featured in a full-page spread in the *Los Angeles Herald* Sunday morning edition on January 15, 1893. The section of the article titled "The Firm of Monaghan & Murphy Known Far and Near" featured the store.

> ... extending from Los Angeles on the West to Denver on the East, and from the sources of the Colorado River on the north to the point where it empties into the Gulf of California on the South, the firm of Monaghan & Murphy is known far and wide, and favorably known, too—not only for the business sagacity of its members, but also for the broad-gauged, liberal policy which its members pursue ...
>
> The firm comprises Frank Monaghan and Daniel Murphy, two as whole-souled, courteous gentlemen as one will meet in a month's journey. Both partners were formerly railroad men, and are well and favorably known in Los Angeles where they have hosts of friends. ... their business has increased until it has grown to enormous proportions. A good share of this increase is due to the popularity of the firm and to the well-known reputation which they have established for square and honest dealing. The business of the firm reaches $200,000 per annum.[17]

The *Bazoo* reported a Christmas holiday tradition that had begun long before they became prosperous:

> The little folks of Needles will never forget Messrs. Monaghan and Murphy the enterprising, public-spirited merchants, who after their days' sales were finished on Christmas Eve, sent all their remaining toys to the Christmas tree for public distribution among the children. The ladies too were each recipient of a nice silk handkerchief with the compliments of the firm.[18]

Dr. Booth, the editor of the *Bazoo*, also wrote, "We are puffing away on a box of beautiful 'Perfect Stock' cigars, thanks to the bighearted firm of Monaghan & Murphy.[19]

As ice production became more common in the early 1900s, artificial ice plants began springing up. A.P. Maginnis, to whom Murphy originally had pitched his idea; copied it and ran with it, building two

Mojave men provided the strength to ice reefers at the Murphy Water, Ice and Power Company in Needles. Circa 1890.

similar ice plants along the Santa Fe route, one in Winslow, Arizona, and another in Argentine, Kansas. Murphy wasn't threatened by this proliferation of ice plants; he could have easily pursued a string of ice plants all along the Santa Fe line to Chicago, creating a huge enterprise that would have earned him a fortune. But his response was much more indicative of Murphy's nature: money was not his primary motivation. He was satisfied having been "in on the ground floor" of the business (plus, he was still making a handsome profit from Needles Ice Company). He much preferred coming up with unique ways to improve the lives of others, be it the Mojave tribe across the river, the people of Needles, or the railroad employees. Devout Catholic that he was, he may have felt so guilty for having more money than his neighbors, perhaps he thought it best to spend his wealth for the greater good. Given his mother's teachings when he was young, this could be closer to the truth. She had read to him from the New Testament so many times: It is easier for a camel to go through the eye of a needle, than for a rich man to enter into the kingdom of God. Getting to heaven may have been Dan Murphy's primary goal.

Murphy's contentment with his Needles achievements enabled him to forgo pursuing other town development assignments, destinations the PLIC badly needed along the rapidly expanding rail lines. Despite his qualifying experience, he was at ease to stay in Needles with Monaghan and their Native American employees.

While he was a PLIC contractor, Murphy helped out friends who wanted to develop their own businesses. To that end, he sat on numerous boards, investing his own money in their companies, which were, in turn, frequently backed by the PLIC.[20] One of these early investments was the Globe Grain and Milling Company, a large flour mill owned by his friend Will Keller.

> The most important men in the world today are those who stand in some vital position with respect to the production and distribution of indispensable material, especially foodstuffs. There is probably no man in California who directs and influences a larger volume of business in the grain and milling industries than Will E. Keller.[21]

Born to a poor farming family in Mississippi, Will Keller cut short his own education at age fourteen so he could help with the family finances. His first jobs were as a wagon teamster, railway postal clerk, and bank clerk. He made his way to Wilmington, California, in 1892, where he set up a feed mill with two partners. In 1898, they built a large flour mill on East Third Street, near the railroad tracks in Los Angeles.[22]

Refrigerated train cars enabled California oranges to be shipped to the East Coast. The first shipment of citrus to the East Coast was in 1885. Murphy's Chicago World's Fair ice making equipment produced large 2' x 4' blocks of ice (see blocks on top of cars).

By 1902, Keller bought out his partners and changed the name to Globe Grain and Milling Company. He expanded this milling operation to more than a dozen rail centers during the first decade of the twentieth century. Keller's Bay Area grain mill burned to the ground in the fire that followed the 1906 San Francisco earthquake. When he rebuilt, he used concrete, and thus created the first fire-proof flour mill in the west. During the 1910s Keller developed a string of ice companies in El Paso, Texas, and in the California towns of Bakersfield, Fresno, and Modesto. Both of these businesses were no doubt facilitated by Murphy. Keller received direction from Murphy who was on the boards of directors for both the mills and the ice plants. The two were not competitors; they were both private contractors for the vast Pacific Land Improvement Company. Murphy usually kept his investments focused on PLIC interests. Milling grain and icing of refrigerated rail cars were relatively low-risk, rail-dependent industries and, for Murphy, sound investments.[23]

Phil Ball, who supplied Murphy's refrigeration equipment, successfully enticed Murphy and Keller into the construction of an ice plant on the Arkansas River to serve the Iron Mountain Railroad. Although this was not an AT&SF line, Ball knew that the experienced Murphy and Keller would be right for the job. In February 1912, Murphy, Keller, and Ball invested $300,000 to construct the Mountain Ice Company in Argenta, Arkansas. Iron Mountain Railroad used the plant's entire ice production to cool its fruit shipments. Ball Ice and Cold Machine Company of St. Louis was happy to have made friends with Murphy and Keller, who would become investment partners in the future.

The fruit packing industry was growing exponentially throughout the South and California. Gustavus Swift and Philip Armour, both Chicago meatpackers, experimented using refrigerated fruit cars (called "reefers") for shipping meat to Eastern cities. There was abundant natural ice, cut from the Great Lakes, and Armour began aggressively buying reefers. By 1900, he owned 12,000 cars. He leased these cars to producers and billed them by the mile. This was the same billing method that had worked so well for Pullman's sleeping car service. The Santa Fe was not interested in developing refrigerated meat transportation cars as it undermined their substantial investment in cattle cars and cattle lots all along the Western rail lines. Nearly every rail stop between Los Angeles and Chicago had corrals for cattle. It was a requirement for the humane treatment of cattle to be offloaded daily for feeding and watering.

Although the refrigerator car invention cannot be attributed to a single individual, Edwin T. Earl was an early developer of these specialized rail cars. In his early twenties, he "began building a business of packing, shipping, and marketing California fruit to eastern markets." Based in

Los Angeles he "shipped oranges from Riverside and Santa Ana on the Atchison, Topeka & Santa Fe Railway."[24] In 1884, the Santa Fe started their own refrigerated car business, Santa Fe Refrigerator Dispatch. The Chicago meatpacker Armour & Company had a near-monopoly on the meat industry and was one of the largest owners of refrigerated rail cars. By 1890, Earl owned 625 refrigerator cars, and in 1901, he sold out to Armour thereby increasing their fleet of cars. Soon a controversy over refrigerated transport broke out regarding price-fixing, rebates, and excessive rate charges. By 1899, refrigerated fruit traffic in the US had reached ninety thousand tons annually. By 1905, "Seventy-five percent of the California fruit market value was absorbed in freight and refrigeration." The Armour Car-Lines, American Refrigerator Transit, and the Santa Fe Refrigerator Dispatch controlled this lucrative market and were referred to as The Big Three. The Interstate Commerce Commission stepped in to apply some order to the situation.[25]

The Santa Fe underwent investigation, which drew into question Murphy's ice contract. Murphy and Holterhoff were called upon to explain that the increase in icing charges was due to an increase in fuel prices and not favorable treatment of Murphy's original 1893 ice contract that had been renegotiated in 1902 between the city of Los Angeles, the county of Los Angeles, the state of California, and the AT&SF. Murphy's was only one of many icing stations along the nation's rail lines.

PDC Ball was the provider of much of the ice-making equipment for the re-icing plants along the nation's trunk lines. He secured the contract to provide ice for the St. Louis World Exposition of 1904.[26] The equipment Murphy purchased from Phil Ball in 1893 continued to perform flawlessly and kept up with the growing numbers of reefers re-iced in Needles. In 1904, Murphy bought out the PLIC interest in his Needles Ice Company. He incorporated the ice company, under the sole ownership, of his brother Tom, Frank Monaghan and himself, consistently looking out for the benefit to his associates.[27]

10

Ahvote

The cool spring air was redolent with desert primrose. Mojave asters, with their sweet lavender flowers, were just beginning to bloom. Murphy took all this in as he admired these bright purple blooms while standing on the boardwalk in front of his store. It was as if he were lord of all when in actuality he was just thanking God for all his great fortune and this glorious day.

Suddenly an Indian boy staggered out of the thicket, looking wounded. He breathlessly ran toward the store. Murphy immediately stepped off the raised boardwalk and hurried toward the kid, who was struggling to shout something.

"Eldorado! Much dead!"

Monaghan, who was standing in the store that was thick with the aromas of coffee and new leather, heard what the young man said. He immediately stepped out the back door with a rifle and saddle in hand. He was consumed with anxiety because his brother Charlie lived alone in a one-room shack in Eldorado Canyon, eighty miles north of Needles. Moments later, Monaghan galloped out of the barn at full speed headed toward the canyon. Murphy turned to go back into the store while a small group of women and children began to gather in the doorway. A nearly seven-foot-tall Indian, dressed in poorly fitting white men's clothes, walked through the door, pushing the women aside without a glance. His stolid face thundered: "Charlie dead."

Gripped with confusion and dread, Murphy ignored the towering Indian. He raced out of the store into the plaza, the sun glaring. Several miners and townspeople were huddled around the trembling Indian boy trying to get out of him what had happened.

"Ahvote!"

"Ahvote killed miners!"

News had already spread. Three men rode up on horses and shouted after Murphy.

"We're goin' up there! We'll get those murderers."

Murphy was stunned. Monaghan and the other men were already out of sight as a dust cloud settled back onto the desert floor. Murphy turned the hand-painted sign on the door to "Closed." He marched out to the plaza and headed to the telegraph office, a shabby little room at the end of the depot's enormous wood platform. He dashed off a telegram to Dora, Frank's wife, informing her that her brother-in-law had been murdered and that he was sending a party out in search of the killer.[1]

Frontier telegraph operators were not concerned about privacy and were always on the lookout for big news. No doubt they got a few coins from reporters who hung around the telegraph office waiting for a scoop. The next day on May 14, 1897, the *Coast Record*'s headline read: "Slain by a Piute: A Posse is in Pursuit." On May 15, *Kingman Daily Miner* multiplied the victim count to seven: its headline read "Murder Most Foul. Ahvote, a Piute Indian, Kills Seven Men. A FIEND RUNS AMUCK." The story sent chills of horror throughout the entire Southwest.[2]

A month earlier, Murphy had taken Eastern investors to inspect the Wall Street stamp mill and mine that he and Monaghan ran on the banks of the Colorado River in Eldorado Canyon. Several bands of nomadic Paiute Indians lived peacefully along the river. Peace had existed with the Paiute tribe since the Indian Wars ended nearly twenty years earlier.

On the afternoon of May 13, 1897, two teamsters had been working all day bringing their loads of ore to the river bank, but they were late returning to the diggings. The foreman was unconcerned as he thought they had broken down along the way. Around six o'clock that evening, an Indian rode into the mill site and told the foreman that a fellow Paiute named Ahvote had a gun and was riding out to kill the white men who were blasting and hauling away their sacred mountains. The foreman immediately sent the Indian up the canyon to see why his men were late returning.

"The man soon returned, and b[r]ought the blood-curdling news that the two poor fellows were lying dead by their horses, below Nielsen's house, on the road between the canyon and the mine, and that Mr. Nielsen himself had also been murdered."[3]

At 3 am the following morning, another Eldorado miner, John Apple was awakened by a messenger telling him that teamsters Lee Franzen, Ben Jones, and "The Swede" Nielson had been murdered by an Indian. Apple saddled up with two of his men and headed out to find the slain men. Before leaving, he had sent a Chinese man to the mill to warn Charlie Monaghan of the renegade Indian. The men were hardly an hour up the canyon when, "the Chinaman rushed up to them, half-dead with terror and fatigue, to impart to them the shocking news that he had found Charles Monaghan dead in his bed, shot through the head."[4]

Upon hearing this, Apple took off for the Paiute Indian camp, unarmed and alone. The other two men continued onward and soon came upon the bodies of Franzen and Jones. They buried them where they were found and brought the team back to the mill. Meanwhile, Apple cautiously approached the Indian camp. He could see about twenty-five Indians in a high state of agitation. They were obviously upset by the killings. Some rode wildly around in circles while others milled about on foot. Seeing they were unarmed, Apple walked fearlessly into the chaos and demanded to know their intentions.

Unable to understand what was going on, one Indian said: "Ahvote must be crazy."[5]

Apple then asked for a boat and two men to accompany him to Charlie's cabin. He wanted to collect the body and take it down the river to Needles. The Indians were appalled because they superstitiously dreaded the idea of hauling a dead body in one of their boats on the river. They motioned anxiously to him, indicating he could take a boat and leave immediately. Disgusted and angry, Apple trudged off to the river where he found the boats. He took the best of the lot and shoved off into the turbulent river. He spotted two prospectors on the bank and yelled for help. He drew near to the shore and worriedly told them of the previous night's murders. The men readily volunteered to go with him.

In the spring, the Colorado was rushing with swirling eddies and whirlpools. It "runs like a mill-race when in flood and with a deafening roar." Courageously, the three men maneuvered with great difficulty down the raging river and reached Charlie's cabin before nightfall. The exhausted men quietly paddled to the bank. All were silent as they carefully stepped ashore. In the darkening evening light, they cautiously approached the ominous-looking mill works. Apple motioned for the men to go around on each side of the building. Meeting at the door of the weather-beaten shanty, they entered the little room. Desert air breezed through the dusty gloom and grit crunched underfoot as they stepped on the wooden floorboards. In the dim shadows, they saw a man, lying on the bed, fully clothed. Somberly they approached the bed, where Charlie Monaghan lay shot in the head at close range. The bed and floorboards were pooled with clotted blood. Lighting the kerosene lamp next to the bed, they observed that he had just eaten his dinner. Seeing his book and pipe still on the bedside table, they determined that he had lain down on his bed to read and had fallen asleep. Poor Charlie was "never to wake again on this side of Time."[6]

It was dark outside, and the only sounds were those of the rushing river. They would have to spend the night in the cabin with the corpse, taking rounds as lookouts. The men were unable to sleep, fearing a repeat of the previous night's horrors.

When day broke, they loaded the body into the tribe's handmade boat and set off downriver for Needles on treacherous waters. They made good time due to the swiftness of the spring floodwaters. No one spoke. They set to the task with the same grim determination they had earned during a lifetime of desert prospecting. Apple and the prospectors had spent the entire night struggling with the realization of their own mortality. A dangerous path lay ahead as they guided the boat with their ghastly cargo. Indians had murdered four of their kind, and they feared they were being followed and may at any moment be attacked.

As two of the men madly maneuvered the boat in the churning waters, the third man had his Winchester trained on the banks in the event of an ambush. After traversing only a few miles, an Indian appeared on the bank, waving them ashore. He had a message that Ahvote had been found and killed. Apple pressured the Indian to get into the boat, to show them the spot where Ahvote lay. He refused, terrified by the shrouded body lying in the boat. They set off without him and continued downriver about seven miles to Cottonwood Island where another band of twenty-plus Paiute Indians camped. Apple approached the camp unarmed and demanded to see the dead Ahvote. The tribe member who had killed Ahvote picked up his rifle and motioned for Apple to follow him.

> There they found the corpse in a dry wash. Ahvote, the fiend, had evidently died hard. He lay, face downward on the ground, his knees and thighs off the ground, resting on the points of his toes and on his breast. After he had been shot, he had dragged his body some twenty feet further and died in agony. He had received two (gun) shot wounds and was stiff in death.[7]

The sky was clear and cloudless as the temperature soared, and the sun beat down on them. The party, somewhat relieved, resumed their river journey to Needles.

Earlier that morning, the entire Mojave Indian camp had come into town from both sides of the river. They presented themselves in front of the Monaghan & Murphy General Merchandise store. The assembled tribe offered condolences and volunteered to seek the murderer. The store owners were well-known and respected by the Indians and the townspeople. Well aware that this event could affect their future and that of the town, each was eager to show support for the two grieving partners.

Murphy was concerned for the people gathered in front of his store.

He fretted about what to say to them. He gazed out the window of the store, with all its neatly arranged sacks of grains, canned goods, and mining tools. He knew he must address the subdued and saddened Mojave crowd while hiding his own grief. Some of the Native women sat in the plaza, keening as they do for their own dead. Soon, local railroad men and miners also began to mill about, all of them much more agitated and talkative than the pensive Mojave.

As always, Murphy was dressed in his three-piece suit. He mustered his courage and stepped out onto the boardwalk. Silence fell over the crowd. He raised both hands, appearing more like he was offering a benediction than a greeting, and proceeded to address the sorrow-filled people he knew so well. Although there is no written record of these days, Murphy recounted the story years later to his trusted secretary Howard K. Bagley, saying he appealed to the crowd's sense of justice and love for their neighbor. He told them it was a senseless act by a single individual against innocent and honorable men. It should not reflect negatively on the good friends, citizens, and law-abiding Mojaves gathered before him. Murphy recognized the solidarity shown him by the great gathering at the plaza. He called for peace and justice and offered a $500 reward for the capture of the guilty party.

Having painstakingly navigated the treacherous river, the trio with Charlie's body arrived back to Needles as evening approached. They delivered the body to the tiny village's morgue, and all the Indians and the townspeople dispersed as an eerie silence descended over the desert.

Several nights after the murder, three Mojave men crossed the plaza and ascended the three steps to the Monaghan & Murphy store asking for Murphy. They "wanted to see him—alone. They had a bundle wrapped in the gunny sack. Murphy greeted them and took them into the backroom. They asked him if he was the one who had offered the reward. When he answered yes, they dumped the sack upside down, and out rolled Ahvote's head, bouncing across the floor like a football. Murphy paled when the head came to rest, the eyes looking right up at him." Aghast and revolted by the Natives' display, he went to the safe and gave them their reward in gold coin.[8]

The Eldorado Canyon operation was jointly owned by Frank and Dan as it included a stamp mill for reducing the ore to the size of gravel for processing. After the tragedy, Tom leased the mine to a San Francisco outfit, which failed to pay the royalties agreed to in the lease, so Tom was forced to evict them. At that point, Dan and Frank closed the mine at Eldorado Canyon, never to return. It stayed idle for the next thirty years.[9]

Naturally, Frank Monaghan was devastated by his brother's murder. He blamed himself. It was he who convinced his brother of the riches in mining and had persuaded him to leave Los Angeles and to come to Needles. What was he thinking when he left Charlie alone at the mill? His overconfidence had influenced Charlie to adopt gold fever. If only he had not left his brother alone, Charlie would still be alive and he would have a brother. Monaghan decided he was through with it all and returned to the loving arms of his wife Dora and the comfort of his children in Santa Ana. He lost all interest in mining and in the desert. Merely recalling the sound of a stamp mill brought him waves of sorrow.

The grisly image of a severed human head rolling on the floor haunted Murphy.[10] He was alone. His companion, partner, and friend had left for Los Angeles on the previous night's train. Neither knew when they would see each other again. Remorse descended upon Murphy and the entire little desert town. Even the sounds of the locomotive's whistle seemed longer, lower, and more plaintive in their modulated wails. Townspeople kept downcast eyes and spoke in softly lowered voices. They all felt the loss and sorrow for Monaghan and Murphy, the men who had shaped their town. The promise and childlike innocence of the once-pioneering town had irretrievably slipped away. Murphy, too, slipped away. He returned to Los Angeles. He was focused on the fact that he would be turning forty in a few months. Alone.

Some historians claim the American Frontier closed in the 1890s. If that is too extreme, certainly western mining changed in the late 1800s. Large corporate mining endeavors supplanted the smaller pioneering mines which could not afford the sizable investments required to extract the minerals from their claims. That Murphy and Monaghan failed to develop their mines is a reflection of the PLIC's failed efforts to make the region's mining industry a success.

There were other failed attempts, most of which were lost to history, but at least one had a lasting impact: A group of investors from Denver, led by a former Standard Oil executive named Isaac Blake, owned mines in the New York Mountains outside Needles. They built a reduction plant to process their ore and established a short line railroad, Nevada Southern Railway, to transport it. Blake founded Needles National Bank to fund all the construction. By 1895, however, Blake turned out to be nothing short of a crook, and as a result, the railway, reduction plant, *and* bank had all gone bankrupt. One suit against the defunct bank, filed by Abner Bowen, ended up in federal courts, and resulted in a change to the Truth in Lending Act, establishing that "a national bank has no power to lend credit to any person or corporation," legal language still used in modern finance and citing the Bowen case as its foundation. Leading the charge in the landmark case was attorney Henry Clay Dillon, who represented the bank and, it turns out, Dan Murphy, who had been named receiver, on behalf of the many jilted locals who suffered when Needles National Bank collapsed.[11]

Although Arizona and California continued into the modern era in the top five mining regions in the nation, their worth came primarily from copper, boron, and Portland cement. Murphy continued to call himself a miner, but his future would be tied to different mineral resources. Not gold, nor silver.

Amid Murphy's depression over the events in Needles and his continuing disappointments with his mining investments, word came by telegram that his friend and colleague Godfrey Holterhoff had married. Neither Murphy nor anyone else was aware that Holterhoff was dating or even looking to marry. In the fall of 1889, after the California Southern Railroad and the Santa Fe merged, Holterhoff was granted a hefty promotion and became treasurer of the Western Division. Shortly after his new position was announced, he married Mrs. Louise Schaeffer Lewis, a divorced woman from his hometown of Cincinnati, who had a daughter, Leila. Leila was blinded when she was only one month old by "a physician's blunder." Her mother Louise never allowed the child to identify as a blind person. She "was sent to find things, to fetch and carry like other kids ... she was not permitted to lay her hands upon people. Instead, the individual was carefully described to her. Furniture was moved without telling her, yet she was not allowed to feel her way about with groping hands ...."[12]

Holterhoff's new wife Louise had a sister, Harriett, who lived in a large home at 1342 West Adams Blvd. in Los Angeles. Harriett Schaeffer Bishop's husband, William, owned the largest bakery and candy company on the West Coast. Godfrey bought a home down the street from the Bishops at 1360 West Adams. Years later William Bishop devised a delivery truck for chocolate bars and cookies that were refrigerated by large blocks of ice, the same way Murphy iced train cars. No doubt Murphy and Holterhoff influenced Bishop & Company in this endeavor.

Holterhoff's benevolence in marrying a divorcee with a blind child made a lasting impression on Murphy and would later influence his own domestic choices.[13]

11

It's a Gusher

"A Great Oil Strike" was the lead story on Sunday morning, December 17, 1899, in the *Los Angeles Herald*.

> Oil spouted hundreds of feet into the air, drenching men, tools, and the derrick. Thursday night, Brea Cañon Oil Company came in to be the largest well in Southern California. The company is under the management of Dan Murphy. It will prove to be the largest gusher to date, in the Los Angeles basin.[1]

How Dan Murphy got involved in the oil business requires understanding what was happening in Los Angeles prior to Murphy's spectacular gusher of 1899. Oil was the hot topic of the day, both with the railroads and with the citizens of Los Angeles. The railroads were anxious to use oil as an alternative fuel to coal, while the citizens were complaining about the oil stench infiltrating their neighborhoods.

On the West Coast, wood was scarce, while coal was expensive and of poor quality. Hot embers from inferior coal escaped from locomotive fireboxes causing fires which, in turn, burned railway trestles, resulting in the loss of lives and costly route closures. On the East Coast, there was an abundance of low-cost high-grade coal, so there was little incentive for Eastern railroads to pursue oil as an alternative fuel.

In the 1880s and 1890s, crude oil was primarily refined into kerosene. Essentially, all lighting in America was by kerosene lamps. The discovery of oil in Pennsylvania in 1859 had set off a drilling boom. This was the same oil boom that had attracted Si Lewis's father to move to California and work in those oil fields (Si Lewis was the manager of the Needles Ice Company). Pennsylvania crude was a lightweight and a less-viscous crude that lent itself to productive refining. In 1870, John D. Rockefeller and Henry Flagler founded Standard Oil Company which quickly became the dominant company refining oil into "standard" kerosene. Until this time, highly volatile impurities in poorly refined kerosene were prone to exploding. Exploding kerosene lamps during the era caused two of every five fires. Rockefeller had improved the refining methods to remove the volatile by-products, making a safe and superior kerosene. The company "standardized" the process. The popularity of standard kerosene enabled Rockefeller to control the vast majority of the country's oil.

By the late 1880s, there were several hundred producing oil wells operating in and around Los Angeles, but there was little use for the thick, smelly, tar-like liquid. Edward Doheny, a feisty prospector from Silver City, New Mexico, moved to Los Angeles in 1891.[2] Depressed and discouraged after years of hard-rock mining that had left him broke, Doheny and his mining partner Charles Canfield hand-dug their first well at Glendale Boulevard (then called Lake Shore Drive) and Second Street.[3] Too poor to afford mechanical equipment to do an appropriate job, the pair dug a 4x6-foot well, using only miners' tools—a pick and shovel. Doheny was keen to get in on the action of the wildcatter's frenzy in the Los Angeles oil field. Doheny said: "I had found gold, and I had found silver, and I had found lead—but this ugly-looking substance I felt was a key substance more valuable than any one of these metals."[4] Doheny was right. So right.

By the early 1890s, individuals—wildcatters, like Doheny—had drilled more than four hundred wells in the Los Angeles oil field, an area which encompassed what is today the southern tip of Dodger Stadium, along Third Street to Vermont Avenue on the west, and passed through Elysian Park, Chinatown, Echo Park, Westlake, and Koreatown.[5] The oil wells initially were concentrated in only a few city blocks slightly north of downtown. "At this pace, the oilmen were putting down about fifteen wells a week, eating up a new city block each month."[6] The drilling and pumping engines ran all night long, and the noise was intolerable. Crude oil pooled on the ground around the wells. The noxious stink of oil and gas filled the air. In response to citizens' protests, the Los Angeles City Council suggested drilling during the hours of 5 am to 7 pm, but the drillers would have nothing to do with it; they were unwilling to accept any limitation whatsoever on their hours. Doheny and the other wildcatters argued defiantly: "The oilmen were putting ten dollars into the area for every dollar they took out."[7]

At the time, crude oil was essentially worthless until it could be refined. There was no market for it aside from its historic use as a waterproof sealant for roofs. Besides, the crude was thick, heavy, and generally of poor quality. With few customers, the drilling frenzy soon stopped and the price of oil plummeted.

A market for crude oil was not established until an efficient oil burner for heating was developed, thus enabling the conversion from coal to fuel oil. Lyman Stewart, the founder of Union Oil, had been repeatedly turned down by SP in his efforts to convert a steam locomotive from using coal as fuel to running on oil. The SP was resistant to developing crude oil as fuel because it had lucrative contracts for shipping coal to the West. But Santa Fe executives, on the other hand, were anxious to take advantage of the low-cost crude oil for its locomotives. Stewart asked the California Southern Railroad, a Santa Fe subsidiary, to lend his company an engine for experiments in switching from coal to oil.

K.H. Wade, an executive with CSRR, agreed to loan Union Oil engine No. 652, a 4-4-0 built by Manchester in 1882, for their oil as fuel tests.[8]

Santa Fe Magazine documented the first American conversion of steam locomotives, in 1899, from coal to oil in a retrospective article written nearly twenty years after it happened:

> It is hard to say who first proved the practical value of oil as a locomotive fuel; yet, according to our present information, a man named Thomas Urquhart, superintendent of the motive power of a Russian railroad, made the first successful experiments ... In the early nineties, K.H. Wade, who was then general manager of the Southern California Railway (under which name the Santa Fe's lines in Southern California were operated), made extensive experiments with crude oil for locomotive fuel use, the first being made with an old switch engine (No. 10), which had been reclaimed from the junk pile at San Bernardino, patched up and put into shape for that purpose ... Successful demonstrations having proved the practicability ... Mr. Wade [needed] to be assured of a sufficient supply at a price that would warrant his changing the engines from coal to oil burners. In this matter, he was largely assisted by E.L. Doheny, who was the discoverer of the Los Angeles oil field, and which field at that time was producing oil of a heavy gravity more suitable for fuel than for refining.[9]

Although he didn't "discover" oil fields in Los Angeles, Doheny enjoyed the misappellation; he thrived on the attention. But he was confident that even though LA oil was heavy and unsuitable for refining, it was perfect—that is plentiful and cheap—to burn as fuel.

Godfrey Holterhoff and A.P. Maginnis, Santa Fe's Western Division officers, were mired in local oil politics in the mid-1890s. Holterhoff was eager to enable Santa Fe to convert all of its locomotives to oil. Because the public found the environmental havoc the drillers were creating to be intolerable, Holterhoff feared Santa Fe would be held liable. Maginnis, who actually owned some of these wells, was also directly involved with Doheny's oil field affairs. To avoid any discredit to Santa Fe, Holterhoff no doubt leaned on Maginnis to do something about the situation. Maginnis, in turn, compelled Doheny to join in a scheme to placate the disgruntled citizenry. Maginnis, the heavyweight in this duo, was a familiar face to the Los Angeles City Council. He had proposed to the council that he and Doheny could replace the noisy engines and their offensive exhaust with quiet, non-polluting electric motors, similar to the ones Dan Murphy had been using to generate electricity in Needles. Doheny and Maginnis, with skeptical approval by the council, tried the new generator for a few months before abandoning the experiment as a failure.

Once word got out that the railroads were contemplating the switch, wildcatters caught the oil-as-fuel fever and started pumping as much as they could. But they had no way to store the oil they produced. They were forced to sell their oversupply at the going price, which had fallen from a dollar per barrel to thirty-five cents a barrel. Clever Doheny started an oil-storage company, building huge storage tanks for the cheap oil he bought from the wildcatters. Not surprisingly, PLIC managers, one of whom was Maginnis, were the original board members of Doheny's thriving new storage company. K.H. Wade, the Southern California railroad manager, also served on the board. Using Maginnis's and Wade's influence, Doheny secured a contract with the California Southern Railroad (CSRR) for twenty thousand barrels per month, plus a full month's supply in reserve.

Doheny was hard-pressed to fulfill that much oil, however, despite the contracts he had with wildcatters. Yet, he continued to sign additional agreements to supply even more oil at an even lower price. When oil production receded, the price of oil spiked as the oil field ran dry. The bank foreclosed on his company. Having cornered the oil market by aggregating the oil from these numerous wells into storage tanks, Doheny refused to admit to the combination of poor management and greed that newspapers were charging him with. In fact, Doheny claimed he was the victim.

By 1895, the California Southern had eighteen locomotives in service burning oil, and each time one was brought into the San Bernardino shops for a complete overhaul, it was converted to oil burning. When Doheny failed, the CSRR began converting locomotives back to coal.[10] In March of 1895, the city council, aided by a geologist hired by the chamber of commerce, limited the size of the city oil field to a few square blocks.

The reality was that Doheny had a contract to fulfill with CSRR. Maginnis, a partner in the foreclosed business, was not about to allow the citizenry—nor any environmental damages—stand in their way. An oil refinery and asphalt plant had sprung up near the oil field. It became a symbol of all that was wrong with the oil business. The city was prepared to prohibit oil refineries within the city limits. In December 1895, Maginnis and Doheny swung into action to defeat the city council's plan. Maginnis complained to the council that the oilmen (himself included) were being unjustly persecuted and unrightfully accused by numerous lawsuits and injunctions. He protested that these complaints were unduly costing them money and were nothing but an annoyance and nuisance to their business. Echoing Doheny's "victim" stance, Maginnis even claimed that they were victims of Standard Oil efforts to limit the competition. He and Doheny pleaded to move the refinery to the CSRR tracks along the Los Angeles river bank.[11]

All of Maginnis's protesting, litigation, and failure to fulfill the railroad's demand for oil came to the attention of the Santa Fe executives in Chicago. E.P. Ripley, who was president of the Atchison, Topeka & Santa Fe Railway, and Chairman of the Board Aldace Walker corresponded about Maginnis, and as Ripley wrote to Walker: "Later on we anticipate making more changes, which will result in relieving Mr. Maginnis of some of his duties, consequently some of his pay." This all came to pass. Maginnis was stripped of most responsibilities, but he remained as the company's tax commissioner.[12]

In an effort to fulfill the fuel needs of the railroad, Doheny obtained two leases on land at the Olinda Ranch near Fullerton in Orange County. In 1897, he began to develop these leases. "Doheny's financial difficulties in no way imperiled his relationship with the Santa Fe. But certainly it made him more dependent on their largess."[13] The railroad wanted total independence from the volatile price fluctuations of the local producers. Within seven months Doheny had two wells at Olinda producing a total of fifty barrels per day. This was only five percent of the demand from the railroad. Over the next two years he had developed nineteen wells, each producing nearly a hundred barrels a day. This brought the Santa Fe closer to their desired independence.

Godfrey Holterhoff, who not only worked for Santa Fe but was also—unfortunately—on the board of Doheny's company, was distraught over the entire situation, especially knowing that Santa Fe locomotives were being converted to use coal again, which to him was a ridiculous step backward.[14] It is highly likely, though not documented, that Holterhoff had discussed his concerns with his good friend and colleague Murphy on one of Murphy's frequent trips to Los Angeles, because in July 1899, as reported in the *Orange County Press*, in a column labeled "Large Real Estate Deals," Dan Murphy did something totally out of character, he bought land oozing with oil:

> ...the largest sale was a tract of 1,214 acres of oil land in the Rancho San Juan Cajon de Santa Ana. This track was sold to Dan Murphy of Needles by George Chaffey, M.E.C. Munday, and R.F. Del Valle, all of Los Angeles for $20,000. This property is known to be rich in oil deposits. A few years ago it could have been purchased for a mere song.[15]

Until that sale, Murphy hadn't been interested in spending his money on businesses that were inherently competitive and risky, like the oil business. On one hand, buying oil land in 1899 wasn't consistent with Murphy's axioms "get there before the newspapers" and "get in on the ground floor." but it was consistent with his desire to help his friends Holterhoff and Doheny out of a difficult position. The oil seep property was just what Santa Fe needed to convert their engines to oil. Murphy certainly could justify the investment because Santa Fe was a ready, risk-free market.

At this critical moment in his life, Murphy used his uncanny ability to get out in front of the market, and he sought out more distant sources of oil. In the same way that he supplied water to a thirsty town and tons of ice to a needy railroad, he once again found a need and filled it. This time, the need was oil.

As sole owner of the property, Murphy incorporated Brea Cañon Oil Company as its president/owner with PLIC board members: C.N. Sterry (SCRR lawyer), A.P. Maginnis (PLIC manager) and W.G. Nevin (another PLIC manager),[16] and of course, E.L. Doheny. Holterhoff was notably absent from the board. Most existing historiography calls Doheny the founder of Brea Cañon Oil Company. But existing deeds clearly show that Murphy purchased the oil-rich land, and those deeds record him as the owner.[17]

Murphy's newly formed Brea Cañon Oil Company committed all of its oil production to the Santa Fe. Doheny's responsibility was to use his prospecting magic to point to the spot where the first well should be drilled.

On Thursday night, December 15, 1899, Brea Cañon Oil Company had the biggest gusher Los Angeles had ever seen. This gusher produced high quality oil that measured a desirable "25 gravity," which compared

Dan Murphy, second from the left, and his crew, at the Brea Cañon Oil Company office at the oil field. Circa 1920.

to the heavier crude ("16–17 gravity") that other producers in the region were pumping out of the ground. The Brea Cañon Oil Company contracted its production for five years to the AT&SF at $1.25/barrel. The railroad realized its goal of independence and was assured of having a good supply of oil at the agreed upon price. The original gusher, well No. 1, immediately produced a thousand barrels per day. However, within two years, the price of oil fell to sixty cents a barrel due to overproduction from new oil fields. "The Santa Fe squirmed, but the contract stood, and all through the [oil] depression, Murphy received the highest price for his oil."[18]

With the production from Brea Cañon Oil Company, Doheny had fulfilled the requirements of the Santa Fe and within a few months moved on to the Kern River oil fields. Murphy soon bought out the railroad men who sat on his board. As soon as Doheny exited, Murphy invited Holterhoff to his board, a seat his friend readily accepted. It was at this time that A.A. Robinson, president of the Mexican Central Railroad, urged Doheny to inspect exuding oil pits Robinson had seen along his rail line. "And so, accompanied by Charles Canfield and A.P. Maginnis, Doheny traveled to Tampico, in a luxurious Pullman car complete with trained chef and willing porter."[19] President Diaz of Mexico gave Doheny full access to develop the country's oil resources. Maginnis followed Doheny to Mexico, becoming one of his oil field superintendents, returning to Los Angeles in 1903 to take up building ice and refrigeration plants along the Santa Fe route. Doheny sold out his oil interests to Santa Fe in 1902, he left California and went to Mexico where he achieved his legendary fame and fortune.

12

WE ASK YOUR BLESSING

Early on the morning of February 25, 1900, Antoinette Sinnott and Dan Murphy sent a telegram from San Francisco to her mother Delia in Leadville: "We leave for LA tomorrow and ask your blessing." It was signed "Nettie and Dan."[1]

Later, about 10 am in the sacristy of Saint Joseph's Church, near The Alameda, the family home she shared with her mother and sisters in San Jose, Reverend Father Walsh officiated at the couple's nuptials. A week later, the *San Francisco Examiner* ran a notice about their union with the compelling headline: "Miss Antoinette Sinnott marries Dan Murphy, a capitalist of Los Angeles." The article that followed was rich with detail:

> Only the bride's sister and Mr. and Mrs. Fred Moore of San Jose were present. The bride's mother was away in Leadville, Colorado. Mrs. Murphy wore a blue serge suit and matching hat. After a brief reception at her home, the pair will travel to Los Angeles to take up residence. Mrs. Murphy was a social belle and enjoyed art and a large circle of friends. Daniel's interests in railroad, oil, and mines have made him well known throughout the state. He has been a frequent visitor to this city and has many friends here."[2]

Needles residents were astonished when news of the marriage reached them. No one had heard of Antoinette Sinnott, nor was anyone aware that Murphy even knew a woman in San Jose. The newlyweds received numerous notes of congratulations. A letter from Needles City Councilman Colonel W.H. Bonsall, summarized the congratulatory comments:

> His marriage was a great surprise to me, and I expect,

Antoinette Eleanor Sinnott (1867–1938). Circa 1887.

to most of his friends, but I'm glad to hear of it. Such a good fellow is entitled to all the good things of this world, and a good wife is one of the best (hear that, Tom?) [a friendly challenge to Dan's brother, Tom].[3]

People were bewildered. Not even Frank Monaghan had known in advance. Murphy knew how to keep a secret and rarely spoke of his private life. The most people knew about anything personal was that his parents lived in Kansas and that he had a sister in Leadville. And certainly no one in Needles knew about the real baggage the new bride brought with her to the marriage.

In the years since Murphy had first met Antoinette Sinnott and her parents at his sister Mary's wedding in Leadville, disaster had struck her family. After a seventeen-year absence, a terribly ill John Sinnott had returned from Colorado to San Jose to be cared for by his wife Delia and their three adult daughters. He died a few weeks later, on September 19, 1897. Eight months earlier, the Sinnotts' eldest daughter, Grace Mae Weber had died of typhoid fever at the family home. Her two children, seven-year-old Helen and Charles Junior, who was just three, were suddenly left motherless.

Before he died, John had told his wife that he had a great deal of faith in his latest discovery, the Famous mine, so much faith, in fact, that he said that he had, "at last, found reserves that would protect them in the days that would come." Delia later testified in court that her husband

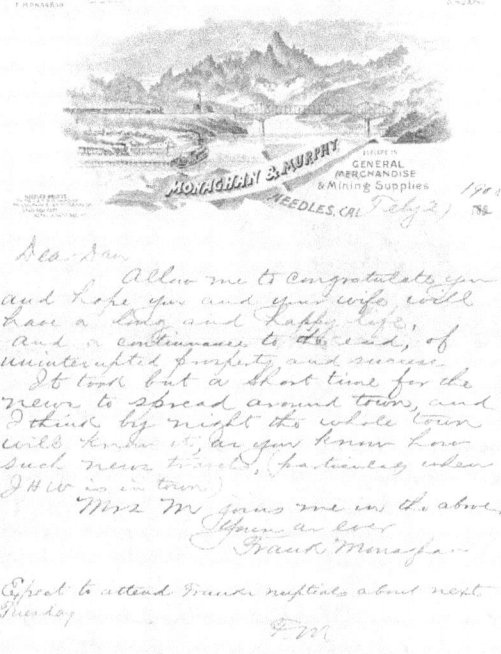

On official Monaghan & Murphy stationery, Frank Monaghan congratulated his business partner Dan Murphy on his recent wedding. 1900.

"showed me the Famous mine books with 617,219 shares of stock."[5]

On July 14, 1898, an article on the front page of the Leadville newspaper reported:

> A very important mining suit involving several millions of shares of the Famous mine's stock opened here today. The heirs of the late John Sinnott are plaintiffs and the directors of the Famous Mining Company defendants. Mrs. Delia Sinnott and her daughters from California are the heirs, and their complaint is that the directors used up the treasury stock and granted a lease to R.T. Root of Denver without the consent of the heirs and that conspiring was entered into to deprive them of their interests.[6]

Transcripts from the trial show that as soon as word of Sinnott's death reached Leadville, his mining partners, Kenneth Mathieson and William Mosher, leased the mine to R.T. Root and sold the treasury stock for a half-cent per share. Root had quickly begun digging at the mine to discover why John Sinnott thought he "finally had something." Indeed the mineworkers found rich ore deposits in a shaft conjoining

Delia Ela Sinnott (1837–1907), the matriarch. Undated.

the Famous and Dolly B mines. Mosher had placated the unsuspecting women for months: "Do not worry everything is taken care of" as tons of high-grade ore was being shipped from the site to the reduction plant. Once they found the strike, they called a board meeting, without a Sinnott present, and reelected a dummy board that promptly changed the bylaws.[7]

Soon after John Sinnott died, Delia and Nettie had gone to Leadville—in the fall of 1897—to check on the business. Unaware of who she was, Mathieson had approached Nettie on the street and offered her stock in her own mine for about three cents per share. This chance meeting tipped off the Sinnott women that they were being swindled. All of John's interest was stealthily transferred to a third party who quickly absconded with the cash. John Sinnott's family was left penniless.

The legal case was complicated because the bylaws of the mining company allowed directors to elect a new board member in the case of a death of a sitting director, a step the board had taken immediately. As plaintiffs, the Sinnott women alleged that high-grade ore had been hauled out of the Famous mine. When the court-appointed inspectors arrived, they were shown only low-grade samples and piles of poor ore stacked about the mine. The mine's high-grade veins had been hidden.[8]

Delia had asked Winters Morrell, a family friend in Leadville, to represent their interests in both the Famous mine and the adjacent Dolly B. mine. Morrell, who was married to Dan Murphy's sister Mary, would have helped, but, as he later testified in court, he believed the business was under control, since the mine had been leased. What he did not know was that the lease had been made without the Sinnott women's knowledge, and they were cut out of the deal.

Antoinette and her mother Delia hurriedly hired a lawyer in Leadville to investigate how this could have happened and to file a suit. The

Delia Sinnott and Mary Murphy Morrell on the porch of Delia's cottage 702 Pine St., Leadville. Mary and her husband Winters Morrell lived a few blocks away at 216 East 9th St., Leadville.

Sinnotts had inherited nearly 90% of the stock and were therefore entitled to legal control. Delia returned to California, and her namesake daughter Delia wrote to John's former partner, Mosher:

> My dear friend, I have been expecting to hear from you any day since our mother's return from Leadville. My lawyer has just returned from the East ... Lawyers are very slow to act. Sometimes it makes me wish I were a man or in a position to get out and act for myself. I realize I have quite a responsibility, on my hands in knowing just how to act in the best advantage for us all, and shall be very glad to take you at your word that you will be a friend to us and work in our interest. ...
>
> We are very anxious to do something with the property that will bring us money, and at as early date as possible. Trusting that everything will be done satisfactorily to all concerned, and with kindest regards to your wife and yourself, I am sincerely, Delia Sinnott.[9]

The trial and questioning continued throughout the summer. The defendant's lawyer and witnesses maligned the women: "It is to the best interest of Mrs. Sinnott to sell, because she is a woman, and can't run a mine."[10]

Much of the questioning was meant to make the women look unresponsive and disinterested in the mine and wholly unable to understand the complexity of a lease, stock transfers, and business in general. To make matters worse, the majority of the papers, clarifying evidence and correspondence that the Sinnotts had in San Jose were all sent by express to Leadville, and subsequently lost. But, they were never delivered or found in the dead-letter box at the post office.

When Winters Morrell was questioned, regarding the critical letter, he said he thought he had "pigeonholed" it. Mary was called to the witness stand to clarify:

> Question: "Do you remember a letter received by your husband from Delia Sinnott?"
> Answer: "I do."
> Question: "What disposition does he make of these letters?"
> Answer: "He generally leaves them around the secretary, and when they accumulate, to a certain extent, I burn them up."[11]

The "stubbornly fought" case of Sinnott vs. Mosher, concluded with Delia Sinnott prevailing on twenty-two counts, each of which the court overruled in her favor. The newspapers reported that the Sinnotts were now in control of the mine "valued at $100,000" (more than $3 million in 2020 dollars). An undated newspaper article regarding the outcome was carefully clipped and pasted into Antoinette's scrapbook, with the notation "Ha Ha!" next to the headline, "Atty. Burchard Won the Case." It was a cynical remark, as the Sinnott's themselves realized very little money. After legal expenses they were nearly destitute.[12]

Delia had already moved to Leadville to be on top of things. Being cut off from all income, save the daughters' teaching salary, she wrote to her widowed son-in-law Charles Weber in Stockton. Delia wrote to Weber: "I have ten dollars left, and I need you to cosign a note to borrow $500 for living expenses."[13]

Weber refused her request.

Mary Morrell felt somewhat responsible for the Sinnotts' situation. She and Winters were called to testify. She kept her brother Dan Murphy apprised of the Sinnotts' impoverished situation. It was eight months after the conclusion of the trial that Murphy struck oil, but given his vul-

We Ask Your Blessing

Grace Mae Weber and her son Charles. Grace was Antoinette's oldest sister who died not long after this photo was made. Dan and Antoinette Murphy wanted to adopt Charles after they married in 1900. Circa 1895.

nerable emotional condition after leaving Needles, he might have heard the pleas of the destitute Sinnott women as a sign from God.

While the trial was going on in 1898, Murphy was still single. He had heard some of the details at the Denver District Court, and he also had heard about Morrell declining to get involved. Morrell had placidly accepted "that everything had been attended to." Murphy's realization that his brother-in-law did not come to the rescue of the Sinnotts, beyond a doubt, greatly distressed him.[14]

Deciding to act, Dan saved the day. In the process, he found a ready-made family. Or, did Antoinette plant that thought in his head? The plan had been for Dan to marry Nettie, adopt her late-sister Grace's motherless son, Charlie, and as a lifelong commitment, he would support the four remaining women of the Sinnott household. He and Nettie agreed this would be the best approach, so they married.

The question of them having children, other than the adoption of little Charlie Weber, must have come up. They must have assumed that the boy was a burden to his now-widowed father, who was also busy with the management of his vast ranch. However, seven-year-old Charlie was in the care of his unmarried Aunt Julia Weber. According to family legend, the question of Charlie's adoption was left up to the seven-year-old boy. In retrospect, it is unconscionable that Nettie didn't know that little Charlie and Aunt Julia would not be separated. Why didn't she know that the now seven-year-old Charlie didn't want to be adopted? He had been living with his forty-seven-year-old Aunt Julia since his mother's

Susan Stone Sinnott (1867–1945). Circa 1898.

death. Nettie did know, after all, that Dan's primary reason for marrying was to have a male heir. Perhaps that point was overshadowed by her primary goal: to maintain the Sinnott family lifestyle at The Alameda in San Jose? The very thought of living in uncultured Needles was out of the question as far as Antoinette was concerned.

At the conclusion of the Denver trial in August of 1900, Nettie left her husband of only seven months and asked her twenty-one-year-old sister Sue to "take the waters" with her at the very fashionable White Sulfur Springs, a spa in the village of St. Helena, in California's Napa Valley. The Sinnott sisters wasted no time living the exalted lifestyle of their dreams on Dan Murphy's bank account.[15]

Widow Delia Sinnott remained in Leadville to look after her family's other mining claims, so she purchased a tiny Leadville cottage at 702 Pine St. Meanwhile, her other daughters—Delia (her namesake), thirty-eight, and Kathryn, thirty-four—continued to live at The Alameda, which was near their work. The younger Delia held a teacher's certificate from San Jose Normal School and taught at the nearby Washington Elementary School. Kathryn, who taught kindergarten in San Jose, had sued the City of San Jose for six months' salary because the city had claimed that the newly formed kindergarten was not part of the school system. Fortunately for Miss Sinnott, the courts found otherwise, and she received her $65 in back pay.[16]

Frank Monaghan and Dan Murphy did not quit the mining industry in Needles entirely. Nor did they abandon their friends in the town they had built. They invested in businesses that their friends were developing. In 1906, Murphy was named president of the Cocopah Copper Company, which was a group of mines about seventy miles northwest of Needles. Murphy organized the company for the PLIC. The Santa Fe had a spur off the Mojave line north to Ivanpah which was within hauling distance of the mine. In 1906, the price of copper had risen enough to make these mines profitable. The ore was hauled by Santa Fe and provided added revenue. The Cocopah articles of incorporation listed E.P. Ripley, president of the Santa Fe, and several PLIC directors, including A.G. Wells and Godfrey Holterhoff as founding shareholders. Dr. Godshall, a Needles businessman and mine owner, became managing director. What was critical to Murphy was that the Cocopah Copper Company and Santa Fe Railroad helped buoy the local mining industry.[17] The following year, both Murphy and Monaghan were appointed to the statewide advisory committee of the California Miners Association.

For several years, Monaghan served as a board member of Southwestern Miners Association (SMA). With its offices in downtown Los Angeles, SMA had several hundred members and was an information clearinghouse for the mining industry. Its membership organized an exhibit of minerals that displayed the riches found throughout the Southwest. The exhibition included many rich ore samples that would be valued at more than $300,000 in 2020 dollars. Monaghan headed a committee of three that transferred the exhibit to the Los Angeles Chamber of Commerce after the miners' association dissolved the organization. A few years later, it was turned over to the Los Angeles County Museum of Natural History where it remains the core of the museum's Gem and Mineral Hall exhibit.[18]

As Murphy and Monaghan busied themselves with mining affairs, Nettie and Sue spent their time visiting their other sisters in San Jose and took occasional trips east to shop. Charlie Weber III's decision to remain in the care of his Aunt Julia changed the direction of a number of lives and the fate of the Murphy fortune. Dan and Nettie Murphy never conceived a child.

13

INDIAN TERRITORY

Brea Cañon Oil quickly turned into an unexpected fortune for forty-two-year-old Murphy. Not since the 1887 strike at his Josephine mine had Murphy experienced such a financial bonanza. This time, however, his oil wealth far exceeded any money he had made mining gold.

By 1899, Murphy had opened his first office on the top floor of Los Angeles's newest office building at 317 S. Broadway. Built for ceramics magnate Homer Laughlin 1896–1898 and designed by the notable Los Angeles architect John Parkinson, the six-story Beaux-Arts style building was Los Angeles's first steel-framed, reinforced-concrete building, and the six-story structure was touted by the press as "California's finest" office building. One of the first things Murphy did was to hire Howard King Bagley as his secretary. Bagley, who worked for Murphy for nearly forty years, continued in the employ of the Dan Murphy Company long after Murphy's death, eventually serving as president of several of Murphy's companies.[1]

Brea Cañon limited its drilling to the acreage under Murphy's 1899 purchase. Unlike most other oilmen, Murphy did not pursue additional oil fields. He just kept drilling on his own land. His second gusher was three years later in 1902. "Well, No. 12 on the Brea Cañon ... gave a surprise party. Shortly after noon without warning, it broke loose, and for five hours it was the best thing in Orange County."[2]

"The well gushed ... 43,000 barrels a day for periods of ten or fifteen minutes, and the first year it flowed an average of 1,000 to 1,600 barrels daily. It is a gusher and never has been put on the pump."[3]

A year after this remarkable well first started to produce, the *Los Angeles Times* ran a retrospective of well No. 12's magnitude.

> "Fullerton Producer Best in America—Record Of Brea Cañon Oil Gusher Can't Be Equaled" ... A prominent representative of the Standard Oil Company ...declared

"Gas roaring" at Brea Cañon. Photo taken by Dan Murphy at the moment that well #28 blew open on the evening of February 5, 1916.

yesterday that the best oil producer in America ... The well referred to is No. 12 on the Brea Cañon Oil Company ... which was brought in over eighteen months ago, and alone has made the company several hundred thousand dollars. The record of this producer places it in the front rank, and according to the Standard man it is the best in the world, with the exception of a few oil spouters in Russia.[4]

Brea Cañon's production far surpassed the Santa Fe's needs, and the excess was sold to Standard Oil. Oil from Brea Cañon and other local producers was transported to Redondo Beach docks by the Pacific Coast Oil Company, so it could be shipped to Standard's refinery. Railroad tank cars were used for this thirty-five mile journey to the coast where it was loaded onto steamships and shipped via the San Francisco Bay to the Standard Oil refinery in Richmond, California, a trip of nearly four hundred nautical miles.[5] Murphy knew that Standard Oil was making plans for a second refinery in California, that would be dubbed El Segundo. Murphy also purchased land around the proposed refinery before the newspapers printed the news of it being built. With this knowledge, Murphy again found himself "in on the ground floor," and in time, became the largest stockholder in Standard Oil of California.[6]

When Standard Oil built the El Segundo refinery in 1911, it was not intended to be the immense plant that it eventually became. The plan was simply to supply Southern California with gasoline and kerosene. When Union Oil president Lyman Stewart heard of Standard's plan to build a refinery he remarked that "this is somewhat of a mysterious move in that Standard has no territory in this vicinity...." In Gerald White's definitive history of Standard Oil Company, *Formative Years in the Far West*, he speculates regarding the installation of the refinery:

> Perhaps Standard had taken options on the crude for which it contracted as El Segundo neared completion. The Murphy [Brea Cañon] production, it is said, was arranged for before construction began, although the exact terms were debated for some months.[7]

What Stewart was questioning is: What brought Standard Oil to Southern California since it had no local source of oil? In addition to Murphy's wells were twelve more wells belonging to William Valentine of the Fullerton Oil Company. Valentine and Murphy were the first to contract their production to Standard. Together they were able to supply three thousand barrels of crude per day to the new refinery. It is realistic that Murphy influenced Standard Oil to build a refinery in 1911 and that all along part of the plan was to install a four-inch pipeline from Fullerton/Brea Cañon to El Segundo. Less than ten years later, Standard sold 1,400 acres of oil leases to Murphy and Valentine.[8]

William Valentine, in addition to owning Fullerton Oil, served, with Murphy, as vice-president of the First National Bank. They both were members of two prestigious private clubs, the California Club and the Midwick Country Club. Valentine is known as the co-founder of San Marino, California. When George S. Patton, San Marino's first mayor, was in Europe, Valentine filled in as mayor. Valentine married Louise Chandler Robinson, whose father was the founder of the J.W. Robinson department store. The Murphy and Valentine families would be close friends for the remainder of their lives.

Godfrey Holterhoff had particular influence over Murphy and was in turn in need of some of Murphy's expertise. The Santa Fe had built a three-hundred-mile-long spur rail line into the Oklahoma Territory. In 1906, the fledgling town of Tulsa was plagued with poor quality water since the town's shallow wells were located too near the river. When Holterhoff heard about the situation in Tulsa, he immediately thought of his friend Murphy who had resolved a similar situation more than twenty years earlier in Needles. Holterhoff succeeded in convincing Murphy to take a look at the situation to see if he could help out.

However, Murphy had mixed emotions about going. The Indian Territory was rife with opportunists taking advantage of the Native Americans. The indigenous people had been forced off their tribal lands and onto this federally designated reservation. Murphy was averse to getting involved, since he was sensitive to the plight of Native Americans from his childhood days in Kansas. Perhaps Dan was drawn to the situation by the belief that he could help these people attain their fundamental human right to freshwater.

At the end of the Civil War, the Indian Territory had been reduced to about the size of present-day Oklahoma. The land was held in common among the Native Americans, referred to as the Five Civilized Tribes: Cherokee, Choctaw, Chickasaw, Creek, and Seminole. Treaties with any tribe that had sided with the Confederates during the Civil War were rescinded, further reducing the size of Indian land holdings. Post-Civil War laws required that each Indian man, woman, and child be assigned a specific 160-acre section. However, if individuals were of mixed tribal heritage, they were required to declare their allegiance to a single tribe, thus reducing the amount of land to which they were entitled. Laws such as these were divisive to the Native people and contributed significantly to the loss of their tribal culture. This was especially ironic, since private ownership of land was a foreign concept to Native Americans.[9]

Cherokee grazing lands had been leased to white settlers for a profit. In 1893, President Benjamin Harrison put an end to this practice, which forced the indigenous people to sell their land at reduced prices and led to the 1893 Land Rush. Anthropologists believe most of the area's Native people were descendants of the Mississippian Culture, which gave rise to the great Cahokia settlement, east of present-day St. Louis. The date of this settlement has been traced as far back as 680 AD, when the Cahokia had grown to forty thousand inhabitants, North America's largest urban center, until the city of Philadelphia exceeded it in the late 1700s.[10]

Upon his arrival in Tulsa, Murphy was surprised to find his old friend PDC Ball.[11] Ball was leasing land in the area for oil development. Murphy set out to improve the water quality, just as he had done in Needles, using Phil Ball's pumps and providing ice using his refrigeration equipment, again, just as he had done in Needles. Murphy, Ball, and two local businessmen acquired the Tulsa Water, Light, Heat and Power Company. According to an oil journal of the time, they were "constructing a four-story icehouse and cold storage plant to cost $300,000, which ought to be the biggest chill on the Arkansaw."[12]

As an oilman, Murphy took an interest in the Indian Territory's oil fields.[13] Earlier in 1899, the Santa Fe ran a rail line into the territory's oil-rich town of Bartlesville, about forty-five miles north of Tulsa. In those days, oil pooled at the surface so much so that the first well produced an abundance of oil at a depth of only thirty feet. Bartlesville was in a frenzy of oil leasing. George Getty, a lawyer from Minneapolis, came to Oklahoma in 1904. He was trading leases in Bartlesville while his twelve-year-old son, J. Paul Getty, was selling newspapers around town. In 1914, the younger Getty, at twenty-four, bought half interest in his first well in Bartlesville, with five hundred dollars. When the well came in a month later, J. Paul Getty sold his interest making $11,000 in profit, and his career in oil had begun.[14] But like Getty, Murphy, too, couldn't help but make money on oil—in the same town.

Government law did not allow tribal members to sell their assigned acreage, so the Native American land owners cleverly leased the land to speculators for oil extraction. To this end, the Los Angeles Cherokee Oil Company was incorporated; Murphy was president with controlling interest along with five officers of the AT&SF-Western Division executives acting as the PLIC, including Holterhoff. On May 19, 1904, *Paul's Valley Sentinel* newspaper splashed a headline that said Cherokee Oil Company "Is Paying Fancy Prices" and reported that "the Cherokee citizens of that community [Tulsa] are in high spirits ... last week $10,000 passed into the hands of the people."

The Los Angeles Cherokee Oil Company deposited $120,000 into its Tulsa bank for use as lease payments to the Native Americans. Prior to Murphy's arrival on the scene, the leasing of oil-rich Native lands had been ongoing for several years. Eastern investors had, over time, lowered the percentage paid to the Native Americans. In contrast, Murphy offered them the same percentage as their original lease agreement, which is a ten-year lease; paying 10% of production on top of $50 per year for each well. It was a square deal for the times and a "fancy price," at that. This venture would prove successful: one year later a Los Angeles Cherokee Oil Company well, located two miles north of Tulsa, started producing fifty barrels a day. True to Murphy's business savvy, he had already started drilling several more wells, which were currently underway.[15]

One day in early February 1916, Murphy was working late at Brea Cañon. Well No. 28 had been drilled down 3,500 feet—oil-bearing depth—but no oil. For several days, the crew had been trying to get the oil flowing by using the usual suction procedure, and they were confident the well would come in at any time. Just after sunset, there was a deafening roar that shook the little wood-framed office where Murphy was sitting. Oil and gas shot thousands of feet into the night sky, and within a few minutes, droplets of oil were raining down over the entire countryside. The sound of the spouting well could be heard for miles around. Drillers and oilmen from nearby properties flocked to the site. Under Murphy's direction, all the boilers and kerosene lamps in the area were immediately extinguished to prevent a tremendous explosion. Oil began to stream down the hillside—the well was definitely flowing. Within hours, the workmen miraculously brought it under control, despite the darkness and overwhelming smell of gas in the air.[16]

The blowing in of Brea Cañon's well No. 28 was reported in the *Los Angeles Times*, and by the next morning, there was a convergence of "automobile parties from many parts of Orange and Los Angeles counties. Visitors could hear the roar of the escaping gas a mile down the canyon before reaching the well." The well was allowed to blow off the gas for several days, after which the oil was flowing at a rate of three thousand barrels a day—even without pumps.[17]

Murphy was overjoyed, but this was No. 28. It had been twelve years since wells No. 19 and No. 20 had let go in gushers. Nine wells later, no

Brea Cañon Oil Company's derricks. Circa 1910.

one from Brea Cañon had recorded how many failures had preceded the big one, but there also were no reports of gushers in between. No. 28 was the fifth and the last gusher reported at Brea Cañon. The first, at well No. 1, in 1899, was at a depth of 1,100 feet. No. 19 and No. 20 came in at 2,100 feet.[18] Five years later, No. 32 was down 4,200 feet with "very little oil."[19] The field was going dry; the oilmen moved on to new land at Huntington Beach and Long Beach. By the time World War I was at its most intense, oil prices had risen steadily since the beginning of the war in 1914. Los Angeles Cherokee Oil Company in Oklahoma was a reliable producer. The financial outlook in 1916 was good for Murphy.[20]

14

Champs-Elysees

At the beginning of the twentieth century, the population of Los Angeles was slightly more than one hundred thousand, having doubled in size over the last decade. The growth of the city from its original pueblo plaza had pushed southward during the 1870s and 1880s. The town's leading citizens built impressive Victorian homes that lined Main and Figueroa Streets to the south. The east–west streets were hardly more than graded dirt trails at the time and they ran westward toward the Pacific Ocean in broad parallel avenues. They had historical names such as Pico, Washington, Adams, and Jefferson.

The topography west of downtown rises gently above the surrounding basin with a marked south-facing slope. In time, the most elegant mansions of the city were built along this ridge with their vast, sloping lawns, sites that took advantage of the sweeping views of the Pacific in the distance. Late-afternoon sea breezes, mountain views, and proximity to downtown combined to make this a highly desirable residential location.

West Adams Boulevard extended from Figueroa Street on the east near Chester Place to Crenshaw Boulevard on the west, a distance of only three-and-a-half miles. This stretch of West Adams estates became the Champs-Elysees of Los Angeles. It remained so until the late 1910s. The Murphys chose this neighborhood for their residence. To appreciate their married life and their social standing, it is essential to see the evolution of this influential district of Los Angeles named West Adams.

Just southwest of downtown on Figueroa Street was a large tract of land that had been donated in 1880 for a Methodist Episcopal Church College, the neighborhood that was to become the University of Southern California. Once the college became established, the blocks around it were developed. Murphy purchased a new two-story home at 2858 Orchard Ave, near the college. Because Murphy had a lifelong hobby as a photographer, he himself usually took the pictures, so only one image,

Dan and Nettie Murphy's newly built first home at 2858 Orchard Ave., Los Angeles. Circa 1902.

taken by a professional photographer, captures the two of them smiling on the stairs of their new home. By the time the photo was taken, Murphy was already enjoying his newfound oil profits and continued to pull in more than a million dollars annually from Monaghan & Murphy General Store in Needles. Yet theirs was a modest home, another example of his humble, unassuming character. In this post-Victorian era, men made the investment and housing decisions.

West Adams Boulevard was the main thoroughfare passing just north of the college. In the late 1890s, it became one of the first streets to have concrete curbs, sidewalks, and shade trees. The same year that Murphy's first oil well came in, an ultra-private, twenty-three-lot enclave opened near the crossroads of Adams and Figueroa, named Chester Place. The exclusive sector sat on land that had once been owned by Murphy's friend Nathan Vail, an eastern sea captain. Murphy, Vail and a few other investors had formed the Redondo Beach Development Company, the very beach where Vail tragically drowned before he could see Chester Place developed. Vail's friend Charles Silent, an Arizona Territory federal judge went on to develop the enclave. Decorative iron gates

Dan Murphy at his new home on Orchard Avenue in Los Angeles. Circa 1901.

and massive stone columns topped with urns marked the entrance to Chester Place. One of the first homes constructed was a French Gothic three-story mansion, at No. 8 Chester Place, built and furnished like a rustic hunting lodge. Edward L. Doheny and his new wife, Carrie Estelle Betzold Doheny bought the twenty-two-room furnished home shortly after it was completed.[1]

Years before Vail and Silent created their gated community, two female luminaries had retirement residences in the West Adams district. First was social justice and women's rights advocate, Caroline Maria Seymour Severance. She had moved to West Adams in 1875 from Boston. She was a devoted suffragist who helped Susan B. Anthony establish the American Equal Rights Association in 1867, but Madame Severance, as she was respectfully called, founded the First Unitarian Church in Los Angeles and began the kindergarten movement. She became known as the "Mother of Women's Clubs," and was especially well-known for her Friday Morning Club, which had its own lending library, classes, and focused on civic reform. Progressives flocked to her West Adams neighborhood home that she had dubbed El Nido (The Nest), after her husband

Dan and Nettie Murphy on the stairs of their Orchard Avenue home. Circa 1902.

died. The Murphys' residence on Orchard Avenue was just around the corner from hers.

Jessie Benton Fremont, wife of California's first senator, John C. Fremont (known as "The Pathfinder"), lived not more than a block away. It is curiously fitting that the daughter of Senator Thomas Hart Benton, the advocate of western movement or Manifest Destiny, should spend her last days in Southern California. John and Jessie's final years were a hardship. Fremont had lost his fortune in the reorganization of the Pacific Railroad, the predecessor of the Atlantic & Pacific Railroad. When he was in the East trying to raise funds, he died alone in a hotel room in New York City in the summer of 1890. Jessie and her daughter Elizabeth were left destitute. But the women of Los Angeles came to their aid by taking up a collection to build a home for Jessie and Elizabeth, just one block off of West Adams at 1107 W. 28th St. There, the women were visited by numerous dignitaries.[2]

Antoinette Sinnott Murphy was having trouble adjusting to life in Los Angeles. She missed her friends in San Jose and especially her sisters. At first, she knew no one, nor was Dan well-known in the city. His friends were railroad and oil men. Fortunately for Nettie, her husband had unlimited free passes on the Santa Fe, so she took full advantage of this benefit and traveled to San Jose as often as she wished. Nettie and her twenty-four-year-old sister Sue not only took shopping trips to Chicago and New York, but it was Sue who had accompanied Nettie on the excursion to White Sulfur Springs spa, soon after her marriage. Sue moved in permanently with Dan and Nettie soon after they bought their home in Los Angeles.

Once Antoinette realized the extent of her husband's fortune, she started pressuring him for a bigger, better home— their new home on Orchard was too modest and diminutive for her. Ever since she had come to Southern California, she longed for a grand home in the very best neighborhood that was commensurate with their ever-growing wealth, a showplace where she could entertain in style. She wanted a place where she could practice her gardening and still have the dignified privacy the couple deserved. So Murphy assembled more than twelve acres on West Adams Boulevard, definitely the best neighborhood in Los Angeles at the time, the chic predecessor to Hancock Park and Beverly Hills. Murphy named their acreage on West Adams "The Antoinette Tract" in his wife's honor. She immediately began interviewing architects and had several draw up detailed elevations of the proposed mansion.

The West Adams district forms a large part of the city's Western Addition, and by 1900, a tremendous building boom was underway there. In time, other unique enclaves took shape just a few blocks east along the boulevard. One of these was the site of homes for the Pacific Mutual Life Insurance Company's board of directors, an area with a village feel called Harvard Heights. The insurance company owned a large interest in the nearby sixty-five-acre Rosedale Cemetery. Pacific Mutual's chairman, Frederick Hastings Rindge, the millionaire son of a Boston wool merchant, owned the thirteen thousand-acre Malibu Ranch. The ocean frontage of his ranch became the playground for movie stars and would later be home to the "Malibu movie colony." But during the 1920s, Rindge built a twenty-five-room faux French chateau in Harvard Heights.[3] Several of his neighbors were associated with either the University of Southern California or the Pacific Mutual Life Insurance Company. Pacific Mutual's president, George Ira Cochran, and its vice-president, Charles I.D. Moore, could trace their heritage to John Wesley, the founder of Methodism.[4] Rindge was also the founder of the Harvard-Epworth United Methodist Church in Cambridge, Massachusetts. USC had incorporated in 1880 by the Methodist Episcopal Church and remained affiliated with the church until 1958.

Several other Harvard Heights residents were trustees of USC. One of them was Harvey Mudd, who was born in Leadville, Colorado, the son of Seeley W. Mudd, a mining engineer with the Guggenheim Exploration Company. Seeley Mudd discovered gold in the same region as Murphy's Josephine mine. His son Harvey mined copper in Arizona at the same time that Murphy was running the Cocopah Copper Company on the California side of the Colorado River. Both Murphy and Harvey Mudd were trustees of the Throop College of Technology, renamed California Institute of Technology (Caltech) in 1920. Although they had much in common, the two families were not socially united. Seeley and his son Harvey were college-educated miners and pursued large-scale, scientific, industrial mining. Murphy, on the other hand, had been more of a prospector/investor type of miner, and by the time he met Mudd, his interests had shifted to oil. The school's interest in Murphy was no doubt purely financial. The insurance company executives and university trustees from Harvard Heights were not part of the social life of the predominantly Catholic West Adams Boulevard neighborhood. In the corridor between elegant West Adams and Pico Boulevard, one mile north, there were eight major Roman Catholic institutions. From east to west: Saint Vincent de Paul Church (1925), Saint Agnes Church (1903), Loyola High School (1917), Saint Thomas the Apostle Church (1904), Catholic Girls High School (1923), Good Shepherd Convent (1904), Saint John's Military Academy (1918), and Saint Paul's Church (1917).[5]

Another West Adams Boulevard family whose fortune came from mining was William Andrews Clark Jr., son of the "Copper King" of Butte, Montana. Clark Sr. was considered one of America's wealthiest individuals. His son founded the Los Angeles Philharmonic orchestra. In 1926, Clark Jr. also built the lavish Clark Memorial Library on his West Adams property, home to one of the nation's largest rare book and manuscript collections.[6] Murphy assembled his twelve-acre plot, nearly opposite Clark's estate on West Adams Boulevard.[7]

Murphy was busy with Brea Cañon Oil. He had sunk twelve wells in two years between his first gusher and well No. 12 which became the "best producer" in the country. This was quite a rapid process for 1902. Daily he would leave his Orchard Avenue home by buggy to get to the Wilmington train line. From there, it was a quick one-hour ride to Fullerton, where he took another buggy for the last few miles to his oil field. He returned at the end of the workday by the same route. To Nettie and Sue at home, it appeared to be a boring routine. For Dan, it was his work and it took him out of the house to be amongst his friends and employees.

Two months after the No. 12 oil well came in with a bang, Murphy received a telegram from his brother Tom in Hays, Kansas. "Father is very low—not gaining—we have very little hope." The telegram was time-stamped 4:21 pm on October 6, 1902. By this time, their parents were a kindly, simple couple in their seventies. They lived in a Victorian two-story home at 226 W. 12th St. in Hays, near Saint Joseph's Catholic Church where they were well-known. Although Murphy had always visited his parents annually, his trip to the Midwest must have felt endless this time. With connections, he was on the train nearly two days.

This was a trip Murphy always knew he'd have to make someday—his father had been in failing health for several years and had been confined to bed since late September. Visits to Kansas had been increasingly difficult for Murphy. He had grown distant from his parents and siblings. They had less in common over the years of separation. Now that he was finally married, they no doubt chided him about when he was going to have his own children. Little did they know the pain these harmless barbs caused him. Perhaps that is why Nettie was not by his side at his father's funeral, or perhaps she simply didn't feel the need to cultivate a relationship with his family.

Neither Nettie nor Sue accompanied him on this particular trip from Los Angeles to Kansas. In fact, there is no record that Nettie ever met her in-laws, and she never mentions them in her correspondence. Murphy thoughtfully sent an optimistic telegram home to Nettie:

> Much improved, counted the hours, then minutes, until
> I arrived and much pleased with [his] condition.
> Signed Dan Murphy, 10:55 a.m. Oct 9-02.[8]

His positive outlook did not prevail. His father died at 7:45 on the night of October 15.

The local newspaper reported in his obituary that Thomas Murphy "waited patiently for the moment murmuring: 'Jesus, thy will be done' and 'into thy hands I commend my spirit.'" The obituary continued: "His house has ever been a social center for all classes and ages of people. Such hospitality and genuine cordiality are seldom combined in so active a life." These were values passed on and instilled in his sons. "It was one of the largest funerals ever held in the county" with scores of mourners, with three priests presiding at the solemn high mass at Saint Joseph's.[9]

There are no extant communications between Dan and Nettie from their years on Orchard Avenue, just a few newspaper clippings and telegrams that Nettie had saved. Dan was slowly relinquishing control of his home life, but at age forty-five, he was in full swing as an oilman, often losing himself in his work. He was dejected over his failed plans to adopt a boy to be his heir, but there was little to interest him at home. He was busy buying West Adams properties to assemble enough land to build the home Antoinette had been harping about. Otherwise, the two women in his household seemed content, more interested in entertaining themselves by making frequent trips to see their remaining two sisters at The Alameda in San Jose, leaving Dan to fend for himself.

15

"Aunt" Sue

In the fall of 1903, the Murphys' homelife came crashing down. It came as devastating news to Dan and Nettie when Sue confessed that she was pregnant. In those days virginity, modesty, chastity, and purity were expected virtues of a single young woman. To her sister and brother-in-law, her pregnancy was an unspeakable disgrace, an enormous shame for a single girl—even though Sue was twenty-seven at the time. Antoinette, who was nearly ten years older, was aghast and furious with her little sister. Murphy demanded to know who the father was. All that Sue would divulge was that he was an Italian prince named Ruspoli, a married man.[1]

The Murphys' social life had barely gotten off the ground in Los Angeles. If word got out, Nettie feared, it would mean the ruination of the entire family name—including that of the Sinnotts who were left in San Jose. The Murphys were desperate to do whatever they could to conceal her pregnancy and avoid scandal. Since abortions at the time resulted in a fifty percent chance of the death for both mother and child, such a drastic step was not an option. Not to mention that the Murphys were devout Catholics.

The emotional upheaval in the household must have been enormous. The disgrace the Murphys felt was only worsened by their religious training. Because Murphy was a generous benefactor of the church, he sought counsel from His Excellency, the Most Reverend Thomas J. Conaty, the newly appointed bishop of Monterey and Los Angeles. The bishop advised sending Sue to a children's hospital and orphanage run by the Sisters of Mercy in upstate New York. He made the arrangements.

On December 9, 1903, Bishop Conaty was returning to Los Angeles from the East, and scheduled a meeting with the Mother Provincial of the Sisters of the Good Shepherd of St. Louis; she met him at the Kansas City depot. He requested that she send nuns to Los Angeles, since he de-

Sue Sinnott. Circa 1920.

termined the city was in urgent need of a Magdalene Laundry, an asylum for wayward women.[2]

Mother Provincial and her assistant arrived in Los Angeles the following month, and the two immediately scouted a site for their home for "fallen women," plus a convent. They found a desirable location, but were concerned that the neighbors may object to their Laundry. Therefore, the bishop asked Murphy to buy the $25,000 property in his name, which he did in January 1904, making a significant down payment of $5,000. The church then covered the remainder of the bank loan, which the Sisters of the Good Shepherd paid back without interest. The original Magdalene Laundry and convent was a four-story red brick building on the corner of Pico and Arlington at 3326 West Pico Blvd. Donations came from the home's women's auxiliary, of which Nettie was named treasurer, but the majority of the repayment was from the Murphy family, who probably deemed the restitution to be a fitting penance to absolve Sue of philandering.

On June 2, 1904, Sue, who had been in New York for her entire pregnancy, gave birth to a baby girl whom she named Bernardine Dan. A few weeks later, Sue left the child in the care of the orphanage and returned to Los Angeles. The family was forever indebted to Bishop Conaty for helping them avert a scandal. No one ever knew the truth except the Sinnott sisters in San Jose. Antoinette and her sisters all agreed not to tell their mother about Sue's disgrace.

During the same month that Bernardine was born, four bedraggled nuns stepped off the SP Sunset Limited after two days and two nights of traveling across the deserts from New Orleans. They had come to Los Angeles to staff the Magdalene Laundry. These white-clad nuns with black veils, Sisters of the Good Shepherd, were on their mission to care for fallen women in the City of Angels. They were given temporary housing at the convent of the Sisters of Saint Joseph at 12th Street at Grand Avenue. Within days they found a vacant home to rent.

Two days after the nuns had settled in, the first client arrived. Wayward girls were sent by the civil courts or they arrived at the door, desperate because they were abandoned or homeless. There was "a Mexican woman abandoned by her husband and sent by the court from the hospital where her child had been born."[3] As soon as the nuns had found their place, donations of household goods began arriving. Many local Los Angeles women "regardless of class or creed" contributed. Nettie's good friend Frances Hampton contributed beds and bedding for the home.

The Sisters of the Good Shepherd's first building was a three-story brick convent, which included a school and dormitory with a chapel. The building was a half-block long and seventy-five-feet deep structure that was blessed and dedicated on June 16, 1905, by Bishop Thomas J. Conaty. After the ceremony concluded, "the cloister was established, and the strict rules of the Order were enforced." From that point on, visiting guests "may be seen and talked with only through the grill of the cloister," therefore no callers were allowed on the grounds themselves.[4]

Of the first forty-five girls housed at the institution, only six were Catholic. Each was assigned a new name to protect her anonymity—or her family's. "Piety, purity, submission, and domesticity"[5] were the virtues taught to the girls.

Family or clergy brought in girls thought to be incorrigible, and others were from the court system. The usual length of stay was one year to eighteen months. Delinquent girls could leave after their mandated confinements were completed; others not under court-ordered time were free to leave at will. "The girls were separated into two classes: preservates [girls at risk for falling] and penitents [already fallen or delinquents needing reform] … Some penitents returned, and some never left." A penitent or preservate who wanted to live a cloistered life under the governance of the order was ineligible to "formally become a professed Sister." Those who chose this way of life were called Magdalens and lived in seclusion atoning for the faults of an earlier life, separated from the nuns and from the other penitents.[6]

The community received some per diem money from the judicial system, families were asked to contribute on a sliding scale, but most of their income came from the commercial laundry facility run by the wayward girls. The Magdalens also baked altar breads and embroidered vestments to earn money.[7]

Antoinette organized a lay women's group to help support the Sisters of the Good Shepherd. It was named the "Good Shepherd Auxiliary." On the day of its dedication, the auxiliary presented a $5000 check to the nuns for the establishment of a laundry facility on the grounds. The girls worked in the laundry, which was an outdoor lean-to with as many as six washtubs. The hand-scrubbed laundry was dried on outdoor clotheslines at the back of the property. Deliveries of soiled linens were made daily from downtown hotels and restaurants. The fresh laundry was picked up the next day after it was washed, ironed, and folded.

The Murphys were earnestly sympathetic to the work of the Sisters of the Good Shepherd. Antoinette and several of her friends joined the effort. These included Marion Barlow, Louise Kerckhoff, Emeline and Suzanne Childs, Gertrude Dockweiler, and the distinguished Madame Modjeska—Helena Modjeska, a noted Polish Shakespearean actress of the 1870s. She had immigrated to California in 1876 and started a utopian community in Orange County. Her interest in the Good Shepherd facility was a boon for Antoinette's auxiliary, attracting many new members.[8] Madame Modjeska said of the girls:

> Those that go into the home come out different through the wonderful influences of the Sisters. I want to see those unfortunate girls who have their lives before them saved from themselves or their associations, not because of creed, you know, but just because they are women.[9]

Antoinette and Louise Kerckhoff chaired a committee to honor Madame Modjeska. They created an event in 1905 which doubled as a fundraiser benefit for the Good Shepherd Shelter. It was held in the lobby of the Mason Opera House in downtown Los Angeles where Modjeska was performing in Shakespeare's *The Winter's Tale*. Modjeska was a frequent guest at the Murphys' West Adams home where she later inspired two neighborhood youths to successfully pursue international music careers.

Ironically, perhaps, Sue Sinnott was not involved in the laundry.

Nettie's mother Delia was still in Leadville where she had been living since the 1900 trial, anxiously looking after mines that remained in her control, mines that her deceased husband Thomas had been working for years: the Famous, Dolly B, and Ida Nice Shaft mines. Most of them had yielded as much ore as was profitable to remove, which is why Thomas had told her that he "at last, found reserves that would protect them in the days that would come."[10] He was referring to the Famous that had been tied up in legal battles for the last three years. By the time

"AUNT" SUE

the case was settled in her favor, it was too late—the mine was no longer profitable. Delia held onto the hope of making "some show."

Delia sent a letter to her son-in-law Dan on March 6, 1906:

> Received the fifty dollars you sent, which part was applied on taxes, I have until twenty-eighth of March to pay the balance due on taxes ... The taxes on Famous are over $100. I am a month behind in living expenses, have tried to even up, so I can get away for the spring months. I get very nervous staying right-along here. The Dolly B. will start up this spring.[11]

Whipple, her lawyer in the 1900 trial, had not paid the taxes, and she was about to lose the property, but her letter changes course:

> I want to ask you about Sue, I want to know her true condition, different ones are writing to me that she is looking very bad. Nettie writes that Sue lacks ambition or does not exert herself. I do not agree with Nettie on this; I wish I were in a position to have her with me for a while. I would have gone to San Jose this month if I had the show [money] to go. I do not like to be wired [telegraphed] here and not able to move when I wish to. I am, as ever, Mother [Delia Sinnott].[12]

Delia's comment about Sue's lack of ambition may indicate that Delia is wondering what is going on with her younger daughter, since she is unaware that Sue had given birth. It also sounds as if Nettie and Sue are having their own issues on Orchard Street.

The day after Delia sent that missive to her son-in-law, she followed up with yet another letter, this time sent to him in Tulsa, where he was attending to problems with the water and the Los Angeles Cherokee Oil Company:

> Letter from Nettie this a.m.... Nettie writes my telegram did not please, first I could not wire you, my reasons for wanting to see you, for they were many ... taxes due on various mines and living expenses. I am ready to resign my position any time, any of the family will take my place ... mining men say this year will be the best year for mining that Leadville has ever had ..."[13]

Delia was advised by her lawyer to release the patent on the mine, thereby enabling her adversaries to take over.

"I'm not such a da_m [damn] fool as they take me for. If I am old, I still have my fair amount of reason."[14]

An experienced mining man, Murphy knew that Leadville had been declining for the last ten years, and the mines were not even worth the taxes she was demanding. She sued the new board of directors of the Famous mine to regain control; the mining operators countered the motion, and litigation continued. With the mines not operating, she had no income, and her San Jose home, The Alameda, was in bad shape.

Murphy had been supporting her life in Leadville, but she was spending the money on taxes and more lawsuits. Delia was, in fact, a "damn fool."[15]

Within a few months, Delia signed over "all mining and other property in Colorado" to her son-in-law for $1.00. No doubt Delia did this with a certain amount of pressure from the Murphy family. Between his mother-in-law, his wife, and her sister Sue, Murphy was rightfully distressed over the women in his life.[16]

On January 26, 1907, seventy-one-year-old Delia Sinnott died. A few months before her death, she had written to Dan worried about the taxes due on her Famous mine and hopeful that her other mines would reopen in the spring. However, in the winter, living at an altitude of 10,000-feet was a challenge, and Delia caught a severe cold. Her friends Winters and Mary Morrell, now retired to Denver, brought her to their home, where she succumbed. After Delia's death, with no reason to keep daughter Bernardine a secret, Sue and Nettie wanted to bring the little girl to Los Angeles. In order to protect her true identity, the Murphys agreed to adopt her legally. The sisters went to New York City by train. This was not unusual as Nettie and Sue often went East to shop. They traveled first class with their Santa Fe rail passes. On this trip, however, the women went straight to Saint Agnes Orphanage in White Plains, New York, where they collected Bernardine, now three years and two months old. On the way home, they sent a telegram to Dan in Los Angeles, at 5:30 pm on August 28, 1907:

"Bernardine is with us. All more than delighted with her."

Signed Nettie.[17]

The women returned to Los Angeles, and their neighbors were thrilled that the Murphys had adopted a child. From that point on, Sue took up permanent residence with the Murphys and helped to raise her own daughter—their adopted daughter—Bernardine.

Little Bernardine Dan Murphy on the garden wall at the Murphy home at 2076 West Adams Blvd. Circa 1910.

It was around this time that the *San Francisco Call* ran an article about Tom Murphy in Needles. The newspaper article reported that Tom was "an inventor who promises to create a big stir in the world." It goes on stating that he had invented steel ribs for women's corsets which he patented and sold that patent for $9,000 (nearly a quarter-million dollars today). When asked how he came up with the idea, he claimed that he was able to study the human body better at Needles where dresses were the exception rather than the rule. He was also working on a lifeboat for ferry passengers. "He has planned a seat which by being turned upside down can be converted into a lifeboat." It would be the size of a bench and equipped with a life preserver. Later Tom's ingenuity as an inventor will come to play an essential role in redeeming his brother with one of his mechanisms.[18]

Dan Murphy split his time and attention between Brea Cañon and his real estate investments. He continued to work on assembling lots for their new home. Although the rampant real estate boom had ended, prices were recovering and profits were being made. He rallied his long-lost partner Monaghan to join him in investing in Los Angeles properties. Together they began purchasing city lots for speculation under the Monaghan & Murphy Company name. They bought sixteen lots in three separate tracts. Ten of these lots were in the Electric Homestead Tract, between Pico Boulevard and Ninth Street.

In 1886, the Los Angeles Electric Railway had built a line from downtown that ran west along Pico Boulevard to Lorde Street—later renamed Harvard Boulevard—on the north side of the Electric Homestead Tract. The verbiage on the railway's promotional poster created a romantic image of the route as it left downtown:

> ... gradual rise to Alvarado Street, and when the latter street is reached the country becomes a beautiful plateau, from which a fine view of the city and surrounding country is obtained. The location being elevated, there is no possible danger of malaria, and the breezes which come daily from the ocean temper the atmosphere and make the warmest days pleasant.[19]

William George Nevin was general manager of California Southern Railroad and one of the original signers incorporating Brea Cañon Oil. Together with Eli Clark, Nevin purchased a large tract of land just outside the city limits. The Pico electric streetcar line comes within a mile of the city limits at Western Avenue. Pico continued west twelve miles to the ocean. At Western and Pico was the 107-acre Los Angeles Country Club golf course.[20] On the south side of Pico was the W.G. Nevin and Clark tract which ran west six blocks to Arlington Avenue. The first two streets in the tract had oversized lots, extra-wide streets, and as marketed, had a high altitude that offered views of Hollywood to the north and the ocean to the west. The remaining streets were more typical in size. Nevin, "a man of charming personality, could tell a good story, and won some very strong friends."[21] Additionally, Nevin and Godfrey Holterhoff worked in the same office at the California Southern Railroad. On January 16, 1904, Murphy purchased the entire west end of the W.G. Nevin tract along Arlington, eleven acres that became the Magdalene Laundry.[22]

Murphy invested some of the money that came pouring in from Brea Cañon into Southern California real estate. The field produced more oil than the Santa Fe contract required. The excess was transferred by pipeline to El Segundo and sold to Standard Oil. The cash that did not go into real estate was deposited in local banks. This brought the obscure storekeeper from the desert to the attention of the directors of the First National Bank of Los Angeles. In 1905, when the bank reorganized as Los Angeles National Bank, Murphy was elected vice president. Conceivably, these Los Angeles bankers may have thought that Murphy was an expert in high finance since the Needles National Bank had, after all, had its case decided in the federal courts in Washington, D.C. He was also nominated to the Los Angeles Chamber of Commerce, a position he accepted. He was now sought after by the very businessmen he had tried to avoid. Murphy served these organizations for more than twenty years without fanfare or issue.[23]

Never one to show his wealth, he found alternative ways to invest his money quietly. Standard Oil stock was his favored investment, despite the fact that the company was manifestly unpopular on the West Coast and especially unpopular in Southern California. Local businessmen believed the giant corporation was undermining their nascent oil industry and they knew little more than what the negative press from the East had been reporting about Standard Oil. This is where the bicoastal Murphy's New York Union Club contacts proved their worth. No doubt Murphy had personal contact with the Rockefellers, since he was the largest stockholder in Standard Oil of California, a distinction he held for many decades. In addition to his stock purchases, Murphy sold Standard any Brea Cañon Oil that was not contracted to Santa Fe. All this stemmed from his relationship with Charles Crocker, who encouraged him to do business on the East Coast rather than sticking with Los Angeles enterprises.

Many of Murphy's actions reveal his preference for doing business with firms located east of his stomping grounds. He stocked his Needles store through direct purchases from enterprises such as luxury goods from Marshall Fields in Chicago, stationery directly from Crane & Co. in Massachusetts, and plumbing supplies from Cleveland Faucet Company.

Initially, his vast fortune brought him regard, but wealth without substance is just that. Seemingly overnight Murphy appears to have become the darling of Los Angeles finance. From railroad man and small-town store owner, he was thrust into the limelight. Once he became known in Los Angeles, these same high-born, college-educated men sought his advice and counsel at every opportunity. Besides board membership offers, he was asked to join the most prestigious clubs and committees. He turned down most of these overtures. A popular publication of the day, *Illustrated Weekly*, referred to Murphy as a "modest businessman who carefully avoids all ostentation."[24] His club of choice was the California Club downtown. Although he was a member of the Los Angeles Chamber of Commerce during some of the city's most turbulent years, he steered clear of contentious issues like the city's water supply. His hands were clean when it came to the Los Angeles aqueduct and the Owens River valley issues. He had the gift to "see around corners," and he avoided all controversy primarily because he lacked greed.

From left to right: Sue Sinnott, Dan and Nettie Murphy at Brea Cañon. Circa 1910.

By all measure, however, Murphy was a success in the oil business—his Brea Cañon Oil had brought him more money than most of the oilmen in Los Angeles. When Edward Doheny came back to town from Mexico in 1907, he was also awash with oil money. There were plenty of black gold fortunes in town, however. Among the most successful were Lyman Stewart, who became the chairman of Union Oil, and Doheny's old partner Charles Canfield, who struck it big in Bakersfield oil. Murphy, Doheny, Stewart, Canfield, Holterhoff, and William Kerckhoff, the city's largest lumber dealer and president of Pacific Light and Power, all joined forces to open San Diego Bank of Commerce and Trust Company.[25]

Kerckhoff was two years older than Murphy, and they initially knew each other through the ice and power business. Kerckhoff was a true industrial pioneer in Los Angeles, who came to town about the same time as Murphy. Kerckhoff went into the lumber business with his father under the name of Kerckhoff-Cuzner Mill & Lumber, and served as president. Lumber was shipped to Southern California by coal-fired steamships from the Pacific Northwest. In 1893, Kerckhoff's company converted the coal-burning ship *SS Pasadena*, to the first oil-burning, ocean-going US steamship.[26] When he later branched into the ice and cold storage business, he used the hydraulic power of the river to run the San Gabriel Power Company. His business partner, Alan C. Balch, was an electrical engineer from Cornell University. Kerckhoff and Balch incorporated San Gabriel Electric Company in 1896, transmitting electricity into Los Angeles.

Kerckhoff's parents were German immigrants who sent their son to Hanover, Germany, for his secondary school education. Murphy, having learned to speak German fluently at home in Hanover, Kansas, quickly developed a strong friendship with Kerckhoff. The friendship was enhanced by the fact that William and Louise Kerckhoff lived in an immense arts-and-crafts half-timbered mansion at 734 West Adams Blvd. Nettie and Louise worked together over the years raising funds for several of the same charitable organizations.

16

Got Nerve

Clearly, black gold had made Murphy a very wealthy man. Their Needles general merchandise store was supposed to have been only a means to an end, but it turned out to be a reliable long-term source of income. After leaving Needles, Frank inherited his father-in-law's acreage in Santa Ana and settled down with his family to make the best of it in oranges. Nearly twenty years after leaving his desert mining operations, Murphy still listed on his US passport his occupation: mining business. Why? Did he think that mining was a better moniker than oil? Perhaps he believed that searching for mineral resources was a higher calling? With his newfound wealth and business stature, Murphy could have pursued any number of paths open to him such as banking, real estate, retail, construction, or even politics. However, he had a passion that existed as early as his days on the Yuma Line. Whenever he left or returned to Los Angeles by train, he passed Slover Mountain, a mountain of pure limestone—no prospecting required.[1] However, it did not meet his requirements, especially since someone had already claimed it, and everyone knew about it. Furthermore, newspapers were critical of it.

But Murphy was haunted by Slover Mountain, a geological landmark rising more than seven hundred feet above the San Bernardino Valley floor: a mountain of pure, high-grade limestone. Throughout history, the mountain had been a landmark for Native Americans and pioneer settlers alike. The deposit is sixty miles east of downtown Los Angeles and the Southern Pacific's Yuma Line passed right by the foot of the mountain. Murphy had traveled past this mountain of lime hundreds of times. In the 1860s, Colton Marble and Lime Company had quarried it for marble. For years "it did a thriving business in marble for ornamental purposes."[2]

The white marble bases for the columns of the California Exhibit at the Chicago World's Fair were of Colton marble.[3] He recalled his days at the Chicago World's Fair with its massive *Germania* statue. He had spent many hours at the exhibit discussing the cement-making process with the German experts. He learned that Germany had perfected the characteristics of Portland cement. Processing limestone to make cement required extremely high temperatures with carefully prepared fluxes, a lot like the process of smelting ore. Limestone was pulverized and ground into a fine powder, just like the processing of ore at the Needles Smelter. Murphy felt he understood it.

In 1891, five people owned the deposit at Slover Mountain. Incorporated as California Portland Cement Company, the plant was built at the base of the mountain using its limestone as raw material.[4] The owners struggled with the production process from the start. To make quality Portland cement, it takes exacting methods.

Bad press plagued the company and their problems were reported in an article titled "Inferior Cement Contractor Has Trouble." Just as the city was pouring their first curbs and sidewalks using California Portland Cement, the newspaper pointed out that the cement never hardened. After several days the concrete remained soft, and pedestrians had tracked through the sidewalk making it uneven and hazardous. The unset concrete had to be dug up and removed.[5]

The original incorporators of the California Portland Cement Company were ultimately unsuccessful because they never mastered the art of making quality Portland cement. The plant had been closed for several years and remained idle. But Murphy comprehended that cement was an expensive commodity and in high demand. "Hundreds of thousands of dollars have been sent out of Southern California annually for foreign cement, shiploads of it are being imported from England and Belgium."[6] In 1901, J.R. Toberman and S.W. Little, took over the California Portland Cement Company with its indebtedness of $80,000. They issued new bonds raising its debt to $280,000, and again in 1903, they increased their indebtedness to $500,000 (That would translate to about $10 million in the first quarter of the twenty-first century). With the ever-growing populace of Los Angeles, there was a significant demand for the cement to pave streets, curbs, and sidewalks. Concrete was also needed for home foundations, driveways, sewers, and spillways. Throughout Southern California, numerous commercial buildings were under construction, and regional dams and flood control channels all were being built with cement. The need far outstripped the company's ability to supply enough material.[7]

Many of Portland Cement's board of directors were boosters of the Los Angeles real estate market. These businessmen were intent on building the city's infrastructure. A reliable source of quality, concrete was vital to the region. They were concerned that "Chicago and Michigan parties held options" on the company, and they could lose the largest cement manufacturing plant in the West to out-of-state investors.[8] Murphy heard about their concerns at a First National Bank board meeting. He realized he finally had the opportunity he had been waiting for many years. Just as he had once told the *Washington Post*, "he waited for the opportunity. Nerve is worth its weight in gold and sometimes more. A man's success depends largely upon the nerve he has got. If a lad gets a job as an office boy, he ought to right then and there decide to be the manager of the company."[9]

Murphy had waited not only for the opportunity to buy the company but also had held off until he had the necessary finances to pull off such a significant acquisition. He would not be a manager, but rather he would become the president with controlling interest in the company's stock. Now he had both the cash and the nerve of a seasoned entrepreneur. With the impending threat of out-of-state investors taking over the largest cement company in the Southwest, Dan Murphy made his move.

As vice president of First National Bank, Murphy brokered the purchase of the California Portland Cement Company, in January 1906. He replaced the previous board, and as the largest stockholder, he also was named board president. William H. Avery, president of Merchants National Bank; Robert Easton, president of American Bridge Company; and Edward W. Gilmore of American Oil & Asphalt, joined him on the board. The *Los Angeles Times* reported: "Expect to Enlarge the Works Fourfold with Over a Quarter Million Dollars," which would've been mostly Murphy's money. Still following Charles Crocker's style, Murphy found talented men, put them in charge, and let them make their own decisions. From the beginning, Murphy made his right-hand man T.J. Fleming, the general manager in charge of operating the plant. Hardships surely followed, but Fleming put product quality first. He employed the finest scientific methods, and raised the quality of the product to its highest level.[10]

Earlier, in 1902, the US Geological Survey had been running reconnaissance trips up the Colorado River from Needles. Murphy heard of these explorations from his friends in Needles. The federal government was finally thinking of building a dam in the same location that he and Monaghan had suggested nearly twenty years earlier.

Murphy once again had demonstrated that he had a gift for anticipating future business needs: from his first inspiration at the World's Fair, to a mountain of ore, to the damming of the Colorado River for a tribe of Indians. This was more than just the luck of the Irish. Over time, California Portland Cement Company was the most important and lucrative investment made by the Dan Murphy Company, an investment that has sustained the Dan Murphy Foundation into the twenty-first century.

17

A Showplace

A seven-acre parcel named the "Antoinette Tract" was the result of Murphy's acquisition of lots from 1903 through 1906. The Murphys chose the noted architectural firm of Frank Hudson[1] and William Munsell to create elevations for their proposed Italian Renaissance style home. The firm was well-known for its Los Angeles civic buildings including the Hall of Records and the Exposition Park Museum, which was still under construction in the early 1900s. Moreover, the firm was designing three other homes of vastly different styles on West Adams Boulevard. Several people in the Murphy social circle employed these architects including the Secundo Guasti family who built a French-style Beaux-Arts villa at 3500 West Adams; Katharine and Fred Flint Jr. at 20 Chester Place; and Murphy's oil-business partner William Valentine of San Marino, all had homes in progress designed by Hudson and Munsell.

Nettie chose Wilbur David Cook Jr. as the landscape architect to create a formal Italian garden on the hillside of their 160-foot by 589-foot property.[2] Their lot extended from West Adams Boulevard south to 27th Street, at the bottom of the hill. Cook was working on her friend Louise Kerckhoff's landscape at 734 West Adams Blvd. while he was designing Nettie's elegant Italianate terraces. He enhanced these estates by employing broad setbacks with formal landscaping to delineate broad, extensive parkland environments. Cook's concurrent installation at Exposition Park may have influenced his residential designs. To exploit the immense size of the Murphy property, Cook devised a thirty-foot sweeping lawn with a semicircular driveway that dramatically separated the home from its spacious frontage along the boulevard.

It is not surprising that the owner of California Portland Cement Company would build his mansion of concrete using Portland cement. The window trims, balconies, cornices, balustrades, and ornamental railings were all fabricated from Mount Slover's white Colton marble. The cost of their new home was $85,000. The average price of a home

Above: Home of Dan Murphy, 2076 West Adams Blvd., built in 1910 Italian Renaissance style using Portland cement as poured concrete, Colton marble door and window surrounds. Hudson and Munsell architects and Wilbur Cook landscape design on six acres. Circa 1920.

Below: Rear view of Murphy home showing pergola and upper terrace. The garden terraces continue down the hill (not shown) to 27th Street where a two-story servants quarters was built in addition to a four-car garage with chauffeur's quarters above.

A Showplace

at that time was $4,000. The extensive, sloping rear garden flowed down from one terrace to the next, following a staircase with a central waterfall. The trickling waterfall was bordered by small hand-set stones, designed to resemble Villa d'Este in Tivoli, Italy. Three outbuildings at the base of the property included a four-stall garage with chauffeur quarters, a duplex servants' house, a laundry, and gardeners' quarters.

At the time, it was by far the largest home and property in the area. Nettie furnished the interior with dark, antique Italian Renaissance furniture. In keeping with Murphy's carefully guarded privacy, there were no interior photos or floorplans published at the time. Interestingly, the Guasti villa which was built at the same time by the same architects filled five pages of the 1912 edition of *Western Architecture* with floor plans and interior photographs.[3] When completed in 1910, the Murphy home was featured in the *Los Angeles Times*. The *Times* writer explained that architects Hudson & Munsell developed a showplace at 2076 West Adams Blvd. and "created a residence of the purest Italian Renaissance."[4]

The Murphys were planning their first trip to Europe, intending to purchase furnishings for their new home and garden. But this would be no Grand Tour of the continent like most people of their social standing took. They were on a mission. They were going to meet the family of Bernardine's biological father.

On April 27, 1909, Murphy sailed to Naples aboard *SS Moltke*, accompanied by Nettie and her sister Sue. They left five-year-old Bernardine with the other Sinnott sisters at The Alameda in San Jose. The Most Reverend Thomas J. Conaty, bishop of Los Angeles and his entourage accompanied the Murphys, who even then were among the biggest donors to the archdiocese. They all were headed to Rome for a private audience with Pope Pius X in the papal apartments in the Vatican.

> I envy you not so much the trip through this most delightful part of the world as the company you are to have. Certainly, anyone is fortunate who could have Bishop Conaty and his equally distinguished brother for traveling companions, and though this were enough, I understand that you are to have also Mr. and Mrs. Hampton with you. It would be a difficult thing to imagine a more delightful set of traveling companions, or a more interesting objective point than Italy, and particularly Rome, and over and above all the meetings which you will undoubtedly have with the Holy Father. I must confess that the whole prospect makes my mouth water. I wish it might be that I could be with you.

April 19, 1909.
T.A. Riordan
Arizona Lumber and Timber Company
Flagstaff, Arizona.[5]

Godfrey Holterhoff wrote the following to Murphy:

> Tell Mrs. Murphy to buy everything she wants for the new house. Harriman has turned "his" oil land interest in California to the Standard [Standard Oil of California] at a reputed price of $66 million ... I talked to Tom [Murphy] this morning to find that the Colton plant sold 56,000 barrels of cement last month and produced 50,000 ... Our Cherokee [Oil] conditions are quite pleasing: May's production 36,580; deliveries to Prairie 18,900 and Texas 13,900. Brea Cañon conditions not quite so good as I could wish. I spent an hour and a half at your house this morning looking over matters and found that there were a number of things to find fault with. I found Frank Hudson [architect] there, with the painting contractor, and Cook [Wilbur] the landscape gardener .... Tom had been giving [them] a jacking up in several directions, and I added a little to the job this morning."

June 26 and 29
Godfrey Holterhoff
Assistant Secretary and Assistant Treasurer
Atchison, Topeka & Santa Fe Railroad Company
Coast Lines[6]

Pius X had been elected in 1903. "The simplicity and near poverty of his earlier life" endeared him to the American people. "He appeared to be a simple man, unaffected and generous—a man not unlike America's great democratic heroes, Jackson and Lincoln ...." It was not until 1908 that the Vatican had finally raised the United States from its former pagan "missionary status." In recognition of the growing Catholic population, Pope Pius X created two new cardinals bringing the number of US cardinals to three. At the same time, he also created fifteen new dioceses in the United States.[7]

When Bishop Conaty arrived at the Vatican Palace to introduce Dan and Antoinette Murphy to His Holiness, the pope was riding a wave of popularity in the United States. Even *Harper's Magazine* reported,

> Pius X is of good height, strongly made, even stout, and has a fine grace of carriage; his dignity is as great as his

Pope Pius X (1835–1914)

position, but utterly without haughtiness of pomposity or pride of office.[8]

Nonetheless, in Conaty's entourage, the men were dressed in morning coats with tails and the women were dressed in black and wore long drooping mantillas. When they entered the tapestry draped Consistory Hall, where private papal audiences are held, they knelt before the seventy-three-year-old pontiff in keeping with protocol.[9] With Bishop Conaty translating, Murphy was introduced and presented the pope with an envelope containing his generous donation, an amount that would compare to $1million at this writing.[10]

For their five-week stay in Rome, the Murphys took a suite of rooms at the Grand Hotel de la Minerve. The Grand Hotel is a seventeenth-century palazzo, which was turned into an aristocratic luxury inn in 1820. Major personalities of papal Rome stayed there right from the start, including hundreds of cardinals and prelates. Pope Pius IX (1846–1878) paid a visit soon after it opened. All this made the Minerve one of the first, if not absolutely the first "great hotels in Rome."[11]

If there is such a thing as an ecclesiastical hotel, it would be the Grand Hotel de la Minerve. In addition to being "home away from home" for visiting cardinals, it also played the role as an entertainment venue for many of Rome's "Black Nobility." Throughout the labyrinth of Italian history, the Catholic Church wielded immense power, but it was the unification of Italy in 1861 that had stripped the papacy of its lands and its rule over Central Italy and Rome. This new government was called the Kingdom of Italy. In defiance, the pope voluntarily became a "prisoner of the Vatican" rather than give the impression of accepting the ruling of a new government and its annexation of the Papal States. For the next fifty-nine years, five consecutive popes never left the Vatican or even appeared at the "papal window" over Saint Peter's Square. Ten or twelve noble families supported the papacy over the century and became known as Black Nobility [black for the color of a cleric's cassock]. From these families came several popes, many cardinals, and the formation of the "Papal Court" and "Noble Guard." Two of the oldest and most influential surnames of the Black Nobility families were Ruspoli and Orsini.

It may have been Prince Alessandro Ruspoli who arranged the Murphys' papal audience, because he held the inherited title of Grand Chamberlain to the Pope, the highest title a layman can hold at the Vatican.[12] The Murphys and Sue were cordially received at the Palazzo Ruspoli in the center of Rome. With spiritual fortitude on his side, Murphy confronted the family with the dishonor afflicted upon Susan Sinnott and, in turn, her child. His intent was to clear Bernardine's name and to have them recognize her with the dignities, honors, and social position she was entitled to because of her noble birth. They were graciously and sympathetically heard by the Ruspolis, who promised Bernardine an introduction to Roman society in Italy.

During the following weeks, Dan and Nettie picked their way through Rome's countless antique dealers and galleries. They searched for and bought furniture, art, and garden ornaments. On this visit, they also purchased marble door frames with massive entablatures to be installed over the double-wide doorways between their entrance hall and living room. Their expenditures included dining room chairs, cabinets, and all manner of decorative items. The travel itinerary also took them through France, England, and Ireland. The Murphys made a side trip of four weeks to Carlsbad, Germany, to "take the waters." Since this was Murphy's first trip abroad, he also chose to visit his father's hometown of Castletown, Ireland. There he met several relatives and fell in love with an Irish Terrier puppy which he brought home to Bernardine. They named the dog Tom Tiddler.

Even though Dan and Nettie had left five-year-old Bernardine with her aunts in San Jose, they sent numerous postcards to her, all of which she kept in her scrapbooks. Of those that survive, most were from Dan, a few from Nettie, and only two from Sue. Dan wrote, "Father misses his Little Miss Sunshine every day, and we wish for you to be with us. Love to Aunt Delia, Kathryn, and Helen from all."

Toward the end of the trip, Sue wrote a postcard from England with a picture depicting a sainted child with a halo: "Happy birthday to Bernardine from Aunt Sue." Another from Sue states: "Dear BeBe: don't you think these little German children are pretty? They all have such

A Showplace

Dan Murphy with puppies from Ireland trip in 1909.

rosy cheeks and brazen yellow curls." Bernardine was always described as "tall and dark with lovely coloring," and soulful brown eyes—hardly reminiscent of the blond and rosy-cheeked children of Germany. From a very early age, Bernardine was self-conscious about her appearance.

The Alameda household where Bernardine awaited her parent's return included her two schoolteacher aunts: Delia, forty-seven, and Kathryn, forty-three, both of whom were single. No doubt little Bernardine was doted upon, and she was always under their watchful eyes. An often-told story among relatives refers to the time period when Bernardine was to begin attending the private Marlborough school for girls in Los Angeles. She had returned home after the first day in tears because someone put gum in her hair. It was more likely that her olive complexion and black hair had aroused teasing from the Anglophile Los Angeles society children. Nettie and Sue were aghast at the incident, and Bernardine never returned to school. She had live-in tutors for the rest of her formal education.[13]

Crates of furniture, marble architectural embellishments, and antique terra-cotta garden ornaments began arriving in Los Angeles from the 1909 European trip. One significant piece they shipped from Rome was of considerable size and weight: an antique three-tiered fountain. Nettie had chosen it expressly for the large terrace positioned halfway down the hillside. Water from the fountain fell into a surrounding basin which in turn flowed under the pavement into a pebble-lined channel that was bordered on both sides by steps. These stairs led to the lowest terrace, where the garages and servants quarters were located. Nettie was particularly proud of this monumental fountain. However, due to an occasional telltale sign of an oil sheen, Murphy always knew there was oil beneath his property. As the landscaping and the gardens flourished, Nettie employed three to five full-time gardeners, depending on the season, to trim, replant, and tend the cutting beds. One gardener lived on the property in one of the cottages at the bottom of the hill.

An early newspaper article written during the first spring in their showplace home described the garden and photographs took up a full half-page.

> ...the layout is entirely formal, but the stone columns of the pergolas, with their entwining vines, possess stately beauty yet rustic appeal. In all parts of the garden are set stone urns, holding rare shrubs and formally trimmed trees, and there are many stone seats hidden in shady angles.[14]

Nettie's extensive gardens were the center of her life. She subscribed to every important horticultural and gardening publication of the day and built a library of gardening books from American and European publishers. She delighted in discussing her plans for the beds with her head gardener as the seasons changed and together they edited plants that failed to thrive. In the ensuing years, their efforts resulted in spectacular displays of seasonal blooms. With the maturing of trees, hedges, trellises, and the restrained serenity of multilevel terraces, the overall effect was that of a long-established garden, a credit to its devoted owner.

Murphy's secretary Bagley had several communiqués from PDC Ball while Murphy was in Europe. Ball was asking him to look in on matters of the Los Angeles Cherokee Oil business in the Indian Territory. Having just returned from his transatlantic voyage and cross-country train trip, Murphy was back on the rails en route to the new state of Oklahoma. In Bartlesville, Oklahoma, he hired a car to drive to the oilfields. The broad flat, treeless plains stretched endlessly across the horizon as he drove the dirt road from the railroad station. A storm gathered in the distance. When he was five miles from the town of Bigheart, a massive funnel cloud dropped from an angry black sky. He watched as it skipped across the grasslands and, to his horror, headed toward the village of Bigheart. Debris, lumber, and dust suddenly shot up from the town.

> Believing that the storm had left death and destruction in its path, he hurried into the town to aid the injured. He found that five persons had been killed and forty injured. The injured were mostly children from the local schoolhouse, the whole end of which was blown in.[15]

Murphy contacted the AT&SF to send a locomotive with a boxcar to the devastated village. Once the train arrived, Murphy helped load the injured into a boxcar. The makeshift ambulance train carried them to Tulsa where they were taken to a hospital. *Tulsa Daily World* led with stories of the disaster and photos of the school and town destroyed by the tornado. Murphy kept his name from appearing in connection with his efforts, but it wasn't long before he was listed at the top of the list of financial donors helping the survivors.[16] On his way to St. Louis the next day to see PDC Ball, the newspaper wrote:

> He ran into another twister. The damage done there was very heavy, but no lives were lost." From St. Louis, he headed to New York City for business meetings. Returning home two weeks later, he witnessed a freak snowstorm in Chicago. "By this time, he was wondering why he had left Los Angeles ... [T]he most pleasant part of his travels was when he passed over the Cajon Pass, into San Bernardino, on his way back to Los Angeles."[17]

18

Dust and Oranges

While Dan Murphy was traveling in Europe, he received letters from Godfrey Holterhoff apprising Murphy of the state of affairs with several of his companies. In one letter dated July 14, 1909, Holterhoff mentioned that Frank Monaghan was selling some of his Brea Cañon stock. Monaghan needed cash to invest in the Southern California Sugar Company in Santa Ana. The company was started in May of 1908, it was the tenth sugar beet processing plant in the state.[1]

The agricultural community in Orange County converted thousands of acres to sugar beet cultivation. Monaghan was in the middle of this movement and bought into a newly formed firm named the Southern California Sugar Company, and quickly became one of its board members. The company's immediate goal was to build a beet processing plant, with Monaghan overseeing its construction. As the processing plant neared completion, in 1910, he became increasingly unhappy with its construction. After the plant failed to meet its designed capacity, Case-Hinze, the builder, claimed that Monaghan had misrepresented the plant's production capacity. Monaghan said the contract stipulated that the factory should process six hundred tons of beets per day, but as configured, it was a challenge to process four hundred tons daily. The board—which also included James Irvine, James McFadden, and A.J. Crookshank—sued Case-Hinze for breach of contract. The courts ruled in favor of the sugar company, but by the time the trial ended, the sugar beet industry was on shaky ground. In a region where there had once been five processing plants serving local farmers whose fields were devoted to sugar beets, price wars forced a collapse and farmland gave way to real estate developers and oil companies eager for more oil fields.[2]

Six months after the sugar beet factory trial ended, Dora Monaghan died. She and Frank had been married for thirty-five years. Their eldest daughter Lillian had married a few years earlier and moved to Oregon. Thirty-four-year-old Frankie Jr., their only surviving son, lived in New

Mexico, and had no interest in his father's mining business. Monaghan and Murphy had asked Dan's brother Tom, who was still in Needles, to sell their infamous Capitol mine in Eldorado Canyon, which had been idle for eleven years, ever since the murder—neither Murphy nor Monaghan had ever returned to the area after Charlie Monaghan died there. Three months after it was sold to its new owner, the Tracy Company pulled gold and silver ore from the mine valued at $400/ton.[3]

> The murder was the cause of the operation of the mine to stop at that time, and it has never been started since, although there has never been any question as to the value of the ore bodies."[4]

Six months after Dora's death, Monaghan and Murphy sold their eponymous general merchandise store. A page-one boxed notice in the *Needles Eye* (formerly the *Bazoo*) on August 5, 1911 announced:

> To the public and our many loyal customers and friends: after twenty-eight years of successful merchandising, during which time we have seen Needles grow from a one-tent town to its present prosperous population of more than 4000 souls, we have decided to retire the general merchandising business and devote our attention to other branches.

Ever since Dan Murphy had married and moved to Los Angeles, Tom had been looking after the family interests in Needles. After arriving in Needles when he was just twenty-three, Tom learned the merchandising business under his brother's tutelage and kept all the books for the Murphy Water, Ice and Light Company, which serviced the Santa Fe operations as well as the rest of the town. Following Dan's consistent style of management, Tom was in complete control when he moved to Los Angeles. After their father's passing, their mother came from Hays to live with him and his sister Margaret. Margaret had been Dan's housekeeper, and now she lived with Tom and their mother. Tom ran the Monaghan & Murphy General Store for eleven years before it was sold in 1911 to William Claypool who rebranded it Claypool General Store.

On June 15, 1915, Tom Murphy, forty-three, married twenty-eight-year-old Anna Marie McDermott, the niece of Bishop Thomas J. Conaty. Tom's brother Dan served as best man. According to the *Mohave County Miner*, the couple "departed for their honeymoon aboard the Canadian Pacific Railway." They returned to Needles, where Tom managed the Monaghan & Murphy Company interests. Later on, Tom moved his family to Los Angeles. In 1925, they built a beautiful 6,100 square-foot, eight-bedroom/eight-bath mansion with a pool at 635 S.

Muirfield Rd., in the fashionable Hancock Park district. In time, Tom and Anna would have eight children, their first-born having been named Dan to honor his uncle.[5]

Tom continued to look after the ice, water, and power business in Needles as well as a few mining sites that were still in operation. The Murphy Water, Ice and Light Company, which had been incorporated in 1904, was sold in 1925 as well as the Monaghan & Murphy Bank.[6]

Monaghan married Gertrude H. Keller in 1911. They lived in Glendale for nearly ten years before he suffered a stroke. He lingered for eleven days before he died on the morning of November 6, 1921; he was seventy-one-years old. Murphy helped the coroner fill out his friend's death certificate. He also wrote the obituary for the Los Angeles County Pioneer Society. In it, he referred to his lifelong partner "whose charity knew no bounds and whose love for his fellow man extended to the ends of the earth. He was a man of the very highest ideals in character, approachable and possessed of beautiful simplicity, integrity, and honesty beyond doubt."[7] Frank Monaghan is buried at Fairhaven Memorial Park in Santa Ana, California.[8] The Monaghan & Murphy Company outlived both of its founders and was not dissolved until the 1960s.

Dan Murphy settled into a comfortable retirement, highlighted by more European travels. Murphy's business life now consisted of attending board meetings and committee meetings at banks, companies, and the various organizations to which he belonged. Among his many investments, the cement plant remained the crown jewel. He had named T.J. Fleming as its manager and allowed Fleming to make the major decisions. But when in town, Murphy never missed the California Portland Cement board meetings. Since his purchase, the plant's output had more than doubled.

> Consistently adhering to a policy of producing a product of uniformly high quality and dealing fairly with everyone, the new company overcame production and marketing handicaps and began the steady rise to industrial and commercial success.[9]

The improvements to the quality of the product were paying off. To dispel the common misconception that only Europe produced the highest quality cement, Portland Cement Company held an invitation-only excursion to its plant. More than three hundred architects, designers, and structural engineers boarded a "special train" to Colton to tour the plant. The train was switched from the Santa Fe's main line at Colton to circle Mount Slover on one of the plant's spur lines. After a two-hour tour of

Frank Monaghan. 1912.

the manufacturing process, guests were taken to a hotel for a banquet replete with speeches by the mayor of Los Angeles and plant executives. Though he was immensely proud of the factory, Murphy usually avoided the limelight, but on this particular trip, he brought Nettie and Sue to Colton "by touring car" to share his excitement.[10]

The large plant, which operated every day and all day, employed most of the citizens of Colton and neighboring San Bernardino. Southern California was experiencing a boom in orange production since the icing of railroad cars had opened the industry to eastern markets. The original navel orange had been imported from Brazil in 1873 and planted at Riverside, just ten miles away. The Colton cement factory was well-established before any orange groves were sprouting, but soon local farmlands were filled with citrus, and the factory was surrounded.

Dust emissions from the cement plant settled on the trees damaging the crops. As a result, in 1910 the local orange growers sued California Portland Cement, seeking an "injunction restraining the Corporation from permitting dust to escape and injure the orange trees."[11] The growers sought damages amounting to $500,000 (today worth about $14 million). The company pleaded for time to install dust-catching devices, but the court ordered the plant to stop all production until the devices were in place. The ruling was challenged but was upheld by the Superior Court of the State of California. The case attracted the attention of cement companies across the nation.[12]

Abiding by the ruling, the plant closed in the summer of 1909. Tom Murphy, who had always been a clever inventor, was called in to devise equipment that would suppress the dust. During July of that year, California Portland Cement installed $300,000 worth of dust collection equipment that he designed.

The first day that the dust controlling plan was in operation, it saved 60 tons of powdered cement ... The dust-controlling device does not prevent the escape of all dust, but reduced the blighted zone to a radius of three-quarters of a mile.[13]

The plant management declared the dust collectors a success, but the growers continued to complain. After four years of litigation and emboldened by their success, the growers filed for an injunction against the cement plant to prevent the noise from blasting and equipment.[14]

For five years the board had dealt with the dust lawsuits. Murphy, true to his principle of allowing managers to make their own decisions, had authorized them to solve the problem, giving Tom time to improve on his dust collection devices. But, Murphy had had enough. Following his faith and Luke 12:58:

> When you are going with your opponent to appear before the magistrate, try to settle with him on the way, lest he turn you over to the judge, and the judge deliver you up to the jailer, and the jailer throw you into prison.[15]

Murphy directed the board of California Portland Cement Company to buy all 125 acres contested by the sixteen growers. The company paid over the appraised value, paying $92,450 for the land, and gave the growers $24,381 in damages. As a result, on July 9, 1914, the courts dismissed all twelve pending suits.[16]

He then gave the company board an additional million dollars to enlarge the plant. The announcement of the buyout headlined the front page of the *Los Angeles Times*: "Million Will Double Colton Cement Plant," announcing the doubling of the plant size, which would raise the production to nine thousand barrels per day.[17]

19

WEST ADAMS

Dan and Antoinette Murphy were appreciative of their home, and enjoyed their companionable neighbors. However, Murphy was concerned that Bernardine, his "Little Rosebud," had few friends since she had been taken out of Marlborough School. His wife and her sister Sue had hired a live-in tutor for Bernardine named Ms. Meinhardt, a stern Austrian-born woman. At Nettie's direction, Ms. Meinhardt had set up a classroom on the second floor of the house. She provided her employers with regular report cards that listed Bernardine's *grandes* in French, German, English, and arithmetic. So the little girl could interact with other children, Nettie and Sue threw luncheons and parties for youngsters of her age whose parents were in their social circle. Two of these kids were the Flint sisters, Muriel and Anna (their other sister Geraldine was too young to attend), the daughters of Frederick and Katharine Flint who lived nearby at No. 20 Chester Place. Murphy and Frederick's father, US Senator Frank Flint, now served together as vice presidents of the Los Angeles First National Bank. Later, both the Flints and the Murphys bought summer homes in pricey Pacific Grove on the Monterey Peninsula.

Another of Bernardine's playmates, Genevieve Maier, was a fun-loving young girl who lived with her widowed mother, Isabel Denker Maier, and grandmother Louise Antoinette Ruellen. Louise had built a sumptuous mansion at 3820 West Adams.[1] A native of France, Louise modeled the new home after Le Petit Trianon at Versailles. The grand interiors were embellished with furnishings imported from France, and only French was allowed to be spoken at home. Together those ladies were the social *grandes dames* of the city. Louise's late husband Andrew Denker was one of the premier hoteliers of the city with the firm of Hammel & Denker, which owned the Cosmopolitan Hotel, where, incidentally, the young Dan Murphy had conducted much of his early business, organizing his railroad commissary car for the Mojave Line.[2]

Bernardine Murphy at ten years old.

Godfrey Holterhoff also had an adopted daughter. Little Leila Holterhoff and Bernardine were especially close friends, since she lived only a few blocks east on West Adams. Leila was an exceptional child; blinded at birth, she excelled at music and linguistics. A tremendously gifted vocalist, Leila inspired Bernardine's love of music, and Leila helped her best friend learn to speak and write French, German, and Latin. It was no surprise to the Murphy family that Leila eventually became a renowned vocalist, acclaimed throughout Europe in the 1920s.

All of these children—Leila, Muriel, Anna, and Genevieve—were among the group of girls who celebrated with Bernardine at her tenth birthday party, held in the spectacular gardens of the Murphy home:

> The huge dining room was like a garden of wildflowers. A maypole of crisp rose-colored paper with broad pink satin ribbons tied to each plate centered the table … upon which danced dainty bisque fairies. To each ribbon was attached the name of the little guest. Later in the beautiful sunken gardens of the Murphy home were gay frocked maids were intent on a peanut hunt. Everyone won prizes, and little Miss Bernardine cut her great sparkly cake for everyone.[3]

Another grand party that Nettie helped organize was a children's fair to benefit the local Children's Hospital fund. She and her fellow board member Catherine Coffin Phillips arranged a benefit circus for the "clever little society girls" and their families to be held on the grounds of Berkeley Square, a gated community near West Adams. Phillips had built an immense brick home, "the largest house in Los Angeles." Nettie and Catherine Phillips organized what the newspapers hailed as:

> ...a whirling circus, with elephants and bears and kangaroos and cow ponies and, Poto the clown, and Charlie Chaplin selling peanuts, and Douglas Fairbanks playing naughty tricks, and Julian Eltinge [a female impersonator] and his dancing girls. Boxing matches, a Japanese wrestler ... a saucy fashion show, too, under the auspices of Vogue [magazine], with professional models who can wear the more daring fashions with greater aplomb."[4]

Little Kathryn Phillips, Hortense McLaughlin, and Katherine Cheney "are going to perform bareback stunts in cowgirl costumes and vie with the professional, Keystone comedy crowd ... Let nobody say our society women are not courageous, it is a tremendous undertaking" by the group that included Catherine Coffin Phillips, Antoinette Murphy, Agnes Connell, Blanche Garland and Anna Cheney.[5] "Oh, can't you picture them [all those animals and stars] marching into the sacred precincts of the select Berkeley Square?"[6]

Although Nettie and Sue tried to entertain the neighboring children the best they could, Bernardine still spent many long days at home surrounded by her elderly adults. They agreed a fundamental change was required, perhaps a governess or a live-in playmate. Bernardine was no doubt in favor of the latter.

Nettie devoted a large part of her time to charitable works. She and Dan donated the acreage for the Sisters of the Good Shepherd to build their convent and a laundry facility for the wayward women residents. Nettie headed the women's auxiliary at Good Shepherd to raise funds to support the enterprise. Madame Modjeska, an enthusiastic supporter, lent her theatrical fame to advance the auxiliary's membership and charitable giving. A year after Modjeska's benefit at the opera house she and the auxiliary organized a second benefit titled "A Visit to Florence." It was presented at the Stimson Auditorium by the well-known European lecturer of the time, Fraulein Antoine Stolle. An article promoting the lecture noted that Good Shepherd now had seventy-two inmates. Modjeska was a frequent visitor to the Murphy residence and Nettie would often open her stately home for entertainment and public benefit affairs.[7]

Madame Modjeska and Antoinette advanced the Murphy home to become a stage that launched the musical careers of two West Adams prodigies to international prominence. Madame Modjeska's influence and encouragement aided Leila Holterhoff, with her superb soprano voice, to later achieve acclaim as a diva on the stages of Berlin, Florence, Paris, and throughout the United States. Leila, in her mid-teens, had taken voice lessons for two years in Florence. She spent six more years studying repertoire and harmony in Berlin before beginning her career touring the great European concert halls. Musically gifted, she could play any piece on the piano having heard it only once. She spoke seven languages, and at the age of sixteen, she had earned a teacher's certificate from the State of California to teach Latin. Frequently when in Paris, the Murphys met up with Leila to hear her perform and visit her mother. By 1920, she was thirty-five and at the height of her career.[8]

Bernardine's neighborhood friend Lester Donahue lived with his widowed mother at 2181 W. 25th St., merely a five-minute walk from the Murphy home. Lester captured Madame Mojeska's interest because he was a keyboard prodigy. In his youth, Lester, with Madame Modjeska's assistance, became a world-class pianist and studied in Los Angeles, Berlin, and Switzerland. Both of these West Adams prodigies traveled the leading European stages between the wars. When they grew up, Lester, Bernardine, and Leila were lifelong friends and would arrange to meet-up whenever they were abroad.[9]

As Murphy eased into semi-retirement, the couple's life outside their family centered on their various charities and their tight-knit West Adams community. As a board member of Children's Hospital, Nettie spent many years actively supporting the facility.[10] Both Dan and Nettie were social friends with Jarvis Barlow, founder of Barlow Sanatorium, a tuberculosis hospital near Elysian Park. Over the years, they and several of their social groups supported Dr. Barlow's facility. Barlow's hospital campus consisted of several airy bungalows donated by various Los Angeles philanthropists. In 1909, the Murphys donated a structure they named Saint Bernardine Cottage. Dan was a life member, and for several decades he served on the Barlow Sanatorium board.[11]

Dan was becoming progressively concerned about his "Little Rosebud" as he affectionately called Bernardine. Coming from a large family of seven children, he was worried about her socialization, so he encouraged Nettie and Sue to find a solution. Concluding that she should have a live-in playmate, they sought help from their sisters in San Jose. As school teachers, the Sinnott sisters were able to introduce Nettie to Frances Coleman of Oakland, California, whose young daughter was also named Frances. For several months each year from 1912 to 1916, Little Frances came to live with the Murphys, so she and Bernardine were constant companions from the ages of eight to twelve. Mrs. Coleman once wrote to Nettie commenting that after her most recent visit to pick-up Frances, she was struck by Frances's love for Dan and how

> despite my presence, she clung to him, and he looked to be as equally fond of her. You and your family seem to be especially born for parenthood. It seems a wicked shame you each haven't a house full of children.[12]

Although Mrs. Coleman thought the Murphys were "born for parenthood," she was mistaken. She was never privy to the true situation. Frances and Bernardine were very fond of Dan and given the ruse of "Aunt Sue," he may have been the only one in the household who fully embraced their childhood. On the other hand, the ever-watchful mothers/sisters kept a skeptical eye on the youngsters and were ready to correct their deportment at any hint of misconduct. The two little girls were fast friends and pined for each other during their separations, which were dictated at the whim of Mrs. Coleman.

20

THE GOOD LIFE

As the spring of 1912 approached, Bernardine's long-awaited first trip to Europe was about to become a reality. This journey was preceded by months of shopping. In addition to shopping for herself, Nettie also searched endlessly for the "perfect little outfits" for Bernardine. There was nothing that Nettie loved more than to dress up her little girl. She was rarely satisfied with the local wardrobe choices. This prompted semiannual trips to Chicago and New York City in quest of the latest styles. As their departure date approached, trunks, passports, and tickets all had to be ready for her daughter's first trip abroad. Eight-year-old Bernardine was well-tutored to converse in French, and she was knowledgeable about the geography and the tourist attractions they would visit.

As part of their departure preparations, Murphy secured letters of introduction from Bishop Conaty. One of the letters, to Bishop Thomas F. Kennedy at the Pontifical North American College in Rome, requested an audience with Pope Pius X. Murphy and Nettie had been introduced to "His Holiness" in 1909, but now they wished an audience for the particular purpose of having Bernardine presented and blessed by the pope. Bishop Conaty wrote in his letter of introduction for Murphy:

> He is anxious also to again testify to his reverence and affection for the Holy Father, and no doubt will do so in a substantial manner.[1]

Over the years, the Murphys made nearly annual trips to Europe. They always included Rome on their itinerary. Murphy would personally present a "substantial manner" donation to the reigning Pontiff. When she grew up, Bernardine would carry on the Murphy custom, donating $1million annually to the Pope.[2]

On the appointed day of their departure Dan, Nettie, Bernardine, and Aunt Sue, were driven to the Santa Fe Depot where they boarded the Santa Fe de-Luxe. The de-Luxe was a brand new train that had been in service for only five months. The train was advertised as "Extra Fast—Extra Fine, Extra Fare." They were bound for New York via Chicago.

Frequently, "a party of fifty or more would come down to the old Santa Fe Depot to see [Murphy] off," and this trip was no exception. Murphy greeted them as always in his cheerful Irish way. He took his secretary Bagley by the arm and led him the length of the train and gave him last-minute instructions.

The veteran locomotive engineer pulling this new Santa Fe train climbed down from the cab and removed his heavy engineer's glove, to shake Murphy's hand.

"Where you going this time, Dan?"
"Oh to Chicago and then over to the other side for a little trip."
"Fine, Dan. We'll pull you through."

According to the trade journal *Petroleum World*, "That was Dan Murphy, loved and honored by all, high or low, with whom he had contact."[3]

Holterhoff had no doubt arranged for their Pullman car reservations aboard this fast train to the East Coast. Murphy could have purchased a private car of his own, but shunned the ostentation and notoriety that such luxury transport brought. He preferred the camaraderie of the club car found on most long-distance trains. It was in just such club cars that a much younger Murphy had made many of his most important deals. But even Murphy must have looked forward to the Santa Fe de-Luxe. It was limited to sixty passengers in six cars, plus an observation car. It consisted of four Pullman sleepers, a club car, and a Fred Harvey Company dining car. These newly designed cars had heavy steel under-framing which vastly improved the comfort of the passengers. In the 1880s when Murphy routinely traveled on trains of rocking, wood-frame cars with coal stoves and smoky lanterns, it was a ten-day journey to New York. The Santa Fe de-Luxe, however—powered by its state-of-the-art, 4-6-2 steam locomotive—boarded passengers only at Los Angeles, Winslow (Arizona, the Grand Canyon stop), and Kansas City, before arriving in Chicago in sixty-three-hours. Travelers from Los Angeles reached New York in five days.[4]

The Murphy family arrived in New York less than two weeks after the *Titanic* sank (April 15, 1912), claiming 1,500 lives, so there must have been some sleepless nights before they boarded the SS *Rotterdam* bound for Naples. Nevertheless, they were soon at sea.

Murphy had arranged for a special menu for dinner in the first-class dining room on April 28, 1912. The setting was opulent: The room was the width of the steamer and ninety-two feet long, with its ceiling reaching the height of two decks and supported by pilasters with capitals hand-painted to look like bronze. Its walls were lavished with pearl-gray lacquer and detailed with gilt. In this posh setting, dress was always formal, requiring white tie and gowns. One of Bernardine's keepsakes from this voyage was a special menu with "Mr. & Mrs. Murphy and Party" printed on its cover. To the diners' delight, they enjoyed dishes such as Filet Mignon Antoinette, Coupe Bernardine, and Omelet Susanne.

Once they arrived in Europe, newspaper clippings noted that the Murphys "keep an automobile in Europe" and will be "motoring" through Rome, Lausanne, Paris, and London before returning to the United States on July 28. Antoinette saved her 1912 to 1913 season pass to the Casino de Monte Carlo, proof that they also stopped along the Cote d'Azur.

In Rome, they took a suite for a month at the Grand Hotel Minerve where they had stayed in 1909. Bernardine had been tutored by Ms. Meinhardt on the classical monuments of Rome, so she looked forward to seeing these works of art in person. Murphy's first order of business was to present his letter of introduction from the bishop to Bishop Kennedy at the Pontifical North American College (which at one time had been a seventeenth-century convent), near the Trevi Fountain. A seminary and graduate school for American priests studying in Rome, the college also serves to assist visitors with requests for papal audiences and tours. Murphy's family was seeking a private meeting with the then seventy-seven-year-old pontiff, Pope Pius X. His Holiness may not have remembered Murphy himself, but he undoubtedly would have recalled the "substantial" (as Conaty called it) donation Murphy had made in 1909. When their private audience was granted, the family presented seven-year-old Bernardine to the pope, who blessed her and each member of the party as they approached his throne and knelt at his feet. For most people, this would have been a once-in-a-lifetime experience, but over the decades, each of these individuals would receive several papal blessings, each accompanied by a "substantial" donation, of course.

Italy had changed since their last visit, which prompted Murphy to write to an American friend, "I cannot say enough about the progress of Italy. Mussolini has made the nation understand the nobility of labor."[5] The month that the family arrived in Rome, Mussolini had just been appointed the editor of the *Avante* [*Forward*], a socialist newspaper.

> Benito Mussolini burst onto the Italian political scene, confounding the country's political establishment with

his unorthodox doctrine and tactics and his outsized personality. A mercurial hothead, Mussolini reveled in his role as a political disrupter. His crisis-mongering platforms contained a confusing blend of socialist and nationalist tenets, trafficking in contradiction and paradox, the better to challenge traditional ideas about politics. Many Italians did not know what to make of Mussolini.[6]

But at this early stage in his career, Mussolini sounded like the answer to the problems of the impoverished Italian peasantry. He was an outsider convinced that the established parties were broken and posed a danger to Italy.[7]

A labor movement was spreading across Europe. Mussolini was not yet in office, but he had a powerful voice against trade unions, favoring nationalism instead.[8] In less than six months, Pope Pius X would issue an encyclical tolerating labor unions but discouraging strikes.[9] Murphy had witnessed the destructive Pullman Strike of 1894 at which more than 250,000 workers were affected before the US Army was called in to halt the strike, an experience that caused Murphy to favor Mussolini's stance against unions.

One of Nettie and Dan's favorite pastimes in Italy was antique shopping. They were familiar with several antique galleries and salons from their previous trip, so they made the necessary appointments. Nettie wrote to her sister Kathryn that they had purchased "some rare specimens of Renaissance furniture." Seven year-old Bernardine spotted a fanciful domed stone gazebo with built-in benches. She fell in love with it. Daddy Dan could not deny her, especially since Nettie believed it would look attractive placed on a lower terrace of the garden.[10]

As their time in Rome came to a close, the Murphys toured other spots in Italy en route to Switzerland. When they arrived in Lausanne, the family took a suite for eight weeks at Beau-Rivage Palace Hotel on the picturesque shores of Lake Léman. This grand Belle Époque hotel, which had been opened in 1861, was redecorated in 1908 in the neo-Baroque style. Surrounded by ten acres of parkland along the lake, it offered a myriad of activities for their young daughter. Bernardine's stay at Beau-Rivage Palace must have been a wonderland of nature, especially after many weeks of touring Italian cities, museums, and churches. It was customary for well-to-do families to take rooms for a month or more in this cool climate. This gave their children ample time to get to know one another. Bernardine developed several close friends during their stay. One little girl remained her pen pal for several years. Bernardine's "classroom French" developed into fluency while at Beau-Rivage. On June 2, 1912, Bernardine turned eight years old. Her parents and Sue arranged with the hotel to throw a birthday party for her in the hotel's glorious dining room overlooking the lake. At the close of their stay at Beau-Rivage Palace, their driver took them motoring in their personal car through Switzerland, to the French Riviera, and on to Paris.

Paris was an opportunity to buy clothing and linens, a hectic time to stock up on both. Quality dresses, gloves, and coats were not purchased off the rack—the fittings required for these garments meant a minimum stay of four to five weeks. Before leaving Los Angeles, they had obtained a letter of introduction from Bishop Conaty to Sister Mary Reeves, an American nun, who was assistant to the Superior General at the motherhouse of the Sisters of Charity on Rue de Bac. With Bernardine in hand, they set out for the convent. Entry into the historic convent and novitiate must have been at once both fascinating and terrifying for the little girl. The convent's chapel was the site of miraculous apparitions in the 1830s: it was here that Catherine Laboure had had several visions of the Blessed Virgin Mary. The visitors had looked forward to seeing this internationally known chapel. At the chapel's side altar, they prayed in front of the incorrupt bodies of Saint Catherine Laboure and Saint Vincent de Paul, who founded the Order of the Sisters of Charity in 1633. Bernardine was enthralled by the sight of the nuns in their gray habits with flying-wing wimples that spanned wider than their shoulders. The nuns appeared to float by in the shadows like swans on a rayless pond.

When Sister Mary received the family, they presented Bishop Conaty's letter:

> Mrs. Murphy is anxious to obtain an intelligent and thoroughly well-recommended French governess for her little daughter, and it may be that you can recommend such a one to her. She particularly wishes to have her little daughter well-grounded in religious instruction as well as in knowledge of French. She will desire to have the governess come with her to Los Angeles.[11]

Nettie also brought with her a letter from the Superior in Los Angeles for access to the Congregation of Our Lady of Charity of the Good Shepherd in Anger, France. An order that was founded in 1641, Sisters of the Good Shepherd are "devoted to the care, rehabilitation, and education of girls and young women in difficulty."[12] Since the Murphys were the primary contributors to the Good Shepherd sisters in Los Angeles,

Wynanspray, the Murphy's home at Pebble Beach, is a 4,500 sq. ft., two-story home (with a 1,300 sq. ft. guest house), sited on 2.6 acres of Pescadero Point, overlooking the Pacific Ocean.

Nettie had a particular commitment to the order. The travelers were no doubt interested in seeing and meeting the sisters at their founding Motherhouse in Anger. No French governess materialized. Back in Los Angeles, Bernardine was still under the tutelage of Ms. Meinhardt.

After a visit to London, the party returned to America. They'd been away for three months. Bernardine sent her Aunt Kathryn in San Jose a letter written in her child's hand,

> I am leaving for home in four days, and I will be glad to see you. I was sorry to leave my little friends in Ouchy. We had such a good time playing. I hope I will not be seasick. Love to all, Bernardine. July 6.[13]

Murphy's favorite getaway was still the Hotel Del Monte in Pebble Beach, a place he had been visiting since his first days in Needles—Charles Crocker had introduced him to the idyllic place. It must have seemed like an unachievable dream to the young Dan Murphy when

The Good Life

Dan Murphy's Mojave and Paiute basket collection is photographed on the driveway of the family's West Adams home. The baskets were later donated to the Southwest Museum now part of the Autry Museum of the American West. Circa 1920.

the Pacific Improvement Company sold a few lots where the wealthy could build summer homes. But time, talent, and good fortune changed Murphy's world. In 1918, Dan and Nettie Murphy bought Wynanspray, a house at 3296 Seventeen Mile Dr., that had been built in 1915 by Joe Ghirardelli, of the San Francisco chocolate company fame. Situated on a craggy prominence called Pescadero Point, this large rustic home was supported by log piers and beams with "stickwork," had an enormous porch that stretched across the front, and had servants' quarters. The roof was shingled with a massive stone chimney.[14]

Wynanspray was an enchanting retreat amongst the windswept cypresses and the crashing waves of the dramatic Pacific Ocean. In early photographs, it "resembled the enclaves of the summer 'camps' built in the Adirondacks by wealthy New Yorkers." Throughout her teen years, Bernardine enjoyed beach suppers, clam bakes, fishing trips, and horseback riding on the miles of groomed bridle paths through the Del Monte forest. Antoinette and her gardener refurbished the existing flower beds and added many more. A serious gardener, Nettie had a vast collection of botanical books and gardening magazines which she studied ardently.

She delighted in giving garden tours at Wynanspray. She would recite the Latin names of each of the specimens along the way. Her gardens were her lifetime passion and consumed most of her time at Pebble Beach.

In love with the house and the beauty of Pescadero Point, Murphy wanted to share the place. He enticed his longtime friend Fred Flint, who was also one of his fellow First National Bank vice presidents, to buy the lot next door.[15] So the same year that the Murphys bought Wynanspray, the Flints built their summer home at 3294 Seventeen Mile Dr.[16] The Flints, who lived on Chester Place in Los Angeles, enjoyed the Murphy family; Bernardine played with the three Flint girls who were all around her age, so together the families enjoyed trips to "the Point."

Pescadero Point, six acres of rocky terrain that seemed to float out into the Pacific, provided breathtaking views and was surrounded by booming waves and foaming surf on three sides. The famous lone cypress tree and "witch tree" were only a few paces away. Lewis Hill, from Saint Paul, Minnesota, was the son of James Hill, the owner of the Great Northern Railway. He owned "most of the hill above Pescadero Point." There he built a winsome, multi-storied, rustic log "cabin"—on twenty-two acres. Lewis was the builder of the Glacier Park Hotel and a great promoter of Glacier National Park. He also had a deep interest in American Indian tribes and collected Blackfoot artifacts. Murphy and he must have passed many an hour discussing this common hobby.[17]

At the time, there were only seventeen homes in Pebble Beach, all clustered near the Del Monte. The Point was definitely priced to be within reach of only the very wealthiest families. Case in point: when the father of Bernardine's playmate Hortense McLaughlin tried to buy a nearby lot "he was so overcome by the figure that it became necessary to secure him a tonic."[18]

21

War Ships

One of the most devastating wars in history began in July 1914. England, France, and Russia opposed Germany and Austria-Hungary. Over sixteen million people lost their lives. Suddenly Angelinos were thrown into turmoil. Never before were Americans asked to ration everything from food to gasoline. Citizens of every stripe stepped up to the challenge. The nation was woefully unprepared for conflict, especially without sufficient ships to aid the Allied Nations. Within the first two years of the war, nearly two thousand ships were sunk at sea, leaving the US government hard-pressed to supply food and grain to British and French ports. Since wheat shipments from the US were the primary relief sent to the Allies, homemakers were asked to use oatmeal, cornmeal, and rye flour while saving wheat for the war effort.

Millions of volunteers joined the Red Cross. Prominent businessmen helped organize the individual chapters as women took to making bandages. Even school children collected money for the relief effort. The Murphy household was immediately distraught and in chaos. One of their longtime servants, Frau Pfaehler, made a hasty return to Germany to be with her family, only to drown trying to save her uncle from a flooded river. For several months, their head butler Joseph and their cook, both from Austria, were agonizing over whether or not they should attempt a return. Fortunately for all concerned, they decided to stay.[1]

On May 7, 1915, the British luxury liner RMS *Lusitania* was torpedoed by a German U-boat and 1,198 passengers drowned, including 128 Americans. President Wilson called for war on Germany in April 1917 when news broke that the Germans were planning to fund Mexico in an attack on the US to regain New Mexico, Texas, and Arizona. With the passage of the Selective Service Act, 2.8 million men were drafted. That same month Congress initiated the Emergency Fleet Corporation to quickly build merchant marine freighters. The Los Angeles Shipbuilding and Dry Dock Company was immediately organized on sixty-nine acres of the West Basin of Los Angeles Harbor. Thirty-five contracts for ships were issued to the company and a dry dock was constructed at a cost of $1.25 million. Dan Murphy was appointed one of five directors and named company vice president.[2] Nothing testifies to Murphy's prestige and respect amongst his contemporaries as much as this crucial appointment during a time of national crisis and war.

While in D.C., Murphy worked hard to broker contracts for the West Coast company to build more ships. His affable and considerate demeanor must have worked. The Los Angeles Shipbuilding and Dry Dock Company soon had $30 million [half a billion today] in contracts for ships and grew to employing five thousand workers. The company broke four world records for construction time and delivery. Even though it began during the Progressive Era, a time filled with contentious labor relations, the shipbuilder was noted for its equitable policies. Murphy, as vice president, reported to Senator Hiram Johnson that they "had met all demands of labor recommended by representatives of the Emergency Fleet Corporation. No labor troubles nor any known to be imminent."[3]

On January 14, 1918, fourteen-year-old Bernardine christened the *Taconia* by breaking a champagne bottle across the prow of the 429-foot steel freighter.[4] This was the fifth freighter launched by the shipyards. Years later, the California state assembly issued a resolution to name one of the ships after Murphy because he "is revered by many citizens of this State who held him in high esteem throughout his life for his high qualities of citizenship."[5]

Dan and Nettie Murphy directed their fundraising work to the Red Cross. Dan helped to organize a "motion picture baseball game" that brought in $8,000 in subscriptions. Nettie, Katharine Flint, Elizabeth Chandler, Louisa Guasti, and Frances Milbank along with several other neighborhood women organized the Enlisted Men's Club where soldiers could relax, read, and get lunch or snacks at a nominal fee. The Enlisted Men's Club even taught French lessons.[6]

Several West Adams homes were directly affected by the war. Hoteliers Hammel and Denker had married the Ruellen sisters of Alsace-Lorraine. Nearly forty years earlier they had escaped the Franco Prussian War. Louise Ruellen Denker believed that this war was a continuation of the one she fled and was, therefore, a dedicated volunteer at Nettie's Enlisted Club. But no one on the street took a more active role in the war effort that the Brunswigs at 3528 West Adams Blvd. Lucien Brunswig was nearly sixty when the war broke out. Nonetheless, he returned to France to offer his support. Brunswig ran a large wholesale drug business and no doubt offered supplies. After eight months in France, he returned to Los Angeles and organized several Franco-American relief societies

War Ships

including the Fatherless Children of France and the Pacific Coast States American Field Ambulance Service. The Fatherless Children of France gave aid to children under sixteen who had lost their fathers. Many US cities formed chapters of this organization. Brunswig was on the National Executive Committee. The American Ambulance Field Service was started by the American Colony in Paris. American college students, artists—young Ernest Hemingway, for instance— volunteer to drive ambulances to the front, to aid the wounded. Hemingway used this experience as the basis for his novel *A Farewell to Arms*. Antoinette donated ambulance No. 613, which was one of the twenty Brunswig had coordinated. At the end of the war, Brunswig presented her with the brass plaque from the ambulance that identified it as "Mrs. Daniel Murphy Ambulance." She treasured the keepsake, which years later was found carefully wrapped among her possessions.[7]

Lucien's wife, Marguerite Brunswig, held a major war-relief benefit on their ten-acre estate on West Adams. Nettie Murphy, Louise Holterhoff, Louisa Guasti, Lenore Chandler, Phila Milbank, Gertrude Monaghan [Frank's new wife], and Katharine Flint of Chester Place were all on Marguerite's committee for this two-hundred-guest affair. Lucien Brunswig would later be singled out and honored for his superb support of France during the war.[8]

World War I ended on the "the eleventh hour of the eleventh day of the eleventh month"[9] of 1918. The armistice was signed between the Allies and Germany aboard a private rail car in the forest of Compiègne, France. No one would have dared guess that twenty-two years later on this same railcar and in the same forest, Hitler and Göring forced the surrender of France.

As the "war to end all wars" came to a close, Antoinette began receiving praise for her work with the Red Cross and the Fatherless Children of France. Cards and letters of appreciation for her service at the Enlisted Men's Club arrived from the many soldiers she had aided, all letters she saved. One came from Sergeant Lyman McFie in France:

> We are all rejoicing that the war is over, but in one sense it doesn't seem quite true—or rather, we haven't had time to quite realize it. I happened to be in the village the night the armistice was signed and was quite amazed at first, at the attitude which the French people assumed. They all seemed happy enough, but yet there was something lacking on such an occasion,

Above: Antoinette Murphy bought an ambulance for the American Ambulance Field Service; neighbor Lucien Brunswig was chairman of this charity which supported France's efforts during World War 1.

Below: Antoinette was very proud of her participation and saved this plaque that was sent to her after the war.

especially for the "wild" Americans. There seems to be just a touch of pathos and on second thought, we realized that there was hardly a family that hadn't given, at least, one son. To them it was *"la guerre est finis,"* and none of them seem to "comphrendie" ... It sure was a contrast however from former nights. Instead of feeling our way along, the street lamps, which hadn't burned for over four years, were again lighted up. On nearly every window sill lighted candles were burning, and with the million and one flags of the Allies suspended from every nook, it seems pretty nice after all.[10]

On the heels of World War I, one of the worst pandemics to ever strike mankind broke out across Europe and North America. Estimates of the number of deaths worldwide range from 17 million to 100 million, at a time when there were about 1.8 billion people on earth. On December 1, 1918, a Sunday newspaper in Los Angeles carried the headline "Hope Held for Dan Murphy's Recovery," announcing that the businessman had taken ill on a train when returning from New York. Dr. M.H. Morrison from the Santa Fe Railway hospital and the Murphy family physician Dr. W.A. Edwards met the train and accompanied him to his home."[11] The *San Francisco Examiner* ran a similar story after receiving a call from Silas Lewis [aka Saint Lewis], the manager of the ice plant in Needles, who noted that he had "learned that Murphy's condition was severe. Physicians and nurses were attending him night and day."[12] The news of his illness "created great concern at the California Club where he is a prominent member and in other club and business circles where Mr. Murphy is widely known."[13]

The family became acutely aware of the fatality rate of the flu when Pat Murphy, Dan's twenty-year-old nephew, died of influenza just two months before Dan became ill. Bernardine, Sue, and several servants were dispatched to Wynanspray at Pebble Beach to isolate themselves from the virus. The symptoms of this 1918 pandemic consisted of a fever of 100 to 104 degrees with a cough, sore throat, severe muscle aches, headaches, and severe earaches. Diarrhea and bloody noses were present in the worst cases. The epidemic came in three waves, beginning in the spring of 1918. By the fall of that year, a second and much more lethal wave began. A third deadly wave struck in the winter of 1918–1919. The influenza outbreak had begun in Massachusetts, but within two weeks, "over 35,000 people throughout California had contracted influenza."

By October, the city of Los Angeles closed churches, theaters, and all other recreational venues. Schools closed and remained closed for four months. The raging illness was most prevalent in Southern California, peaking in November, with more than 115,000 cases.[14]

At the time, herbal concoctions were the only treatments available, since vaccines and antibiotics had not yet been invented. It would be more than ten years before the scientific community isolated the influenza virus, learning for the first time that the disease was not caused by bacteria, as previously believed. The only treatment was the newly introduced Vick's Vapo-Rub. Murphy's doctors were still practicing the medieval treatment of blood letting, using leeches, which was confirmed by a receipt for twelve leeches from the Piuma's Italian Pharmacy ($9.27 with tax).

The week after the newspaper accounts of Murphy's flu, businessmen, friends, ten to fifteen per day visited his home. His doctors kept visitors at a safe distance and Dan saw only thirteen of these in his sickroom. Silas Lewis and George Briggs came to visit him from Needles. Other visitors included his good friend, William Valentine, and two Standard Oil men from El Segundo. The majority of those who stopped by were club men, lawyers, and judges from downtown Los Angeles. Most believed they were paying their last respects to their dying friend. Joseph, the butler, kept a list of the callers—there were seventy-six in all. However, soon afterward, the papers announced, "Murphy Rallies: Condition Improved." It took nearly a year for Murphy to recover, if he ever fully recovered, but his near-death experience remained with him for the rest of his life.[15]

As Murphy struggled to regain his health and the war ended in 1918, PDC Ball again contacted Murphy and convinced him to partner in the construction of yet another ice plant. This time, the plant was in Chicago and it was named the Federal Ice & Refrigerating Company. This ice plant was the largest in the country, and when completed, it had the ability to produce six hundred tons of block ice daily. The enormous plant was strategically located on the Belt Railroad that serviced the Chicago area. Ball, Keller, and Murphy along with two local businessmen had negotiated for the purchase of twenty-five acres of land on Chicago's south side between Halsted, Racine, 114th Street, and 140th Street. The Belt RR "reaches all parts of Chicago where ice can be delivered in carload lots on switch tracks everywhere, and delivery can be made in one night." The ice plant was three stories high with a storage facility sized to the plant's production. The cost of construction was one million dollars.[16]

In 1922, the partners sold the Federal Ice & Refrigerating Company to a Cleveland company at a handsome profit. They may have seen the advent of home refrigeration looming on the horizon—some five thousand refrigerators had already sold by 1921—and believed that railroad icing would also be replaced by individual refrigeration units on train cars.[17]

Although Murphy maintained his investments in several different ice and cold storage facilities for many years to come, this was his last construction of an ice plant. In Needles, where Tom had been managing the Murphy Ice, Water and Light Company, the citizens were rallying for a municipal water company. The issue went to vote in 1925 and passed, thus turning the water system over to the city for $60,000, half of its value.[18]

22

My Warriors Fell Around Me

As the "Roaring Twenties" roared in, Dan and Nettie hardly felt roaring. He had recovered from his death-defying battle with the flu, and Nettie's stomach ulcers were causing her to resort to a bread-and-milk diet. The war had precluded any travel to Europe, and now with Dan's recovery underway, they were longing for a stay at the German spa at Bad Nauheim where a clinic was located. The Murphys received treatments at the clinic on their 1912 trip. William Kerckhoff had recommended the place. Will and Dan were both under the care of the renowned cardiologist Dr. Franz Groedel. Numerous times over the decades they took the cure at Groedel's clinic. The treatment plan required at least a three-week stay at the luxurious spa where strict daily routines were followed, including customized diets, exercises, and thermal pool therapy. Dan and Nettie were both under Dr. Groedel's care, he for a heart ailment and she for those stomach ulcers and high-blood pressure.

By 1921, Sue and Bernardine were living in Rome while the seventeen-year old studied at the American Academy. Back in Los Angeles, the Murphys were worried about them. Dan was rightfully concerned about his "little Rosebud" living in Rome. Bernardine dutifully wrote home saying "there is only one road to success, and that is the uphill road of work that leads to glory."[1] This statement was in reference to her sculpting classes at the academy where she was nearing her completion of a bas-relief of Dante.

Italy's finances, post-World War I, were in shambles with the Liberal government owing vast sums to England and the United States for helping finance the Italian war effort. The Italian middle class had lost 30% of its purchasing power. The working-class blamed the Liberals for poverty, hunger, and the poor outcome of the war. The Socialist movement encouraged a revolution similar to Russia's. The noble classes naturally blamed Socialists for the failing economy. Hundreds of nobles were deposed by the war and flooded the capitals of Europe, especially Berlin, Rome, and Paris. Art, culture, music, fashion, and technology all changed radically. The displaced aristocrats had lost their fortunes and many eligible bachelors turned their attention to wealthy American debs. General societal mores turned from a life that was decorative, where courtesy and refinement walked hand in hand, to new social liberalism. Between the wars France and Italy were teaming with these deposed princes, counts, and dukes, many with money, but even more in search of it. It was in this mêlée that Dan found his "little Rosebud" living in Rome. They were rightfully concerned.

The Murphys set about making plans for their third trip abroad. This time they would be accompanied by their friends Louise and William Valentine from San Marino. On the way, they stopped in New York City for the wedding of Godfrey Holterhoff's daughter Leila and lawyer Bernard Heyn at the Plaza Hotel. The Murphys, Holterhoffs, and the Valentines all celebrated at the Plaza before boarding the luxury liner SS *Conte Rosso*, bound for Genoa, Italy. The newlyweds joined the voyage for their honeymoon on the Italian Riviera. The *New York Times* reported that SS *Conte Rosso*, the newest liner since the War, was "the last word in luxurious travel by sea." Leila's marriage to Heyn was not to last. In a few years, the very talented and self-sufficient Leila would sue for divorce on the grounds of "indifference."[2]

The Murphys took a suite at the Grand Hotel in Rome. As always their first priority was to secure their audience with the Holy Father, this time new pope, Pius XI, and again to make their "generous donation." They politely showed interest in attending the beatification of Thérèse of Lisieux and were given preferred seating for the event in Saint Peter's Basilica. Pius XI was elected to the papacy in February of 1922, succeeding Benedict XV who had reigned for only eight difficult years. Benedict had been elected a month after the outbreak of World War I. His reign was noted for his humanitarian and diplomatic achievements while he had continued advocating non-violence, with pleas for peace. October 28, 1922, marks the date of the Fascist "March on Rome."[3]

Throughout Mussolini's governmental control, he always appointed one of the members of the Black Nobility as governor of the Italian state. In the early days of Mussolini's rule, the Vatican and most Catholics believed that he would restore the country after the devastating effects of the war. "Hundreds of millions of Catholics throughout the world looked to Rome as their spiritual home, he [Mussolini] said, this [Fascism] was a source of strength that Italy could not ignore."[4] It was up to Pius XI to deal with the Fascist state. Compared to his predecessors, Pius XI was cold and curt. Given the dignity of his office, he refused to talk

My Warriors Fell Around Me

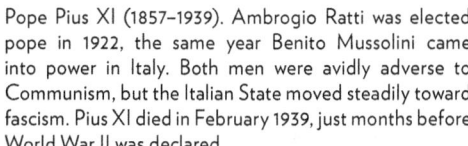
Pope Pius XI (1857–1939). Ambrogio Ratti was elected pope in 1922, the same year Benito Mussolini came into power in Italy. Both men were avidly adverse to Communism, but the Italian State moved steadily toward fascism. Pius XI died in February 1939, just months before World War II was declared.

on the phone or pose for photos with guests. He also insisted on eating alone. (It would be seven more years until Mussolini and Pius XI signed the Lateran Treaty (1929) which stated that the Vatican recognized the Kingdom of Italy and in return was recognized as a sovereign state, thus ending the "prisoner of the Vatican" stance by the pope.)

At Mussolini's March on Rome, Bernardine was photographed on an outdoor platform crowded with uniformed military officers. The photo appeared in a newspaper with the caption that noted "Miss Murphy is the niece of General Ruspoli," who was also on the dais. She preserved the clipping and her ticket to the event as keepsakes. More importantly, it identifies her birth father as a member of the noble family of Ruspoli.[5] This explains Sue Sinnott's and Bernardine's rapid access to the aristocratic families of Rome's Black Nobility.

Unaware of what Bernardine was up to romantically in the Eternal City, the Murphys left Sue and Bernardine and continued on their customary route from Rome to the Beau Rivage in Lucerne, and then on to Bad Nauheim in Germany for the cure. They lingered a month in each place to cure their spirit, soul, and body. Before heading back to Los Angeles, they stopped in Paris for a few weeks of consumer therapy, where Bernardine and Sue would join in the therapy session.

Dan wrote to Father Ruppert S.J. regarding this European trip:

> We are all feeling much benefited from the trip as well as the treatments, and I think I am in better physical condition than I have been during the last fifteen years, for which we are all very thankful. ... When in Rome, it was our good fortune to be there during the Beatification of the Little Flower of Jesus [Saint Thérèse of Lisieux], which was attended by over 140,000 people from all parts of the world ...The singing from all parts

of Saint Peter's ... and the carrying of the Holy Father [Pius XI] before the multitudes, one of the most beautiful and effective scenes that those present, I know, ever had witnessed ... one can imagine the breathing of the saints in heaven could be distinctly heard. ... knowing your great devotion and faith in the Little Flower of Jesus ... [you] remained fresh before me during the Beatification services. I have a medal of the Saint, blessed by the Holy Father, and hope to present [it to] you in the near future.[6]

Just two weeks after the Murphys had witnessed Saint Thérèse of Lisieux's Beatification at Saint Peter's, Godfrey Holterhoff died. He collapsed from sudden heart failure on May 15, 1923, at his home at 1360 West Adams Blvd. He was sixty-four years old. Dan's brother Tom stood in as a pallbearer in Dan's absence. Holterhoff had been of immeasurable comfort and support to Murphy from his earliest days on the commissary car. Godfrey had helped to secure the land and approval for Dan's first ice plant and had encouraged him to purchase Brea Cañon. For fifty years, their lives ran parallel to each other, like the ribbons of steel rails on the railroads they had served. The rails had brought them together professionally, socially, and fraternally. Holterhoff had come to California hoping to improve his failing health when he was only nineteen. He had landed his first job in California as secretary for the emerging California Southern Railroad. With only a high school education, he had become the most powerful man in the Western Division of the Atchison, Topeka & Santa Fe Railroad in addition to being the officer or director of more than thirty corporations. Now, Dan's two closest companions, both Frank Monaghan and Godfrey Holterhoff, were gone. Godfrey was interred in the Great Mausoleum at Forest Lawn in Glendale, California. There his tomb remains at the end of the long "Coleus Corridor" next to a window where the sounds of whistles from the nearby Amtrak trains on the old Santa Fe mainline tracks still can be heard.[7]

On their return voyage aboard the RMS *Berengaria,* Nettie wrote to Bernardine in Rome:

> It was almost darkness, the sun, a big ball of gold, disappeared in a dark cloud—Mrs. Holterhoff, Father, and I stood watching it at the end of the ship. Much to my surprise—Father recites this poem beautifully.
>
> You have taken me prisoner with all of my warriors.
> I am much grieved.
> I had hoped,

Godfrey Holterhoff Jr. As an executive of the Pacific Land Improvement Company and Western Division of the Santa Fe Railway, Holterhoff was one of the most powerful and influential men in Southern California.

> if not defeated to hold out much longer
> and give you more trouble before surrendering.
> But your guns were well aimed,
> and the bullets whizzed by our ears
> like the wind through the trees in winter.
> My warriors fell around me.
> And I saw my evil day at hand.
> The sun rose dim on us in the morning
> and at night it sank in a dark cloud
> and looked like a ball of fire.
> That was the last sun to set on Black Hawk.
> For his heart was silent
> and no longer beat fast in his bosom.

The widow Holterhoff wept, and, later on, said, 'I know Dan Murphy is a grand man.[8] The grieving Murphy recalled this touching poem from his childhood. Memorized from his reading primer *McGuffey's New Juvenile Speaker*[9] from his elementary school days in Hanover, at the time representing his love for Native Americans, but now recalled as a testament to his love for his fallen comrade Godfrey Holterhoff.

In the fall of 1923, Dan and Nettie returned to a very changed Los Angeles. It was changed primarily for Murphy, since his last good friend and confidant of days past was gone. Holterhoff had been an integral board member for many of Murphy's companies and, to Murphy, was irreplaceable. It was a lonely time at home since only Dan and Nettie were together each night at the dinner table.

Nineteen-year-old Bernardine and Aunt Sue returned from two years in Italy for Bernardine's début to Los Angeles society. Before leaving, Bernardine wrote to Nettie:

Bernardine Murphy was twenty at the time of her debut. Circa 1924.

> Your baby has found some very good looking clothes here, some Chanel and Lanvin models. We found a very, very good looking beaver fur coat that I walked right into. [It] was a little over $300, can you believe it? We are delighted, and it is very stylish and becoming ... The life of my friends in Los Angeles sounds so empty; I suppose Hortense [McLaughlin] doesn't think so.[10]

Once everyone was back in Los Angeles, the big event took place on January 24, 1924. And a society writer from the *Los Angeles Times* was on hand to detail the story covering the event at their palatial home at 2076 West Adams Blvd.

> Amid the myriad of blossoms and surrounded by the most attractive matrons and debutantes ... each room had been transformed into a floral bower, roses of rare varieties forming the decorative motif. The Murphy home is particularly adaptable to decoration and on this occasion, many beautiful combinations were used. In one instance, an arrangement of natural oranges and marigolds ... Russell Roses and American Beauties were used in the drawing-room ... pink shaded blossoms formed a rich background for the receiving line. The modest little debutante, clad in silver, looked like a Correggio. Her dark tresses framing her features of cameo daintiness ... a beautifully simple imported Lan-

vin model, of silver lame trimmed with silver lace and she carried Lilies of the Valley ... a young girl of rare charm and accomplishment. She already speaks four languages fluently and is a gifted musician.[11]

Bernardine's coming out was also announced in the *San Francisco Examiner*, indicating that neither Nettie nor Aunt Sue shared Dan's publicity-shy approach to life. One of them, at least, wanted Bernardine properly introduced to society throughout the state. The guests at the two o'clock tea "included many distinguished personages and members of old California families." Antoinette was assisted at the tea by Louisa Guasti, Lillie MacGowan, and Miriam Clark, all from West Adams Boulevard. Susanna Bryant of 15 Berkeley Square and Katharine Flint of 20 Chester Place also helped out, as did several other family friends. Bernardine's childhood playmates and fellow debutantes in attendance were Misses Eleanor MacGowan, Cecile and Susanna Bryant, Susan Valentine, Hortense McLaughlin, and Genevieve Maier. On such an auspicious occasion, sixty-one-year-old Murphy must have been beaming at the sight of his "little Rosebud."

Like many fathers, a daughter coming of age caused Murphy to contemplate the years that Bernardine had been in their household, and to recall the anguish he felt when perpetuating the lie about her true parentage. However, he and Nettie finally must have felt a sense of accomplishment on this celebration day. The lack of a male heir had haunted him since the bungled adoption of Charles Weber years before. Like most businessmen of his era, Murphy probably expected that his daughter would marry a man who would be able to carry on his business legacy. He and Nettie also expected that Bernardine would be able to pick and choose from many marriage proposals, since in addition to her family's status, the society pages of newspapers throughout the state had cast her as "the most beautiful young girl in Los Angeles society ... dark hair ... delicate coloring, and brown eyes with heavy black lashes."[12]

But Bernardine had other ideas.

The month after the coming out party, Nettie had yet another event planned. The Murphys had been asked by Bishop John Joseph Cantwell, the current bishop of Los Angeles, if they would host a dinner in honor of the visiting papal nuncio, Pietro Biondi, upon his first visit to California. The nuncio is the Vatican's ambassador to the United States, and he maintains an embassy in Washington, D.C. A visit by the papal nuncio to California required the utmost planning and fanfare from San Francisco Archbishop Edward Joseph Hanna as well as from Bishop Cantwell of the Los Angeles-San Diego archdiocese. Nettie was called upon to provide dinner at her home for the entourage and invite a few Catholic luminaries from the city. Over thirty guests were at the table, including six bishops, ten other clergy, and thirteen local professionals and industry leaders. Cantwell wrote in thanks "for the high-toned and elegant manner in which you opened your home to entertain His Excellency."[13]

Later that spring, the Murphy family was granted a papal indult by Pius XI, a very rare privilege authorizing a mass to be celebrated in the private chapel at their home, complete with a tabernacle that held the Blessed Sacrament used in holy communion. The only other private chapel with a papal indult in Los Angeles was in the home of Estelle Doheny, the widow of the oil tycoon, Edward Doheny.[14]

Within a few weeks, Sue and Bernardine left Los Angeles and returned to Rome. Bernardine's voice and sculpture lessons awaited. Unbeknownst to the Los Angeles household, Bernardine had more romantic missions to attend to in the Eternal City.

Sue and Bernardine took a suite of rooms at the Hotel de Russie, an imposing nineteenth century structure just off the Piazza de Popolo. The family of the last czar of Russia was frequently in residence. Sue and Bernardine enjoyed hosting other well-to-do Americans who were touring Italy in these fine accommodations. Bernardine began keeping an infrequent diary, noting her excitement and wonder at living in the Eternal City. Long a devout and religious young woman, she was fascinated by the papacy. She and her birth mother Sue were fortunate to obtain tickets in the "Diplomatic Tribune" seating section at Saint Peter's. As Vatican etiquette required, they wore black dresses, below the knee, with high collars covering the neck, and black lace veils over their faces. They entered the cathedral from a side door, and

> as soon as we showed our tickets, everyone bowed lo[w], and we were shown quickly to the "Tribune." It was just beside the statue of Saint Peter, and the throne for the Pope was directly opposite ... the Pope was carried in on the Sedia Gestoria ... he wore the most marvelous lame and the triple crown ... it was [an] unforgettably interesting and beautiful occasion.[15]

Attendance at papal masses in Saint Peter's Basilica was harmless enough, but because her parents back home were concerned, they had asked old family friends to look in on her and Sue. Randolph and Tulita Huntington Miner lived at 649 West Adams Blvd. During the war, Tulita Miner was appointed the head of the Navy American Red Cross. She and Nettie worked together on the Red Cross campaign. When peace was declared, the Miners moved to Rome, where Tulita's sister

Mamie Wilcox Longstreet had been living since her divorce in 1898. The family of the two sisters, Tulita Huntington Miner and Mamie Wilcox Longstreet, could trace their ancestry back to California's Spanish Colonial era and the founding of Los Angeles. In 1814, their great-great grandfather Jose Argüello was the acting governor of California. In 1852, their father Captain Alfred Henry Wilcox was one of the founders of the Colorado Steam Navigation Company—long before the Southern Pacific Railroad had reached Yuma. When Monaghan and Murphy bought the paddlewheel business, Tulita's husband Randolph Huntington Miner was an investor in the venture.[16] He was also a distinguished Annapolis graduate. The Miners' Los Angeles home was inside the gates of the very exclusive Chester Place. When they left it to live in Rome, it was occupied by a string of silver screen entertainers, including Theda Bara, Rosco (Fatty) Arbuckle, and Joseph Schenck and his actress/wife Norma Talmadge. The notoriety and loud drinking parties at the Miners' previous home disgusted the residents of stuffy Chester Place. Ed Doheny's widow, Estelle, began buying the homes in the sedate park to prevent the re-occurrence of similar behavior.[17] Since they were longtime friends of the Murphy family, Randolph and the two sisters took Bernardine and Sue under their care in Rome.

Bernardine's attendance at the American Academy allowed her to meet well-connected Romans in addition to her introductions to the noble Ruspoli family. She soon had an admiring retinue of continental men inviting her to events, teas, and formal dinners. Among these distinguished admirers were the Marquis Leo Lagegren of Sweden; Prince Lelio Orsini of Rome, and Prince Federico Borromeo of Milan. This was the time "between the wars," when Europe was rife with young single male royals looking for American heiresses to marry, most not expecting to meet such a renowned beauty as Bernardine.

On Friday, November 27, 1925, Bernardine wrote her parents. Her newsy letter may have reflected how excited she was, but its contents had her parents worried:

> I have just returned from a most delightful luncheon given by Mr. and Mrs. Miner and Mrs. Longstreet—at the palatial Grand Hotel ... the guests were Prince and Princess Orsini, his brother Prince Don Lelio Orsini, Prince Orsini's daughter, Isabella—a Count Moroni, the grand-nephew of Pope Leo XIII, Guy O'Sullivan, and Mr. and Mrs. Bevini ... I [sat] on one side of Mr. B. and Prince Don L. Orsini, on my left. He is extremely handsome, has a very kind but sad face, and he

> speaks no English. I had a good time speaking Italian … Neither he nor his brother are not the sleek type of Italian, but very strong and healthy-looking men, quiet and simple in manner … Count Moroni is a painter and invited me to his studio next week to see some of his work … Prince Don L.O. is a member of the Noble Guards at the Vatican, and he said he would be happy to get anything for me, in the way of audiences or whatever we would like to have."[18]

Bernardine was featured in a fawning article leading up to her debut.

> Bernardine had an alluring foreign type of beauty. Tall and statuesque … when with her intimates, a surprisingly keen sense of humor is revealed, she's extremely clever and brilliant … a linguist of note, she is just as much at home in speaking French, Italian, or English … can discuss any subject with great authority … she's charitable to a fault, but few people become aware of it … she is constantly doing unselfish charming things for people. Nothing can be too much trouble for friends, and she goes to untold lengths to please with gifts and surprises.[19]

"Charitable to a fault but few people become aware of it" is the same description that would have applied to her devoted father, so she probably modeled his manner. Even in her early twenties she could hold her own at the lavish palaces and dinners, she attended.

While in Rome, the twenty-one-year-old wrote in her diary:

> December 1925, Hotel Russie, Rome. Am wondering what we will have for [seats in Saint Peter's] on the twenty-fourth, Lelio is getting us [Bernardine and Sue]. He is really such a dear. We went out to the Orsini Villa for luncheon today. They sent their Rolls-Royce for us. Marchesa Camponari [of Russian royalty] came in a taxi. Princess Orsini was very sweet and simple—looked very pretty in a velvet frock. Domina Isabella was also there and her sister Hilda … Soon Prince Orsini started shaking cocktails, he is a charming host and says he does not care for society and social affairs. Lelio was my shadow. Sue and I enjoyed ourselves and stayed quite a while.[20]

The Orsinis next invited Bernardine and Sue to visit Castle Bracciano, a property that once belonged to the family and overlooks a lake of the same name. The following week, Sue, Bernardine, Lelio and his sister-in-law Frances Orsini motored nineteen miles northwest of Rome to the fortress, which was where Charles VIII of France encamped on his way to sack Rome In 1419. In 1494, the sons of Pope Alexander VI, Giovanni Borgia, and Cesare Borgia, unsuccessfully besieged the Orsini stronghold. In later years, Paolo Orsini and his wife Isabella de Medici, daughter of Cosimo I, redecorated the castle and lived there briefly.[21]

Bernardine gushed about the history—and about Lelio:

> Lelio was so intent on showing me everything. It was the first time he had been there in ten years, and he said his father went there rarely, when alive, as it made him feel so bad that it no longer belonged to his family. Lelio and I went up on one of the towers and stood in the breeze watching a heavenly sunset. Lelio slipped his arm through mine. That was the first sign of affection and his handsome sad face and velvet brown eyes, I shall never forget ... When we came down and joined Princess Orsini and Sue, they looked rather relieved. I felt simply bewildered and everything and everyone rather unusual. December 21, 1925.[22]

She also let slip another important fact: "Prince Orsini told us how [the castle] was to have come back to him, but through some legal means, he lost it. He is very out and out."[23]

After morning mass at Saint Peter's and an afternoon concert and dinner, Bernardine and Lelio returned to the Hotel de Russie, always accompanied by their chaperones, Sue and Frances.

> After [Frances] left, Lelio and I had a long talk in one of the small salons downstairs. He asked [me] to be his wife, which was a perfect surprise to me. I wanted to say yes immediately, but common sense came to my reason, so I will think it over. Lelio says he has been looking for a real-life companion, and everyone that has interested him in the past has only been half his ideal, and now, at last, he has found the woman that is more than all of that and for whom his title is not half enough.[24]

Two days later Sue and Bernardine went to Lelio's apartment for tea. His apartment had a side entrance to the palace.

> ... He had a long talk with Sue about his affection for me. I had to translate, which was rather embarrassing

Prince Lelio Orsini (1877–1952), of the ancient and powerful Orsini family of Rome, proposed to Bernardine Murphy in 1925. He signed this keepsake photograph to her: "*A Bernardina*, [from] Lelio, *Natali* [Christmas] 1925."

… he went on to explain that he was talking with her as my father and mother were not there. He made his position very clear and said that he had saved enough from the wreck of the family's fortune, but, of course, did not have enough to keep up a big establishment as his position called for. He had always said he would never marry for money. He had seen too much unhappiness. Tears would come to his eyes as he talked.[25]

He then gave them tickets for premier seats on Christmas Eve at Saint Peter's for the closing of the Holy Door by Pius XI, ending the Holy Year, which is celebrated every twenty-five years. She finished this entry with, "He is forty-seven years old."[26]

Among the Murphy papers is a letter, probably never mailed, or perhaps it was a draft, written in Murphy's hand, but it gives rare insight into his thinking and is therefore provided here in its entirety:

Dear Don Lelio Orsini:

Your letter of December 27, asking me for the hand of my daughter, Bernardine, reached me just as I was leaving for San Francisco. As I wish to consult with my wife, I delayed writing until my return.

From what Bernardine and her Aunt Sue have told me, I am convinced of your deep affection for her. And that she cares for you. But would it not be better for us to wait until we meet to have a perfect understanding? I appreciate the honor that you wish to bestow upon Bernardine, and I have no wish to oppose the marriage but want to be assured that neither you nor she are making a mistake. Her happiness has always been most precious to us and our first consideration.

As we have never met, I am sure you realize my position and my not conceding immediately to your request. That it would be a great sacrifice, for her mother and me, to give her to one who lives so far away, you must know. I am now endeavoring to arrange my affairs so as to sail directly to Italy the last of March. My family joins me in warmest greeting.

Hoping soon to have the great pleasure of meeting you and that you will pardon my delay in replying to your request. I beg to remain most cordially yours,

Dan Murphy January 22, 1926[27]

Bernardine introduced her parents to Prince Lelio Orsini on their 1926 trip to Italy. Compared to the tone of the letter Murphy had written to him, the visit did not go well. The couple never married. Their age difference alone would have been enough to squelch the union—he at forty-seven and she at just twenty-two. But perhaps more important, everyone in Los Angeles, including Bernardine and her parents, knew that Lelio's brother Prince Domenico Orsini had two years earlier married a wealthy Angeleno named Laura Rowan, a local widow.[28] Were these brothers gold-diggers? The letters among Bernardine's papers never explained the whole truth. But two years later, in 1928, Lelio married a thirty-year-old Italian noblewoman. Lelio died in 1952 at the Grand Hotel Minerve in Rome.[29]

Not long after Prince Orsini faded from her world, Bernardine and Sue returned from Italy after nearly two years of absence. Bernardine fell ill. In her diary, she noted:

> I have reread all the letters that I wrote since meeting Lelio, and it is interesting to see how blindly I might say you read them. I knew when writing them that they were (not telling the whole truth) the only one I could think about, night and day, had to be ignored, and that was Lelio. I regret now the course I chose with regards to telling you about him, for what I thought would avoid your ever been [being] jealous of him, made you think I did not really love him ... You could say that I was not frank with you and such was the case, but I was so afraid that if I wrote from Rome, how I really felt towards him, you would have sent for Sue and me to come right home. I feared that you would get upset and misunderstand us, but as it was due to your illness or lack of understanding, you did not realize I adored

Sue Stone Sinnott (1865–1945). Circa 1920.

Lelio, and I do to this day.[30]

On March 28,1927, in a fit of melancholy and while recovering from bronchial pneumonia, she asked herself "What is life?" and wrote:

> My heart I gave to man,
> having confidence in God's creatures
> I allow them to call my heart there's [sic],
> so for these twenty-three years
> they have caressed and flattered it,
> with what time have proven,
> to be hypocritical affection.
>
> At various times in my life my heart has been wounded, but last year it died after being pierced by the arrow aimed by Cupid which had been dipped in poisonous "truth."
>
> The pain was excruciating and after one supreme effort to beat—it died. All this was done by loving humans.[31]

She admits to her diary that she lied to her parents "about how I really felt towards him." She knew her parents would not approve of her seeing a man twenty-five years older than she. But what is the "poisonous truth"? Had she, at the age of twenty-two just found out about her true biological parents? Is she accusing her parents of "hypocritical affection"? And who does she think is "jealous of him"? Does she believe her parents are jealous of her love for Lelio?

23

THE PUMP IS BUSTED

By 1930, at home in Los Angeles, Murphy settled into a daily routine, taking the train from downtown to Fullerton where he drove to Brea Cañon. Thomas R. Lee, who was called "Tommie," at the time, was a Union Oil employee. He wrote his recollections of Murphy in an article for the industry magazine *Petroleum World* in 1940:

> [Murphy would greet the workers] always with a friendly wave of his hand to us "pipeliners" hanging around the old pump station. He'd sit around the battered old office talking to Bill Farrand, his foreman, or getting statistics from Walt Munday, his field bookkeeper; drift over to "old man Enock's" boarding house for lunch, and drive seven miles back to Fullerton to catch "the five o'clock" as it came through for Los Angeles, he'd stand a little back from the track, raised two fingers in salute to the engineer, swing with a "Brakeman's flip" on the steps of the "parlor car" coach as it rolled by. Dan never forgot he'd been a railroad man.[1]

The Brea Cañon workman marveled at how Murphy came to own the most productive and best-quality oil in the whole canyon. Tommie Lee noted that

> It's strange that the two hundred acres he acquired at the mouth of the canyon happened to be the only land that produced any amount of oil in the old days. Practically every well drilled by Brea Canyon [sic] Oil was then called a gusher. It must've been more or less Irish luck because they say Dan never hired a geologist in his life.[2]

Lyman Stewart, the founder of Union Oil, leased the land surrounding Brea Cañon. Both companies had water tanks to supply the steam engines that pumped the oil. A string of these tanks was set high on a ridge for each company, all connected by a single two-inch pipe. Union Oil ran the pump that supplied the tanks. Tommie Lee, the Union Oil employee in charge of the water pump, was told by Stewart "to see that the Union always had water." When the pump broke down and water was in short supply, Tommie cut off Brea Cañon.

> That morning, Dan Murphy drove out as usual from Fullerton. In the afternoon, he sent for me. I went, a kid of twenty-one, scared to death. He looked a little hard, but was still smiling.
>
> "Tommie, why can't we get water?" [Murphy asked Lee]
>
> "The pump is busted!" [Lee responded]
>
> "Yes, but why can't we get our share?" [Murphy]
>
> "Because I got orders to give what water there is to Union Oil." [Lee]
>
> Steel came into his eyes and he ceased to smile.
>
> "Who gave you orders?" [Murphy]
>
> I told him.
>
> "All right Tommie, you obey your orders. Always obey your orders. I'm an old railroad man, and I know. That's all I wanted to see you about." [Murphy]
>
> I turned to go.
>
> "Tommie!" [Murphy]
>
> I stopped. The old pleasant smile came back.
>
> "I don't blame you for this." [Murphy]
>
> That night at eight o'clock I got a call from my foreman to see that the Brea Cañon Oil Company did not run out of water, these orders came from the top. How Dan Murphy accomplished this, how he inveigled the top man of the Union Oil to issue an order to cut themselves off from their own water supply, I don't know. That was Dan Murphy's way. He got what he wanted—and made men like it! That was why I climbed the old hill after dark and turned the water into his tank with real pleasure. It was a pleasure to serve Dan Murphy![3]

Tommie Lee went on to say, "Yes, he was lucky and certainly a smart businessman." Murphy was one of the first employers to materially do a little extra for his men. Every employee received a turkey, ham, or a bottle of whiskey each Thanksgiving and Christmas. That was one of the reasons they all like to work for Murphy.

He, like most Irishmen, was a good Roman Catholic.

THE PUMP IS BUSTED

The priests at the old cathedral on Main Street in Los Angeles could tell many a story of his charities—boxes of canned goods, barrels of flour, thousands of Christmas baskets for the down-and-outers. The name of the good Samaritan was never allowed to be used.[4]

H.K. Bagley, his longtime secretary, said, "He took his losses like a good sport, and with a wave of the hand, would simply say—whether it was a dollar or $100,000—charge it [to] profit and loss."[5] The years from 1926 through 1929 were Dan's peak earning years (He was clearly a very rich man: by 1928, he was earning the equivalent of $13.8 million per year, in 2020 dollars). In a small leather vest pocket ring binder with tabs from A to Z, Mr. Bagley had meticulously recorded yearly dividend totals for each of Dan's investments. Under "I," the annual "Dividends and Miscellaneous Income," from all the other pages, were totaled—one line per year from 1908 through 1934. These figures represent only the dividends from investments and do not include profits from ice, oil, or mining:

1908—1917 averaged $155,000/year
1918—1923 averaged $274,000/year
1924—1931 nearly $900,000/year
1927—1929 over $1 million/year[6]

In 1922, Murphy filed the articles of incorporation for Dan Murphy Company. Holterhoff, Bagley, and Murphy's lawyer, Richard J. Dillon sat on the board. Although Bagley first worked with Murphy as his secretary, after nearly twenty-five years of faithful service, he was now a key figure in Murphy's affairs. (All of Murphy's various companies were transferred into Dan Murphy Company by 1938.) Creating the company had protected Murphy from a large portion of personal income tax, but the new entity paid corporate taxes of considerable size. There is no record of Murphy's reaction to these new tax laws. Over the next twelve years, Murphy transferred all his interests to this one company.

Murphy had no male heir to take over the company, so in a move somewhat rare for the era, he named his adopted daughter Bernardine to replace him as chairman of Dan Murphy Company in case of his death. He incorporated the company the year after his lifelong partner Monaghan passed away. It appears as if Murphy was tidying up his affairs.

Murphy had a minor car crash at a residential intersection not far from his home, breaking several ribs. Since the accident, he relied upon his chauffeur to take him downtown to where Howard Bagley maintained his office in the Kerckhoff building at 560 S. Main St., a ten-story Morgan and Walls building built in 1910. At least monthly, he went to Colton to attend the California Portland Cement Company board meetings. By the late 1920s and into the early 1930s, his time was spent attending various board meetings and socializing at the California Club.[7]

In 1929, Nettie had her own chauffeur, a young man who was not very experienced driving in an era when lanes, crosswalks, and signals were new and controversial. But she had her own interests and meetings to attend, so she needed her own driver; this man lived above the four-car garage at the foot of the family's property.

Always a dedicated gardener and horticulturist, Nettie took great pride in landscape design. Her existing West Adams garden had been written about often in the local newspapers. In 1920, the Southern California Chapter of the American Institute of Architects listed Antoinette's garden as one of the top five gardens of Southern California. In that listing, Huntington Botanical Gardens in San Marino, near Pasadena, received only an honorable mention.[8]

By 1928, Nettie was ready to renovate and redesign sections of the now fourteen-year-old landscaping. She contracted with Florence Yoch, the renowned landscape architect from South Pasadena. Yoch is credited with having set the distinctive style of California gardens of the 1920s and 1930s. She interpreted Nettie's classic Italian villa and European gardens to fit the Southern California landscape. Yoch also designed gardens for Henry Huntington, George Cukor, Jack Warner, and David O. Selznick. Nettie would not have been influenced by any of these Hollywood people, but she knew a good landscape architect when she saw one. Antoinette had been quite content with the exemplary job done by her original designer, Wilbur Cook, but the mature landscape was in need of work.[9]

By now West Adams Boulevard had been paved, and motor traffic had increased. Nettie wanted a privacy wall along the frontage of their estate to block the street view of the vast green lawns that flowed uninterrupted from the street to the home. She installed a four-and-a-half-foot-high brick wall covered with white stucco to blend with the white stucco house.

She contracted with Florence Yoch for a half-million-dollar upgrade that included a dozen large trees: five cypresses, three peppers, two magnolias, and two pines, as well as twenty-four olive trees, and an English Laurel. The mature trees alone cost $25,000. Yoch and Nettie included 274 boxwoods and pebble pavements in the new garden design.

With the relandscaping set to begin in April 1929, Nettie was in need of a visit to the clinic at Bad Nauheim. Her stomach ulcers were giving her trouble and the diet at the spa always appeared to help. Although doing better than in the past, Dan was intending to see his doctor

The Pump Is Busted 241

It was common for affluent women to shop for pairs of natural pearls to add to their "string." Antoinette Murphy and her daughter Bernardine were both fond of this hobby. Upon Bernardine's death in 1968, these four strands (a combination of Antoinette's and her own pearls) with a diamond-and-platinum clip, were donated to the County of Los Angeles and are on permanent display in the Gem and Mineral Hall of the Los Angeles Natural History Museum, where Frank Monaghan, representing the Southwest Miners Association, deposited the collection which is the basis of the museum's mineral display.

there to check up on his high blood pressure and his knee pain. Leaving Florence Yoch in charge of the landscaping, the family set off for Europe. This time, Bernardine took her car. That meant it was sent by train from Los Angeles to the docks in New York and then into the hold of the ocean liner, to the port of Cherbourg, France. After a week shopping in Paris the family split up, Dan and Nettie went to their health spa at Bad Nauheim. Sue and Bernardine motored on to Rome.

Their return to Bad Nauheim in April 1929 was particularly sorrowful for Murphy. His compatriot Will Kerckhoff had died at the spa the month before his arrival. Will had been suffering for years with heart trouble. Murphy and Kerckhoff had been fast friends since 1907, when they had opened the San Diego bank (along with Holterhoff, Doheny, and Canfield). It was Kerckhoff who originally introduced Murphy to Bad Nauheim's cardiologist Dr. Franz Groedel. Bad Nauheim was home to the luxurious spa with effervescing natural hot springs which were rich in minerals. It was particularly noted for treating heart diseases and nervous disorders. Doctors reviewed their daily progress and adjusted their activities accordingly. Dr. Groedel was the leading cardiologist for the clinic at that time. Murphy's first visit to Groedel was in 1909. Dan had been seeing him every other year since. Murphy and Kerckhoff sat on many of the same boards including those of California Institute of Technology and First National Bank. Murphy sold natural gas from Brea Cañon to Kerckhoff's gas company. Moreover, they and their wives were close family friends. Nettie and Louise Kerckhoff had for years done charity work together for the Good Shepherd Sisters and the Red Cross. The Kerckhoffs had adopted twin girls who were a few years older than Bernardine. Their adoption, however, was under very different circumstances. This was a secret that Nettie or Dan never shared, even with close friends.

 Many of the same people made their annual pilgrimage to the mineral spring resort, so over the years, the Murphys, had made several friends there. Two men Dan particularly looked forward to seeing were Joseph and Auguste Pavin de Lafarge, who were from southern France. They were the owners of a large Portland cement factory on the Rhône River, south of Lyon. The factory had supplied the lime used in the construction of the Suez Canal. In 1833, the Lafarge family built the first lime kilns in France. As the largest and oldest manufacturer of cement in France, the Lafarges had a great deal in common with Murphy.[10] Together they whiled away the hours chatting on their prescribed walks through the parks of the spa town.

24

Gentleman In Question

After a refreshing and rejuvenating stay in Bad Nauheim, Dan and Antoinette traveled to Paris their final stop before the long Ocean voyage and cross country trip home. On the morning of October 9, 1929, the Murphys read in the International News the most crushing news: their daughter was to marry Prince Federico Borromeo of Milan. In one fell swoop, Murphy's lifetime of assiduously keeping his name out of the newspapers came to a sudden end.

In the International News and the *Los Angeles Examiner* the headline read "Bernardine and Prince May Wed—The Betrothal Rumor Persists In Rome." A large photograph of Bernardine Dan Murphy accompanied the article.

> Rome, October 8—a marriage of international importance between a young Los Angeles heiress and the successor to one of Italy's most famous princedoms will be solemnized here within the near future, it was revealed tonight ... The engagement of young Prince Borromeo and Miss Bernardine Murphy, daughter of Daniel Murphy, a wealthy Los Angeles banker, will be announced shortly, it is reported tonight ... Prince Borromeo, the heir to his father's two palaces and magnificent Lake Maggiore estate, is said to hinge upon the outcome of negotiations to be carried on in Los Angeles by a high American prelate who is now in Rome, but plans to return to the United States in November ... The Borromeo family is extremely well-connected at the Vatican, being directly descended from Saint Charles Borromeo at whose church the present Pope celebrated his First Mass. ...The youthful Prince is heir to the worldwide renowned Borromeo Island on Lake Maggiore, which is reputed to possess some of the most beautiful gardens in

the world. His family palaces at Milan and Genoa and a Castle near Pavia are not less famous."[1]

The article was written by Prince Valerio Pignatelli, husband of the *Los Angeles Examiner* reporter, Princess Conchita Sepulveda Pignatelli, a close friend and confidant of Bernardine. Conchita was from the prominent Sepulveda family, one of the founding families of Los Angeles, and was a society columnist. She had married Prince Valerio Pignatelli, an Italian noble. The article was copyrighted by Los Angeles Services Incorporated and sent globally by "Special Cable."

The Murphys were immediately contacted by the United States Italian consulate at their Paris hotel. At 8:05 that morning, Murphy responded by telegram to the Italian counsel: "Cable great surprise report absolutely erroneous my daughter has never met the gentleman in question. Regards Dan Murphy."[2]

Neither Dan nor Antoinette had ever heard mention of Borromeo, nor did they know much about Bernardine's socializing in Rome. Even though they had just spent a month in Rome with Bernardine, she had not mentioned this "gentleman in question." The "high prelate" upon whom the "negotiations hinge" was undoubtedly Bishop Cantwell. "October 10-dateline Barcelona, "Bishop John Cantwell of Los Angeles, arrived here today for a visit to the Barcelona Exposition. He came from France and will tour Spain." The words "came from France" were underlined in red on the clipping preserved in Bernardine's papers chronicling these events. That indicated the discrepancy between Pignatelli's article from Rome and the actual travels of Cantwell. Bernardine was uncertain of the source of the leak. Shortly after the response from a blindsided Murphy, the truth became apparent.

Their daughter's name and theirs had been splashed across newspapers—not only in Los Angeles but also internationally. Three days later, the Sunday *Los Angeles Examiner* ran another article in its society pages. "Bernardine Murphy's Betrothal Hinted In Message From Italy: Isn't Cupid on the Warpath," wrote Cholly Angeleno, "in comes a rumor, relayed through our social underground from a transatlantic cable, that Miss Bernardine shortly may become Princess Borromeo." Even the *Needles Nugget* front page announced: "Bernardine Murphy betrothal to Prince of Italy." This made her father's humiliation complete.

Dan and Nettie returned immediately to the United States. Even aboard the ship, the bad news continued. On October 24, 1929, the stock market crashed.

The Borromeos were livid and equally in the dark. Angry letters from the Borromeo Palace, Piazza Borromeo, Milan, were hurriedly dashed off to Vatican City and to the Italian consulate in the United States. Count Cesare Gradenigo, the Italian consul, immediately traveled to Los Angeles to await the Murphys' return. Murphy responded from New York City by telegram: October 28, 7:02 p.m. to Count Gradenigo at the Ambassador Hotel in Los Angeles "Appreciate your kindness we arrive, Los Angeles, Saturday evening will be pleased to see you at my home. Kindest regards Murphy."

At nine o'clock on the evening of November 2, Count Gradenigo was scheduled to arrive—the very day the Murphys were coming home. Dan and Nettie called in their neighbors Secundo and Luisa Guasti to help with protocol and translation, since they were well connected in Italy and had on numerous occasions advised the Murphys about traveling in Italy. Secundo had been honored by the King of Italy on two occasions and had also received a title from Mussolini, a friend of Guasti since 1922. Not surprisingly, the Guastis knew Count Gradenigo; in fact, he had visited their home.[3]

The outcome of this meeting is unknown. No letters or communications passed directly between the Murphys and the Borromeo family. Bernardine and Count Gradenigo communicated directly since he was close friends with Federico and his family. On March 6, 1930, a letter from Gradenigo to Bernardine relayed five questions that the very cautious and skeptical Borromeo family had asked about the House of Murphy.

Bernardine replied to him:

> I have not mentioned to my parents receiving this letter from you. I'm afraid they would not understand—they would become annoyed at the Borromeos' curiosity. However, I understand that according to the old idea of [sic] these questions must be asked and answered. I would rather you write to me in Italian from now on.
>
> Mr. Murphy has one brother.
>
> Mrs. Murphy has two sisters and only one daughter
>
> The Murphys live a very family-oriented life and are a most devoted family. Their social standing is very high and causes tremendous respect.
>
> Mr. Murphy is a capitalist and philanthropist who has a national reputation for being a most brilliant businessman and is honorable, honest, and most generous. His interests are vast and varied, and he was among the first to discover and develop some of this countries [sic] famous oilfields [sic].

Gradenigo rewrote these responses from Bernardine as his own and added comments to pinpoint what was truly important when talk turned to a union of two aristocratic families:

> Splendid residence, a beautiful villa on a large and expensive piece of land.
> Remember two points about Bernardine:
> 1. I know nothing regarding her feelings for Federico.
> 2. Loyal, iron will, and unchangeable spirit. A young woman who knows what she wants.
> I wish finally to mention the material wealth of the House of Murphy of which Bernardine is the sole heir.
> I wish to give you some advice. If the engagement will take place, tell Federico to offer anything and ask for nothing. Ideal wife. Someday you will thank me."[4]

Gradenigo was clearly determined to see this marriage take place. Yet Bernardine wanted him to communicate in Italian so that her parents could not read it.

Secreted among Bernardine's papers was a small white envelope with the single word "Receipts" written in her hand. Inside was a handwritten letter on letterhead stationery: "Rosebank, White Plains, New York." There was no date, no salutation, and no signature—just a single, concise paragraph:

> We found that the records could not be changed and that even though a handwritten copy was made, leaving out the occupation, it would be of no value without the seal and signature of the Health Department of New York. I am enclosing the Certificate of Baptism, which would be all that is required, provided Bernardine marries an American. So sorry, but we did all we could.[5]

Rosebank was the orphanage, presumably where Bernardine lived until age three. This note refers to her birth certificate. It is not known at what time in Bernardine's life she knew that her biological mother was actually the woman she had known for so many years as "Aunt Sue." That she was an adopted child was the concerning issue. The aristocratic Borromeo family knew that she was of Ruspoli blood [the reason for the letter to the Vatican]. Both families were "Black Nobility" [loyal to the Vatican, as opposed to the Republic of Italy]. However, enmity existed between the two families since the Renaissance.

Bernardine was nearly thirty-years-old before she stopped thinking solely of herself and took full measure of her situation and responsibilities. Under Italian law, if she were to marry an Italian, she would be required to surrender her US citizenship. But worse, she would surrender all her assets to her husband. Because of her social standing, she was well-aware of—and often exposed to—numerous wealthy American women who were exploited by fortune-seeking Italian men who had been stripped of their nobility after the war.

Murphy must have been heartbroken after the embarrassing publicity of Bernardine's proposed engagement to Prince Federico Borromeo. Add to that, she had concealed her romantic relationship with Italian men—not once, but twice. Nettie and Dan did not stand in the way of Bernardine's wishes and had written to her that they would rather she marry an American man, but that they would honor her choice. Always the wise businessman, however, Murphy was not about to turn his life's work over to a foreign son-in-law, since he had designated Bernardine to be chair of the board of the Dan Murphy Company after his death.

Gradenigo continued to serve not just as a go-between for Bernardine and the Borromeo family, but seemingly as a very determined matchmaker. After the death of their mother and with their father in poor health, Federico's sister Margherita took over the Borromeos' investigation of Bernardine's family. As Margherita wrote to an unknown prelate in the Vatican:

> The precious information about Bernardine has confirmed my doubt and it is a real sorrow for me not to be able to know the name of her parents and their condition and social position. Should Your Excellency be able to learn anything among your numerous acquaintances, I would be very grateful to you if you would deign to communicate with me. Although Bernardine might have had a splendid education and training, Your Excellency can understand how in the future this mystery might cause wonderment. I see, however, that Your Excellency did not find any difficulty in the marriage between Bernardine and my brother."[6]

In 1933, the Borromeo family invited Bernardine and Sue to Isola Bella where their fifteenth century palace, surrounded by its magnificent terraced gardens, is situated on its own island. The fairytale-like island and palace appear to be floating on Lake Maggiore.[7] Sue and Bernardine's stay at the palace was "too short" according to Margherita, but it was long enough for Bernardine to attend the yacht races with Federico and take a few snapshots while they all had lunch on one of the many terraces.

Bernardine and Federico were anxious to have the Murphys meet his family. During the spring and summer of 1933, after the Murphys took their usual trip to Rome and attended their audience with Pope Pius XI, they traveled to Milan where the introductions would occur. The Borromeos, once the ruling family of Milan, still used the family's thirteenth century Palazzo Borromeo as their primary residence. There the Murphys and Sue were guests of the Borromeos. The *Paris Tribune* reported having seen the families frequently dining "substantiating certain rumors that may shortly be confirmed by a formal announcement."[8]

There never was an announcement of an engagement or wedding. There is no indication or record of what transpired at this meeting. It was all very cordial with return invitations offered as indicated in Margherita's letters to the Murphy home in Los Angeles. But there never was an announcement of an engagement, and there was no wedding. Based on Margherita's note to the prelate, the Borromeo family is aware that Bernardine is adopted, and the family wants to know the true identity of her birth parents. Perhaps the centuries-old rift between the Ruspoli family of Naples and more affluent Borromeos of Milan stood in the way of Bernardine and Federico's plans to wed, but why they never wed remains a mystery. Nevertheless, Bernardine and Federico corresponded frequently, albeit in Italian, fearing the letters might fall into the wrong hands in the Murphy household. Sue Sinnott was totally silent about the whole affair. Socially, in Los Angeles, the entire subject slipped into obscurity, as Bernardine moved into her thirties.

25

KNIGHT COMMANDER

As the turmoil of 1929 settled and the quiet life at home returned, a commemorative book was issued that honored Murphy and a few of his contemporaries. For several decades he had served on the Board of Regents at Loyola University. He was also a regent at the California Institute of Technology in Pasadena. Both academic institutions were recipients of numerous private benefactions from him. Murphy's gifts to these universities were from the heart. He hoped that future generations would not experience the pain he felt over his lack of degrees. Murphy gave generously to education. In 1931, Murphy was one of six men awarded honorary doctor of law degrees from Loyola University. The announcement from the university noted: "Dan Murphy is an outstanding figure in Los Angeles civic affairs, noted for his philanthropic and educational interests."[1] The other recipients were judges or lawyers.

Early in 1931, four men and six women were bestowed honors from Pope Pius XI by Bishop John J. Cantwell at the Cathedral of Saint Vibiana which was packed with attendees. This was the first time the ceremony had been performed on the West Coast and one of the highest honors granted to a Catholic lay person. The four men were made Knights in the Equestrian Order of the Holy Sepulchre, a ceremonial honor dating back to 1099. Dan Murphy, Ed Doheny, Joe Scott, and Patrick O'Neill all received the honor. Becoming Noble Dames of the order at the same ceremony were Antoinette Murphy, Estelle Doheny, and Louisa Guasti plus three other Los Angeles women.[2] The seventy-three year old Dan Murphy was singled out to receive the additional title of Knight Commander of Saint Gregory with Star. Unfortunately Dan was too ill to attend and received his honors *in absentia*.[3]

Despite all the honors and accolades he received over the years, Murphy was proudest of the fact that early in his career, he and his dear friend and business partner Frank Monaghan had determined the need to dam the Colorado River. He was prouder still that after Monaghan's passing,

Dr. Dan Murphy, after Loyola University awarded him an honorary doctorate of law at a special ceremony. Photo taken in his West Adams gardens. 1931

he was able to fulfill their dream by providing some of the cement to build Boulder Dam. His only regret was undoubtedly that he could not share the achievement with his departed partner.

In 1918, the Federal Reclamation Department, had "ordered a thorough investigation of the Boulder or Black Canyon sites." More surveys ensued between 1919 and 1920. Exploratory drilling at potential dam sites began in late 1920 and continued for three more years. Finally, in 1924, three years after Frank Monaghan's death and after several years of investigations, the Bureau of Reclamation recommended the construction of a high concrete dam at the site in Black Canyon.[4]

An opinion article in the *Los Angeles Times*, February 13, 1927, was titled "Enemies of the Republic." It fretted that Congress would not pass the Boulder Dam bill.

> I think Frank Monaghan and Dan Murphy of Needles are the original Boulder Dam advocates. Long years ago they operated the Capitol Mine at El Dorado, very near Boulder Canyon … Monaghan & Murphy will live, I believe and hope to see our enemies defeated and the dam built, for its construction means as much to the West as did the opening of the Panama Canal.[5]

Although the writer R.J. Leonards's wishes did not come true for Monaghan, Murphy did live to see the project completed. Controlling the flooding was born from his compassion for the Native Americans along with his sympathy for the hard rock miners who needed a smelter to make a profit, the dreams he had envisioned for them all did not come true. However, he and Frank were the first Caucasians to identify the best location for the dam.

At the dedication of Boulder Dam in 1935, Franklin Roosevelt said: "This is one of the greatest undertakings in the history of the world. A

Boulder Dam (renamed Hoover Dam) as completed in 1936. Dan Murphy identified the site in Black Canyon in 1883. He tried to convince the railroad to build a dam to control the flooding at Needles to protect the indigenous Mojaves' farmland.

definite opening of a new era, with respect to conservation, which means a prudent use of all our natural resources to the greatest good for the greatest number of our people."[6]

During the Boulder Dam construction, the Portland Cement Association of America held its annual meeting in Los Angeles. Eighty-five delegates from across the nation attended the conference in the spring of 1934, at the Biltmore Hotel; itself built using concrete from California Portland Cement. With Murphy's planning, the representatives took an excursion train to view the ongoing construction at the dam site. The dam was built with more than five million barrels of cement. No single company could provide that much cement to this massive project, but undoubtedly California Portland Cement supplied a big portion of it to the consortium of firms who were constructing the dam, called the "Six Companies."[7] Between 1931 and 1934, Murphy received over $1.1 million in dividends from California Portland Cement, equivalent to $19.6 million today, proof positive that Murphy's firm was a major supplier.[8]

The consistently enigmatic Murphy, then seventy-six, did not take center stage at the Cement Association conference. Neither did he pose for any publicity photos at the convention nor later at the Boulder Dam dedication ceremony. He encouraged California Portland Cement's vice president and general manager, Ernest E. Duque, to speak for the company.

Few if any of those in attendance at the dedication of Boulder Dam knew that the quiet, unassuming man in the corner was the first to conceive of the entire plan to dam the Colorado River. The "true gold" manifested in the construction of Boulder Dam came from Dan Murphy making the connection between Black Canyon and lime deposits found at nearby Slover Mountain. His foresight about bringing life-giving waters to the Southwestern United States changed the region forever. He was "in on the ground floor." It just took a lifetime to get there.

After the convention, the delegates traveled by train to Santa Barbara where they were entertained at Ernest Duque's Montecito estate. The following day, they continued up the coast by train to the Hotel Del Monte in Pebble Beach where Murphy entertained them the same way Charlie Crocker had entertained him so many years before. This event completed the full circle of Murphy's life on the West Coast—from meeting Crocker at the beginning of his career to participating in the largest cement project in the West, his crowning achievement.

With the newly refurbished gardens and grounds at 2076 West Adams Blvd., Nettie enjoyed a favorite form of entertaining guests: presenting lecture-recitals. One of her most successful events was "An Hour with Beethoven" by Madame Nina Koshetz. Before she fled the revolution, Koshetz's accompanist was the famed pianist, Vladimir Horowitz. She had traveled the world and was with the Chicago Opera in the early 1920s and retired in Los Angeles. In 1934. This noted Russian diva had worked with Rachmaninoff in Petrograd, and to Antoinette's delight, she was singing in the Murphys' home. Koshetz thrilled the guests at two concerts given fourteen days apart. Dr. Alexis Kall, a music history professor from the University of Petrograd, gave a lecture after each performance.

> The magnificent home of Mrs. Daniel Murphy ... to be able to sit and listen to such music amidst the charming and consistently beautiful surroundings of Mrs. Murphy's home is a rare privilege indeed. Masses of white flowers, nearly all Easter lilies, filled the rooms, and the contrast of white against the dark rich woodwork of the drawing-room was most artistic.[9]

Dan Murphy in his Los Angeles garden. Note the gazebo Bernardine bought in Italy on her first trip abroad in 1912. Circa 1937.

Even a celebrated opera singer performing in the living room, followed by an oration by a world renowned music professor could not compare to the joy Antoinette displayed when she was surrounded by flowers. On the heels of a 1936 convention in San Francisco, delegates from the Garden Club of America came to Pebble Beach specifically to see Antoinette's Wynanspray gardens. There "they saw 7000 tulip bulbs in bloom—it was a never-to-be-forgotten sight."[10] Gardening had been Nettie's lifetime passion. From her teenage years painting flowers on china plates, to her adult days spent refining her West Adams grounds where she cultivated the region's most elaborate garden in Southern California. Antoinette had devoted her life to horticulture. Such glorious praise from the Garden Club of America must have been, for her, the highest honor, a tribute to her lifelong pursuit of the quintessential landscape.

26

Our Dan

As the 1930s progressed, so did the Great Depression. Following the stock market crash of 1929, unemployment soared to more than twenty percent. Hoovervilles, shantytowns filled with homeless people, sprang up all over the country. As waves of bank failures swept the nation, President Hoover attempted to support the banks with government loans. When Franklin Roosevelt was elected president of the United States in 1932, he began several programs to address the nation's financial problems.

By the time the Depression descended on the world, the Murphys were elderly. Dan was in his seventies and Nettie her sixties. Nettie settled into enjoying their flourishing gardens and directing the gardeners in creating evermore glorious displays. Dan spent even more time at his men's clubs downtown. The couple divided their time between living in the city and their coastal retreat at Wynanspray. The trips to Pebble Beach required extensive planning and usually lasted a month or more. The couple typically made this three hundred twenty mile trip in Dan's chauffeured automobile, while the cook and maids left ahead of time in Nettie's car with her chauffeur. Caravanning two vehicles normally involved at least one flat tire along the way and took all day. They arrived by sunset, if all went well.

Frequently Bernardine would drive her own car to Wynanspray at Pebble Beach. Next to the main house was a two-bedroom, two-bath cottage with a fireplace, which she used as her personal retreat because of its calming views of the ocean that she could see through the towering, windswept cypress. She filled the little place with "Tyrolean and Swiss peasant furniture of the seventeenth and eighteenth centuries."[1] Her passion for the antiques developed when, as a young girl, she and her family stayed at the Beau-Rivage Palace Hotel in Lausanne, Switzerland. The peasant furniture was either carved with folk geometric shapes or painted with fanciful designs. In the living room of her cottage were the antique bookcases, armoires, chests, and two daybeds she treasured. Each bedroom was furnished with a pair of four-poster beds, one painted yellow, the other green.[2] "A peek in this little cottage has delighted many members of the Pebble Beach colony and not least among its attractions are the bright hued peasant costumes hanging in the wardrobes."[3] Bernardine would spend long, undisturbed hours in the cottage, with only the sounds of the ocean and the wind in the trees.

Neither Dan nor Nettie were in the best of health. His vision had been failing for years due to cataracts caused by decades of the glaring desert sun. He also suffered from bad knees and high blood pressure, both of which had been treated over the years by Dr. Groedel at the Bad Nauheim clinic in Germany. Nettie's hypertension and ulcers lead to much concern in the household, frequently causing her to resort to radical diets. Their butler Joseph, and his wife, who was the head housekeeper, had been with the family since before the war and were of great consolation to Nettie and Dan. Several young housemaids, usually recent immigrants from Ireland, came and went. In general, the household staff remained around five to six individuals. Joseph and his wife remained at the home for the duration.

The aging Murphys continued to fight their failing health. Nettie wrote to Bernardine at Wynanspray:

> This morning found me writing before daybreak. The first time in a long time, I am sleeping better from [Dr.] Purcell's shots. My blood pressure is down from 154 to 128—but my pulse yesterday was ninety—so she has not quite fixed me up yet. Must wait until the first of the week (when he returns home) to see how father is. He does not show the "comeback" as usual after an illness. I think for some reason we cannot see, he does not respond to the camphor and other shots. I wish Doctor Groedel were here ... It keeps one worried and yet I feel each day he must show a return to vigor—I know he is worried about himself.[4]

That fall, Princess Conchita Pignatelli wrote in her, column:

> ... truly a thing of beauty and joy forever. This thought ran through my mind the day Mrs. Daniel Murphy, in the most informal manner, called a few intimate friends (Mrs. Joseph Sartori and Mrs. Godfrey Holterhoff among them) to join her for a cheery cup of tea and a stroll in her luxurious garden, that they might thrill at the exquisiteness of the chrysanthemums.

Words fail me in an attempt to describe the glorious effect of these thousands of blossoms when the setting sun shone upon them, and their colors ranging from chalk white to deep rusts and bronze, become vibrant and dazzling.

The nine-acre estate of Mrs. Murphy, which is in the heart of the fashionable West Adams District, is famous even in Europe and this delightful lady personally supervises the placing and knows the name of every flower and plant from the formal English garden to the tropical section of the grounds.[5]

Murphy was delighted when Nettie finally agreed to allow the Hollywood cinema crowd to use her gardens for filming. This had been a long time coming since West Adams residents originally had disdain for people involved in the movie business. Bernardine convinced Nettie that her gardens belonged on the big screen and worked a deal to make it happen with the help of her childhood friend Genevieve McDonald who lived down the street with her mother Isabel Denker Maier. Genevieve's Aunt Leontine was married to Dr. Attilio H. Giannini, brother of the founder of the Bank of Italy (later renamed the Bank of America) and an early financier in the Hollywood film industry. Cecil B. DeMille and Louis B. Mayer would park their car in front of their home on West Adams Boulevard, waiting for Giannini to arrive for lunch with the Denkers. DeMille would sideline him on the lawn to pitch his latest movie that needed financing. Louise Denker, married Allan DeMille, Cecil B.'s son.[6] Some of the films shot in Antoinette's garden were: *The Great Desire* (1933) with Katharine Hepburn, *Sisters under the Skin* (1934), *Annie Oakley* (1935) with Barbara Stanwyck, and *Colleen* (1936) with Dick Powell, Ruby Keeler, and Joan Blondell.[7]

The aging Dan had plenty of diversions at home beside the occasional filming in the gardens. Sue and Bernardine took up the task of founding and publishing *The Dove*, a quarterly magazine of the Sisters of Social Service for the promotion of social advocacy. Bernardine and Sue were more-or-less housebound and deferred any travel as both were committed to caring for Dan and Nettie. *The Dove* was voluntary work that the two women took on to help the Sisters. Having witnessed the social upheaval in Europe between-the-wars, they felt compelled to perform some sort of assistance here in America. The Sisters helped supply articles for the magazine while the Murphy women did the editing and layout. With all this activity at 2076 West Adams Blvd., Murphy had numerous diversions from his aches and pains. One such occasion was when the Superior General of the Sisters of Social Service, Sister Margit Slachta of Budapest, visited Los Angeles. The Murphy women hosted a tea at their home in her honor. The women's Auxiliary of the Good Shepherd Shelter and their friends were invited to meet the distinguished visitor. Sister M. Slachta was the first woman member of Parliament in Hungary. Between 1939 and 1942 she would use her political power and religious influence among Catholics to rescue thousands of Jewish families from the Nazi regime.[8]

Nettie promised Dan and Bernardine that the 1938 Pasadena Flower Show would be her last, since she had won top awards in previous years. Her entry "South American Reverie" was awarded the Sweepstakes Prize at the opening ceremony on April 1. Her display also received a special award for the variety of chrysanthemums exhibited. "This exhibit was 300 square feet and portrayed a white waterfall emerging from hills, with the terrain about it composed of bronze, red, pink, and other colors of potted chrysanthemums." Additionally, "rare colored begonias, and antirrhinums [snapdragons], and a luxurious, interwoven background of luxurious tropical tree ferns," completed the South American look.[9]

The strain and anxiety from the preparation for the show sent Nettie to the Metabolic Clinic in La Jolla, San Diego. Her dear friend Virginia Milbank wrote to her:

> I'm so glad to hear such very good news of your return to health. I had such a delightful afternoon at the Pasadena Flower Show last Saturday and am writing now to tell you how beautiful your exhibit was. I don't wonder that you received the Sweepstakes Prize. Your Gloxinias were the largest and most gorgeous ones I ever saw—they were the only ones in the show.[10]

As spring faded into summer, Bernardine became alarmed at Dan's deteriorating health and wrote to Dr. Franz Groedel, from Bad Nauheim, telling him of his condition. Dr. Groedel, who was born to Jewish parents and converted to Catholicism, had been forced to escape Bad Nauheim in 1933 to avoid the Nazi Regime. He was at the time practicing medicine at 829 Park Ave., New York City. He wrote back to Bernardine:

> I am very sorry to learn that you all have not been well and that your father complains more, feels weak and depressed.[11]

He also telegrammed from New York to Bernardine.

> Extremely sorry to learn your father again worse … Arriving Thursday STOP if you wish me to come earlier wire immediately and will come, at once …

On June 5, Dr. Groedel responded to a letter from Bernardine who was complaining:

> However, I realize that he has enough discomfort to endure, that he will often be depressed in spite of the fact that he has his philosophy and the good care you give him ... It is a pity that you're [sic] Aunt has cause to complain. I am sorry for her, and yourself have so little time to think of other things than sickness.

Two months later, at 7 pm on June 16, 1938, Nettie died at home of a stroke. She was seventy years old. Her obituaries celebrated her:

> Of extremely charitable nature, she helped to organize many of the cities' institutions for the aid of children, the aged and helpless, among them the Children's Hospital and the Barlow Sanatorium. She was President Emeritus of the Sisters of Social Service and had a long list of private charities which she concealed with invariable modesty.[13]
>
> A notable patroness of the arts, Mrs. Murphy was one of the founders of the Los Angeles Symphony, and her gardens surrounding her home were among the show places of the city. Mrs. Murphy was one of three women in Los Angeles to be named Lady of Holy Sepulcher, an honor awarded for outstanding service to the Catholic Church.[14]

On Friday, the rosary was said at 10 am. Her funeral was conducted in her chapel at 2076 West Adams. She was interred in the family crypt in the Doheny Memorial Mausoleum at Calvary Cemetery.[15]

Murphy never recovered from the loss of his wife. In July 1938, their beloved Bernardine noted in her diary:

> When I slept I dreamed of beauty
> When I woke, I found that life was duty.

On September 14, 1939, one week short of his eighty-first birthday, Dan Murphy passed away at home from a heart attack. Archbishop John J. Cantwell officiated at the Solemn High Requiem Mass held at the Cathedral of Saint Vibiana. This is the same church with the cornerstone inscribed D.O.M. where many years before his friends had joked that those letters stood for "Donation of Murphy." Cardinal Roger Mahony said "the Dan Murphy Foundation is the largest donor to the American Catholic Church" and that "they have given more than any other family or organization to the American Catholic Church." Such a statement by an American cardinal establishes the very private Murphy family of the West Coast as more generous donors than even the very well-known Joseph P. Kennedy clan (the family of President John F. Kennedy) on the East Coast.

Murphy's forty-seven honorary pallbearers included Jefferson Chandler, Joe F. Sartori, Joe Scott, T.A. Riordan, Robert Chambers, Howard Bagley, William Workman, Lucien Brunswig, Harry Chandler, William Valentine, Eugene McLaughlin, J. Wiseman MacDonald, Frederick Flint, Norman Sterry, Asa Call, William Flint, and William Garland.[16] His internment, beside Antoinette, was at the family crypt at the Doheny Memorial Mausoleum in Calvary Cemetery. The front page of the *Los Angeles Times* referred to him as a "pioneer, civic leader, courageous and foresighted." "In the American tradition, he was a self-made man."[17]

A beautifully hand-bound tribute book was presented to Bernardine by the California Portland Cement Board of Directors. In elegant calligraphy, it described Murphy: "His friendship was staunch and true; he was sincere, kindly, and charitable to all. He was courtly and dignified in his bearing, typifying the best elements of a cultured gentleman."

Our Dan.

Epilogue

By the early 1940s, most of Bernardine Murphy's friends and neighbors on West Adams Boulevard had sold their estates and moved to newer, more exclusive developments in Hancock Park and Beverly Hills. This left Bernardine and Sue alone at 2076 West Adams. As nearby mansions went up for sale, Bernardine bought them and donated the structures to Brothers of Saint John of God, which converted the houses into nursing homes and living quarters. Bernardine spent a great deal of her time visiting residents who were near the end of life.

Bernardine continued to watch over her father's businesses by presiding over the California Portland Cement Company's board of directors and serving as a director on boards of his other companies at a time when few women sat on corporate boards. She and Sue took several vacations, driving through New England and the Southeast.

An aging Aunt Kathryn moved into the Murphy mansion to help Bernardine care for Sue who had fallen ill in 1944. The following year, sixty-five-year-old Sue succumbed to a heart attack. Surely by this time, Bernardine was aware that Sue was her birth mother, but she always called her "Aunt Sue." Upon her mother's death, Bernardine sent a telegram to Rosebank, the orphanage in White Plains, New York, announcing her death.

Kathryn developed leukemia, and Bernardine cared for her until she died in 1951. With a small staff, Bernardine was suddenly living alone, dividing her time between business meetings, the Sisters of the Good Shepherd Convent, and the Saint John of God nursing home.

Bernardine and Federico Borromeo continued corresponding for more than twenty years, until the early 1950s. In his letters, he professed his unfailing love and devotion, without mentioning why they never married.

The last building venture in Needles by the Monaghan & Murphy Company was the 1933 construction of a row of shops on the 100 block of F Street. The shops rounded the corner onto Front Street, comprising a large part of downtown Needles (the stores were extant in 2020). The last act of generosity by the company was in 1954: the donation of five lots, comprising several acres, to the local school district for the expansion of Grace Henderson Elementary School.

Also in the early 1950s, the Los Angeles archdiocese focused its combined attention on Bernardine, a single, middle-aged heiress who was living alone in her parent's mansion. Pius XII, soon after his election to the papacy, appointed Francis J. Spellman to be archbishop of New York in 1939. Later, Spellman elevated James Francis McIntyre (a former Wall Street "runner" who was ordained a priest at age thirty-five) to be his personal secretary. In 1941, with more than five thousand people in attendance, Archbishop Spellman consecrated McIntyre as auxiliary bishop at a ceremony in New York City's Saint Patrick's Cathedral. More than sixty-eight prelates were in attendance, making this one of the largest Roman Catholic ceremonies ever assembled in the US. At the suggestion of the newly elevated Cardinal Spellman, Pius XII appointed McIntyre as archbishop of Los Angeles, replacing Bishop Cantwell who had died in 1947.[1] Daniel J. Donohue Jr., the son of one of Spellman's college friends who had become a brother of Saint John of God on July 19, 1946, took the name Brother Kevin and moved into 2025 West Adams Blvd., one of the homes Bernardine had donated. Bernardine and Brother Kevin became friends on her frequent visits with the elderly residents.[2] Shortly after Bishop McIntyre was elevated to cardinal by Pius XII in 1953, Brother Kevin's vows were absolved. And on January 16, 1954, forty-nine-year-old Bernardine Murphy quietly wed thirty-five-year-old Daniel Donohue in a private ceremony, celebrated by Cardinal McIntyre at his rectory at One Fremont Place in Los Angeles.

From photographs, greeting cards, and personal correspondence, it is evident that Donohue brought joy to Bernardine. For the first time, photos show her laughing and lighthearted. The newlyweds immediately made plans to move from 2076 West Adams to an estate designed by famed architect Bernard Maybeck at 3441 Waverly Dr. in the Los Feliz area of Los Angeles. They purchased this eight-acre hilltop property from the estate of her father's old friend Earle C. Anthony, the famed Los Angeles car dealer.

At great expense, and to the amazement of the Los Angeles citizenry, Bernardine had helicopters airlift the Roman statuary, her gazebo, and many rare and mature trees from her mother's gardens to Waverly Drive. The couple then razed the entire West Adams mansion and gardens, "scraped clean to the lot," which was no easy task since the grand home had been made entirely of concrete, using California Portland Cement,

Epilogue

of course. The Donohues donated the property to the Los Angeles archdiocese which leased it to an oil company named Freeport-McMoRan Incorporated. For more than a half century, wells have pumped "black gold" on the site. As of 2017, there were twenty-two active wells and seven injection wells used for fracking oil, all less than two hundred feet from a densely populated inner-city neighborhood.[3]

Together the Donohues made numerous trips to Italy to furnish their new medieval-style home on Waverly Drive. In 1955, they also purchased a condominium in Rome, not far from the Grand Hotel de la Minerve where her parents had stayed when they were in the city. The Donohues continued to use the Grand Hotel salons for occasions when they entertained prelates and clergy.

In 1957, they formed the Dan Murphy Foundation and transferred the entire holdings of the Dan Murphy Company into the foundation.

Bernardine continued in her father's footsteps, donating sizable amounts to Pope Pius XII's charities and the Vatican. Her generosity was not overlooked. Bernardine was the recipient of many high honors: the pope named her a "Lady Commander with Star of the Order of Holy Sepulchre and the Grand Cross of the Order." However, her highest honor was bestowed in 1960 by Pope Saint John XXIII. He bestowed upon her the title of "Papal Countess," an extremely rare honor (the only other American women to receive the title were Rose Fitzgerald Kennedy, mother of President John F. Kennedy, and Estelle Doheny, Edward Doheny's wife). A few years later, Daniel Donohue was named a "Gentleman in Waiting to His Holiness the Pope," the highest honor ever bestowed on an American layman. Notably, this is the same title held by Prince Lelio Ruspoli decades earlier, and because Bernardine was involved, it seems to be hardly a coincidence. Over the years, Bernardine tired of going to Rome with Daniel. She said that it had changed so much and that she preferred to remember Rome as it was before the war.

In June 1966, the couple hosted the largest and most extravagant dinner party ever held at the staid California Club. The fête celebrated their dear friend His Eminence James Francis Cardinal McIntyre, archbishop of Los Angeles, on his eightieth birthday, twenty-fifth year as a bishop, and forty-five years as a priest. Special guests arrived in eighteen limousines, waiters in medieval dress passed hors d'oeuvres, among towering ice sculptures and dancing jesters. Even Cardinal Spellman of New York, who attended the gala, said, "Now, I have seen it all."[4]

Bernardine Dan Murphy Donohue died suddenly of a heart attack in Los Angeles in 1968, at age sixty-four. Her husband Daniel moved to their twelve-acre estate in the exclusive village of Montecito, near Santa Barbara, California, which the couple was in the process of remodeling when she died.[5] He gave the Waverly Drive compound to the Sisters of the Immaculate Heart.

In 2002, with the completion of the Cathedral of Our Lady of the Angels in downtown Los Angeles, the bodies of the Murphy family—Dan, Antoinette, Sue, Kathryn, and Dan's sister Margaret—were removed from their family niche in the Doheny Memorial Mausoleum at Calvary Cemetery and transferred to the "Mausoleum Central 'Jerusalem Cross' Sarcophagus," directly beneath the main altar of the cathedral. The grand room in the mausoleum where they lie in perpetuity with bishops and cardinals is dominated by Bernardine's massive red marble tomb, which is centered directly beneath the cathedral's main altar. The birth year for Dan Murphy is inscribed as 1859, although documents including his birth and death certificates and his passports list his birth year as 1858. After his death on December 3, 2014, Daniel Donohue was interred by Bernardine in the central mausoleum of the cathedral.

In 2016, the endowment of the Dan Murphy Foundation amounted to more than $200 million in assets. Each year the foundation donates a million dollars to the pope's personal charities, and more than $10 million to various religious orders, colleges, social service agencies, and medical institutions.

The Sisters of the Immaculate Heart continued living in the Waverly Drive property as their numbers dwindled to only five. In 2015, the nuns signed a contract to sell the property with the intent to enter a rest home and give the remaining proceeds to their order. The archdiocese challenged the legality of the ownership. The archdiocese prevailed over the nuns when a Los Angeles County Superior Court judge ruled that the sisters' deal to sell the property for $15.5 million was "clearly invalid." The archdiocese then sold the property for $14.5 million to the international pop singer Katy Perry.

Epilogue

Dan Murphy and his daughter Bernardine Dan Murphy. Circa 1935.

Appendix A

MINES

All of these mines were recorded at Kingman, Arizona Territory. Kingman is the seat for Mohave County. Most of the claims filed in 1891 were within the Minnesota Mining District of Mohave County. Furthermore, the 1891 claims were recorded in the month of October, in the names of both Murphy and Monaghan. There are no records regarding the productivity of these mines.

1886	Black Metal	1895	Hidden Hill
1887	Josephine	1895	Golden Queen (Queen)
1891	Minahaha	1896	Prince of Wales
1891	Itata	1896	Eagle
1891	La Junta	1896	Golden Eagle
1891	Balmaceda	1896	Bald Eagle
1891	Independence	1897	Red Hill
1891	Juniata	1897	Sheep Tail #2
1891	Juvenile	1898	Bonanza King
1891	Black Jack #1	1900	New London
1891	Black Jack #2	1902	Capitol Mine
1894	Eagle Tail	1905	Copper World (Ivanpah)
1894	South Wing	1905	Mohawk (Ivanpah)

Appendix B

COMPANIES FOUNDED BY DAN MURPHY

This list of corporations represents the companies in which Dan Murphy was one of the incorporating (usually one of five incorporators) signers of each firm's "Articles of Incorporation"; in a few cases, he was a member of the board of directors. The companies are in chronological order of their founding. Some companies were incorporated long after their founding, i.e., Monaghan & Murphy Company founded in 1883 and incorporated in 1901. Murphy began working in Los Angeles in 1900. Many of the companies founded after that date are corporations which were in the interest of the Pacific Land Improvement Company, the real estate arm of the Atchison, Topeka & Santa Fe Railroad.

1883	Monaghan & Murphy Company
1885	Murphy Water, Ice & Electric Company (Inc. 1904)
1887	Los Angeles Pressed Brick Company
1893	Needles Land & Cattle Company
1894	Needles Smelting Company
1894	Rock Springs Cattle
1894	Hidden Hills Mining
1896	Monaghan & Murphy Bank
1899	Brea Cañon Oil
1902	Holmes Supplies
1902	Globe Grain & Milling
1903	Octave Oil Company
1903	Colorado Steam Navigation
1903	Pacific Redwood Company
1903	W.N. Best International Calorific Company
1904	Los Angeles Cherokee Oil
1905	Avalon Hotel Association
1905	Kings County Land Development

1905	Hawthorn Improvement Company
1905	Western California Land Company
1906	Cocopah Copper Mine
1906	Los Angeles National Bank (Murphy served as vice president)
1906	Redondo Villa Tract
1907	Riordan Investment Company
1908	Arrowhead Health Resort
1910	Artesian Land Company
1910	Factory Site Company
1910	Sunset Park Land Company
1910	Valley Ice Company
1911	El Segundo Land & Oil Company
1916	Ivanpah Copper Incorporation
1916	Needles Ice Company
1917	Los Angeles Shipbuilding and Dry Dock
1919	Federal Ice Refrigeration
1920	Murvale Oil
1922	Murphy Dillon Company
1922	El Segundo Home Building
1922	Dan Murphy Company
1931	Murphy – Dillon Pipelines LTD

ENDNOTES

EPIGRAPH
1. Poem by T.C. Stevens, Sept 21, 1916. Ryan, Joseph Francis. Joseph Francis Ryan Research Collection on Daniel Murphy and Family, Approximately 1900–2012. 1900. Bancroft Library, Berkley, CA.

INTRODUCTION *Pages 15 to 20*
1. Quotation. Interview with Cardinal Roger Mahony, Sep 19, 2016.
2. "People Met in Hotel Lobbies." *Washington Post*, May 24, 1907. This is the only known newspaper interview of Dan Murphy.
3. Richard J. Orsi, *Sunset Limited: the Southern Pacific Railroad and the Development of the American West, 1850–1930* (Berkeley: University of California Press, 2005). Orsi's breakthrough book shed new light on this era. He used primary source material to change this commonly repeated history. His work explained the significance of the Pacific Improvement Company.
4. "People Met in Hotel Lobbies." *Washington Post*, May 24, 1907.
5. Thomas "Tommie" R. Lee, "Deacon Dan" *Petroleum World*, May 1940, 118.

CHAPTER 1 *Pages 21 to 33*
1. Quotation: "Mineral Park." *Mohave County Miner*, Jun 4, 1887; see: "Came West Penniless and Dies a Millionaire," *Reformatory Press*, Oct 16, 1915. Dennis Sullivan 1837–1915. Born in New York, he amassed a fortune in Colorado and the Southwest mining. When he died in 1915, he was worth $5 million (which would compare to about $1.2 billion in 2020 dollars). Revered by the citizens of Denver, they erected the Sullivan Gateway at City Park Esplanade, which consists of twin monumental columns, each bearing a statue, one depicting "Agriculture," the other "Mining."
2. *Deed of Mines. Book 1* (County Recorder, Mohave County, Territory of Arizona), 551–552.
3. "Notice of Forfeiture," *Mohave County Miner*, May 30, 1891.
4. Hiram C. Hodge, *Arizona As It Is, Or, The Coming Country: Compiled From Notes of Travel During the Years 1874–1875, and 1876*, (New York: Hurd and Houghton, 1877), 65.
5. US Census Bureau: Eighth US Federal Census, 1860, Pennsylvania.
6. US Census Bureau: Ninth US Federal Census, 1870, Illinois.
7. Abraham Lincoln signed the Homestead Act of 1862 into law. By paying a

small filing fee, a settler could claim 160 acres of public land in return for building a home and farming the land for five years, after which the settler received clear title to the property.
8. US Census Bureau: Ninth US Federal Census, 1870, Kansas.
9. The One Hundred Year History of Hanover, Kansas. "Hanover Centennial: 1869–1969." http://www.ksgenweb.org/washingt/hanoverc.htm. Viewed Sep 4, 2020.
10. The One Hundred Year History of Hanover … ; US Census Bureau: Ninth US Federal Census, 1870, Kansas; *Plat Book of Washington County, Kansas: Containing Carefully Prepared Township Plats, Village Plats, Analysis of US Land System, Leading Farmers Directory*, (Des Moines, Iowa: Brown-Scoville Publishing 1906).
11. "Boy Who Flunked In School Here Made Fortune Estimated at 50 Million." *Hays Daily News*, Oct 10, 1943. Vertical Files. Ellis County Historical Society.
12. J.M.G. van der Poel, *Gospel Hill: a History of Saint John the Baptist Church, Hanover, Washington County, Kansas, 1868-1978*. John M. Poell, 1978.
13. "History of Hays." Hays Kansas Visitor & Convention Bureau. http://www.visithays.com/118/History-of-Hays. Viewed May 9, 2020.
14. Tom McHugh and Victoria Hobson, *The Time of the Buffalo* (Lincoln: University of Nebraska Press, 1972), 261.
15. McHugh and Hobson, 285.
16. McHugh and Hobson, 286.
17. *Kanhistique: Kansas History and Antiques* Vol 7 No 9, Ellsworth, Kansas, Jan 1982.
18. "The Locust of the West—The Plague of Grasshoppers in Kansas." *New York Times*, Aug 17, 1874.
19. Alexandra M. Wagner, "Grasshoppered: America's Response to the 1874 Rocky Mountain Locust Invasion," *Nebraska History* Vol 89 (2008), 154–167.
20. "Grasshopper Plague of 1874." *Kansapedia*. Kansas State Historical Society. https://www.kshs.org/kansapedia/grasshopper-plague-of-1874/12070
21. Chuck Lyons, "1874: The Year of the Locust." *Wild West*, Feb 5, 2012.
22. Cecil Woodham Smith, *The Great Hunger: Ireland, 1845–1849* (New York: Penguin, 1991), 242.
23. "The Irish Are Repaying a Favor From 173 Years Ago in Native Americans' Fight Against Coronavirus." *Washington Post*, May 13, 2020.
24. A.T. Andreas, *Compendium of History, Reminiscence, and Biography of Western Nebraska Containing a History of the State of Nebraska* (Alden Publishing Co., 1912), Chapter IV, 90-91.
25. "Playful Nimrods or the Hazards of Railroading." *Atchison Patriot*, Oct 13, 1877.
26. *The Commercial and Financial Chronicle*, Jan 27, 1872, 140; "Railroad Troubles, the Saint Joseph and Denver City Road—Stormy Meeting of Bondholders: A Committee of Five Appointed to Protect Their Interests." *New York Times*, Aug 27, 1873.
27. James Ford Rhodes and Allan Nevins, *History of the United States from the Compromise of 1850* (Chicago: The University of Chicago Press, 1966), 36.
28. Catherine Rampell. Economix (blog). *New York Times*, Oct 3, 2008; Justin Fox "What Alan Greenspan Has Learned Since 2008," *Harvard Business Review*, Jan 7, 2014. Economist Alan Greenspan, who chaired the Federal Reserve from 1987 to 2006, said the Sep 15, 2008 crash was more like the Panic

of 1873 than the 1929 stock market crash, and he noted, "The necessary condition of a crisis is nobody expects it." Fox went on to say that what happened in 1873 is similar to the 2008 panic which suggests a further shift—from the United States to China and India.

29. "We Hope It Is True." *Leavenworth Weekly Times*, Jan 21, 1875. The article went on to say, "This is one of the best strikes for Washington we have ever known and a vast fortune for hard-working honest Tom Murphy."

CHAPTER 2 Pages 35 to 46

1. Bill Yenne, *The History of the Southern Pacific* (New York: Bonanza Books, 1995), 6–11.
2. Oscar Lewis, *The Big Four: The Story of Huntington, Stanford, Hopkins, and Crocker, and of the Building of the Central Pacific* (New York: A.A. Knopf, 1951), 68.
3. J.N. Bowman, "Driving the Last Spike: At Promontory, 1869." *California Historical Society Quarterly* 36, no. 2 (1957), 97–106.
4. Stephen E. Ambrose, *Nothing Like It in the World: The Men Who Built the Transcontinental Railroad, 1863–1869* (New York: Touchstone, 2000), 366.
5. Lewis, 105.
6. Richard J. Orsi, *Sunset Limited: The Southern Pacific Railroad and the Development of the American West, 1850–1930* (Berkeley: University of California, 2007), 18.
7a. Orsi, 19.
7b. Bancroft, *The Works of Hubert Howe Bancroft...*, 613.
8. Hubert Howe Bancroft, *The Works of Hubert Howe Bancroft Vol XXIV: History of California Vol VII, 1860–1890* (San Francisco: The History Company Publishers, 1890), 613.
9. Mike Johnson. "Ferries of the Lower Colorado River (or the Red River of the West). Otherwise Known as Taylor's Ferry II. Tripartite Fall Clampout." *E. Clampus Vitus*, Oct 1997. "A rope or cable is stretched across a river and a boat is suspended from it by lines attached by pulleys so that one end of the boat is further upstream than the other; the force of the river will force the boat sideways and thus across the river. By reversing the angle of the boat in the stream, it will return to the other side. No motive power is necessary."
10. "Yuma Arizona. A River Runs Through It." *Yuma Arizona Centennial 1914–2014*. Yuma Visitors Bureau. 2014. https://www.visityuma.com/about-yuma/history/#river
11. Keith L. Bryant, *History of the Atchison, Topeka, and Santa Fe Railway* (New York: Macmillan Publishing Company Inc., 1974), 90.
12. Quotation: Kathy Weiser. "Canyon Diablo—Meaner than Tombstone." *Legends of America*. http://www.legendsofamerica.com.
13. Neil S. Weintraub, "The Johnson Canyon Abandoned Railroad Grade: A History of 9.3 miles of Treacherous Railroading in Northern Arizona." Presented at 1993 Arizona History Conference in Kingman, Arizona.
14. Bancroft, *The Works of Hubert Howe Bancroft...*, 593–594.
15. Quotation: "Brother Frank Monaghan." Historical Record and Souvenir (Los Angeles: Times-Mirror, 1923), 170.
16. Charles Crocker Correspondence. Huntington Library: MSS Crocker-Huntington Correspondence. No 386, Vol 1, Apr 23, 1882.
17. "Reassessing the 'Octopus.'" *Los Angeles Times*, May 31, 2005.

18. Orsi, 115–116. The original company formed by the Central Pacific Railroad was the Contract and Finance Company, which was succeeded by the Western Development Company.
19. Stuart Daggett, *Chapters on the History of the Southern Pacific* (New York: Ronald Press Co. 1922), 132.
20. Orsi, 115.
21. Daggett, 135.
22. Orsi, 116
23. Charles Crocker bought the grounds in 1879 from Jack's Ranch at Monterey, which was about 4500 acres and Gonzalez Ranch, near Salinas, about 3500 acres. From a handwritten letter from C.P. Huntington to F.S. Donaty, secretary of Pacific Improvement Company, dated Sep 24, 1847. Special Collections and University Archives, Stanford University Libraries, PL 17 B1 F33.
24. The town of Monterey dates back to 1770 when Junipero Serra founded a mission there; it was California's first capital. When the PIC purchased most of the peninsula, the company developed the area's water supply, Del Monte Resort Hotel, the Pebble Beach community, and the village of Carmel-by-the-Sea.

CHAPTER 3 *Pages 47 to 57*
1. Doyce B. Nunis, *The Founding Documents of Los Angeles: A Bilingual Edition* (Los Angeles: Historical Society of Southern California, 2004).
2. Quotation: Bill Henry. "By the Way." *Los Angeles Times*, Apr 21, 1940.
3. Steve Fraser. "The Misunderstood Robber Baron: On Cornelius Vanderbilt." *The Nation*, Nov 11, 2009. https://www.thenation.com/article/misunderstood-robber-baron-cornelius-vanderbilt/
4. See: Tom Sitton, *Grand Ventures: The Banning Family and the Shaping of Southern California* (San Marino, California: Huntington Library, 2010),109. The LA&SP became part of Southern Pacific in the agreement to divert its proposed transcontinental line through Los Angeles. This short line railroad was built by Phineas Banning and made two runs daily, hauling wool, wine, lumber, and passengers to and from the harbor. Also see: http://www.railswest.com/history/californiabeginnings.html. Viewed Oct 17, 2020. The site explains that Banning's line had two locomotives, each a four-wheel narrow gauge engine built by Vulcan Iron Works of San Francisco. The locomotives had been purchased second-hand from Napa Valley Railroad. When SP took over, the line was re-tracked to standard gauge and named the Wilmington Line.
5. Quotation: "Brother Frank Monaghan." Historical Record and Souvenir (Los Angeles: Times-Mirror, 1923), 170.
6. Guthrie Genealogy. Ancestry.com.
7. *List of National, State, and Local Commercial Organizations*. Interstate Commerce Commission, Feb 1898. Washington, D.C., 66.
8. Southern Pacific Railroad timetable. *Los Angeles Herald,* Jul 17 1878.
9. David F. Myrick, *Railroads of Arizona* Vol 1 (Glendale: Trans-Anglo:1984), 18.
10. "Brother Monaghan." Historical Record and Souvenir (Los Angeles: Times-Mirror, 1923).
11. Neill Compton Wilson and Taylor J. Monaghan, *Southern Pacific: The Roaring Story of a Fighting Railroad* (New York: McGraw-Hill, 1952), 103–104. Hopkins's wife, Mary, had been overseeing the completion of her Nob Hill man-

Endnotes

sion. When she left San Francisco, she put her adopted son Timothy in charge of the business. She went to New York City where she married her youthful interior decorator Edward Searles. Thirteen years later, she died, leaving her estate to Searles. Lawsuits were filed, and Searles settled out of court by sharing part of the inheritance with Timothy.

12. Richard J. Orsi, *Sunset Limited: The Southern Pacific Railroad and the Development of the American West 1850–1930* (Berkeley: University of California, 2005), 422 note 63. Orsi refers to the papers of William Mahl, saying he knew Huntington as well as anyone. "Huntington's genius as a manager" was to allow "qualified men to make their own decisions once he gave them the task." Crocker passed on this management style to Monaghan and Murphy.
13. Stuart Daggett, *Chapters on the History of the Southern Pacific* (New York: Ronald Press Co., 1922), 133.
14. Steven Ambrose, *Nothing Like It in the World: The Men Who Built the Transcontinental Railroad 1863–1869* (New York: Touchstone, 2000), 44.
15. Hubert Howe Bancroft. *The Works of Hubert Howe Bancroft Vol XXIV: History of California Vol VII, 1860–1890* (San Francisco: The History Company, Publishers, 1890), 546.
16. "Conveyances." *Los Angeles Herald*, Jun 15, 1882.
17. Murphy at the Cosmopolitan Hotel. "Personal Mention." *Los Angeles Herald*, Feb 5, 1882, Mar 8, 1882; GC 1056. Register Cosmopolitan Hotel, Oct 11, 1882, Nov 7, 1882. Seaver Center for Western History Research, Los Angeles County Museum of Natural History.
18. GC 1139, Benjamin Cummings Truman Scrapbooks, Box G. Seaver Center for Western History Research, Los Angeles County Museum of Natural History.

CHAPTER 4 *Pages 59 to 70*

1. "What kind of food did they eat?" Key Questions. *Chinese Railroad Workers in North America*. Project at Stanford University. https://web.stanford.edu/group/chineserailroad/cgi-bin/website/faqs/ Viewed Oct 19, 2020.
2. GC 1139, Benjamin Cummings Truman Scrapbooks, Box G. Seaver Center for Western History Research, Los Angeles County Museum of Natural History
3. "Report of Our Operations at the Front for the Year 1882." Smith, F.W. General Manager, Atlantic & Pacific Railroad Company (Western Division). Albuquerque, N.M. To Henry C. Nutt Esq. President, Atlantic & Pacific Railroad Company, Boston, May 9, 1883. Kansas Historical Society. Lands at Needles 1883–1895. MSS 789. Box 318.
4. "The Needles." *Los Angeles Herald*, Jun 6, 1883.
5. "The Needles."
6. J.C. Ives and A.A. Humphreys, "Camp 41 Mojave Valley Feb. 10." 36th Congress, 1st Session Senate: Ex. Doc.; *Report upon the Colorado River of the West: Explored in 1857 and 1858, by Lieutenant Joseph C. Ives, A Humphreys, Capt. Topogr. Engin., in Charge*; By Order of the Secretary of War (Washington, D.C.: Government Printing Office, 1861), 59.
7. Richard E. Lingenfelter, *Steamboats on the Colorado River, 1852–1916: A History of Steam Navigation on the Colorado River and Its Tributaries, 1852–1916* (Tucson: University of Arizona Press, 1978), 82.
8. Lingenfelter, 82.

9. "Cussedness" *Mohave County Miner*, Jun 3, 1883.
10. "The Disease at Needles." *The Daily Morning Astoria*, Aug 3, 1884.
11. "Needles." *History of San Bernardino County* Vol 1, 632.
12. Arthur Humphrey, *Arthur L. Humphrey* (Pittsburgh, Pennsylvania: privately printed, 1911).
13. Richard J. Orsi, *Sunset Limited: The Southern Pacific Railroad and the Development of the American West 1850–1930* (Berkeley: University of California, 2005), 116.
14. Carolyn Dougherty, "Southern Pacific Company, Sacramento Shops." *Historic American Engineering Record*, Aug 2002.
15. "Wholesale Ledger Monaghan & Murphy." William A. Claypool Collection. John M. Pfau Library. California State University San Bernardino.
16. Quotation: "Needles" *Los Angeles Herald*, Aug 16, 1883.
17. "Needles." *History of San Bernardino County* Vol 1, 635.
18. Stuart Brushey (ed.), *Preliminary Report of the Inland Waterways Commission: Message from the President of the United States, Transmitting A Preliminary Report of the Inland Waterways Commission* (New York: Arno Press, 1972), 161.
19. "Brother Monaghan." Historical Record and Souvenir (Los Angeles: Times-Mirror, 1923).

CHAPTER 5 Pages 71 to 85

1. "Indian population." *Bazoo*, Aug 31, 1889.
2. J.C. Ives and A.A. Humphreys, "Camp 41 Mojave Valley Feb. 10." 36th Congress, 1st Session Senate: Ex. Doc.; *Report upon the Colorado River of the West: Explored in 1857 and 1858, by Lieutenant Joseph C. Ives, A Humphreys, Capt. Topogr. Engin., in Charge*; By Order of the Secretary of War. (Washington, D.C.: Government Printing Office, 1861), 66.
3. Ives and Humphreys, 66.
4. L. Burr Belden, "Needles Begins With Railway, Highway Follows." *San Bernardino Daily Sun*, Nov 10, 1963.
5. L. Burr Belden. "Needles Founded When Railroads Race for River." *San Bernardino Daily Sun*, Mar 14, 1954.
6. Belden, "Needles Founded…"
7. Murphy's Vest Pocket Notebook. Ryan, Joseph Francis. Joseph Francis Ryan Research Collection on Daniel Murphy and Family, Approximately 1900–2012. 1900. Bancroft Library, Berkley, CA.
8. Luther A. Ingersoll, *Ingersoll's Century Annals of San Bernardino County 1769 to 1904: Prefaced with a Brief History to the State of California, Supplemented with an Encyclopedia of Local Biography and Embellished with Views of Historic Subjects and Portraits of Many of Its Representative People* Vol 1, (Los Angeles: L.A. Ingersoll, 1904), 632.
9. Ingersoll, 632.
10. David F. Myrick, *Railroads of Nevada and Eastern California* Vol 2 (Reno: University of Nevada Press, 1992), 771.
11. L. Burr Belden, "Needles Boys Wrecked Little Nine Railroad." *San Bernardino Sun-Telegram*, Aug 23, 1959.
12. Belden, "Needles Boys Wrecked…"
13. Belden. "Needles Boys Wrecked…"
14. *Mohave County Miner*, May 18, 1888.
15. Mohave County Arizona. Index to Mines 1885–1897.

ENDNOTES

16. Charles Battye, "Old-timer Recalls Indian Experience with Mojave tribe." *San Bernardino Sun*, Apr 21, 1939.
17. Battye, "Old-timer Recalls…"
18. Battye, "Old-timer Recalls…"
19. Battye, "Old-timer Recalls…"
20. Battye, "Old-timer Recalls…"
21. "Scenes at the Cremation of a Mojave Chief." *Aspen Daily Times*, Jun 29, 1893. A reporter meets Dan Murphy by chance in the bar of San Francisco's Palace Hotel and shares their fascinating conversation.
22. Ives and Humphreys, 69.

CHAPTER 6 *Pages 87 to 94*
1. Newton H. Chittenden, *Health Seekers', Tourists' and Sportsmen's Guide to the Sea-Side, Lake-Side, Foothill, Mountain, and Mineral Spring Health and Pleasure Resorts of the Pacific Coast* (San Francisco: C.A. Murdock & Company, Publishers, 1884), 20.
2. Glenn S. Dumke, *The Boom of the Eighties in Southern California* (San Marino, California: Huntington Library, 1944), 22.
3. Atchison, Topeka & Santa Fe Corporate Records. Kansas Historical Society: MSS 789. Box 103.
4. Donald Duke, *Santa Fe: the Railroad Gateway to the American West.* Vol 2 (San Marino, California: Golden West Books, 1997), 431.
5. *Los Angeles Almanac*. http://www.laalmanac.com/weather/we13.htm.
6. Richard V. Dodge, "The Fallbrook Line." *The Dispatcher* No 17, Apr 10, 1958. *The Dispatcher* is available on the website of the *Journal of the Railway Historical Society of San Diego*. http://sdrm.info/history/cs/calsouth.html. Viewed Oct 28, 2020.
7. The Cajon Pass is not a gap between two mountains, but rather, it's a passage between two mountain ranges: the San Bernardino Range to the east and the older San Gabriel Mountains on the west.
8. Dumke, 22–24.
9. Godfrey Holterhoff Jr., *Historical Review of the Atchison, Topeka, and Santa Fe Railway Company (With Particular Reference to California Lines)…*, (Los Angeles: Railroad Commission of the State of California, Jun 1914), 5–7.
10. *Press Reference Library: Notables of the Southwest, Being the Portraits and Biographies of Progressive Men of the Southwest, Who Have Helped in the Development and History Making of This Wonderful Country* Vol 1 (Los Angeles et al.: International News Service, 1913), see "Godfrey Holterhoff Jr.," 718.
11. "Holterhoff, Godfrey, Jr., 1860-" California Biography File. Western History-Material questionnaires, 1909–1910, undated, Los Angeles Public Library.
12. Godfrey Holterhoff, (miscredited to "E. Holterhoff")"A Collector's Notes on the Breeding of a Few Western Birds." *The American Naturalist* Vol 15 No 3, Mar 1881, 208–219. Viewed October 20, 2020. http://www.jstor.org/stable/2449354; for a list of Holterhoff's other articles see: Joseph Grinnell, *A Bibliography of California Ornithology* (Santa Clara, California: Cooper Ornithological Club of California, May 15, 1909.)
13. Holterhoff's title belies his true position with the AT&SF. He was "assistant" to the corporate treasurer in Boston but was viewed by the board of directors as the authority in the Western Division.
14. Letter to A.F. Walker, Chairman of the Board. New York, Mar 4, 1898. "1-3

Miscellaneous Los Angeles Office: Miscellaneous Correspondence." Kansas Historical Society: MSS 789. Box. 14.
15. Example of Code: D.L. Gallup, Letter to E.P. Ripley, president of AT&SF. New York, Oct 5, 1904. "Executive and Board Communication." Kansas Historical Society: MSS 789. Box 22
16. Dumke, 24.
17. Dumke, 24–25.
18. Dumke, 25.
19. Spencer Crump, *Ride the Big Red Cars: How Trolleys Helped Build Southern California* (Los Angeles: Crest Publications, 1962), 29.
20. Remi A. Nadeau, *City-Makers: The Story of Southern California's First Boom, 1868–76* (Corona Del Mar, California: Trans-Anglo Books, 1977), 155
21. Dumke, 43–48.
22. James Marshall, *Santa Fe: The Railroad that Built an Empire* (New York: Random House, 1945), 194.

CHAPTER 7 *Pages 95 to 99*
1. "Frightful Railway Disaster. A Train Plunges Through a Burned Bridge." *Daily Alta California*, Feb 28, 1887.
2. Arthur Luther Humphrey, *Autobiography of Arthur Luther Humphrey 1860–1937* (Pittsburgh, Pennsylvania: privately published, 1911), 113–116.
3. Humphrey, 113–116. Twenty-four years after this tragedy, Humphrey came to visit Murphy in Los Angeles. Together they recalled the total number of amputations and setting of broken limbs to be more than thirty.
4. *Railroad Commissioner Report on Mojave Line* Dec 27, 1884 (San Francisco: Superintendent State Printing), 3.
5. "Needles, Cal. Feb. 28." *Arizona Weekly Citizen*, Mar 5, 1887.
6. *Mohave County Miner*, Apr 16, 1887. Reports first snow in sixteen years.
7. "Mineral Park Our Mineral Park Correspondent tells what is being done in that Lively Camp." *Mohave County Miner*, Jun 4, 1887.
8. "Needles Fire." *Mohave County Miner, Aug 8, 1887.*

CHAPTER 8 *Pages 101 to 108*
1. Jane C. Harper, Craig W. Leavitt and Thomas J. Noel. *Colorado Newspapers: A History & Inventory, 1859–2000* (Westminster, Colorado: Colorado Press Association Foundation & Center for Colorado and The West at Auraria Library, 2014), 262.
2. Harper, Leavitt, and Noel, 263
3. "Morrell - Murphy." *Leadville Daily and Evening Chronicle*, Dec 24, 1887.
4. "The Keramic Show." *San Francisco Call*, Dec 9, 1896.
5. "New Companies" *Fairplay Flume*, Mar 4, 1880.
6. "A British Bulldog: The Part It Took in a Fight Between Sinnott and McKenzie; The Latter Gets Winged in the Leg and the Former is Arrested." *Leadville Daily Herald*, Dec 14, 1884
7. Charles Weber was a member of the first emigrant wagon train into California with John Bartleson, John Bidwill, Joseph Chiles, and Jesuit missionaries led by Fr. Pierre-Jean DeSmet. See: Doyce B. Nunis, *The Bidwell-Bartleson Party: 1841 California Emigrant Adventure: The Documents and Memoirs of the Overland Pioneers* (Santa Cruz, California: Western Tanager, 1991).
8. George P. Hammond and Dale L. Morgan, *Captain Charles M. Weber: Pioneer*

Endnotes

    of the San Joaquin and Founder of Stockton, California (Berkeley, California: The Friends of the Bancroft Library, 1966).
9. "Indian Curiosities." *The Bazoo,* Jan 26, 1889.
10. "On the Trail of Geronimo" was a popular expression of the day taken from the title of a book written by Edward Ellis and published in 1889.
11a. Joseph Howard Jr. (ed.), *The Union League Club Historical and Biographical 1863–1900* (New York: Union Historical Association and J.J. Wohltman, 1900), 64, 74.
11b. S.L.M. Barlow Papers, mss. BW, Box 193, Mar. 22, NYC. Huntington Library, San Marino, CA.
12. "Great White Hurricane: 60 MPH Wind that Left 50 Feet of Snow in its Wake." *New York Herald,* Mar 14, 1888.
13. Arizona Territory. Kingman County. Record of Claims. Book I, Oct 8, 1891, 660–662. These claims are in the mining districts named Wallapai, Minnesota, and San Francisco, which are located in the Arizona counties of Mohave and Yavapai.

CHAPTER 9 *Pages 109 to 125*
1. *Glimpses of The World's Fair; A Selection of Gems of the White City Seen through a Camera* (Chicago: Laird and Lee Publishing, 1893).
2. Hubert Howe Bancroft, *The Book of the Fair: An Historical and Descriptive Presentation of the World's Science, Art, and Industry, as viewed through the Columbian Exposition* (Chicago and San Francisco: Bancroft Company, 1893); quotation from Preface. Buildings description, 129–135.
3. Bancroft, *The Book of the Fair,* 480.
4. Bancroft, *The Book of the Fair,* 480.
5. Bancroft, *The Book of the Fair,* 489
6. Bancroft, *The Book of the Fair,* 339. This five-story building is in the style of a Moorish palace. There was even an ice-skating rink on the top floor. On Jul 10, at 1 p.m. with more than 50,000 fairgoers in attendance, the decorative Moorish tower (which disguised a chimney for the steam engines that ran the refrigeration equipment) caught fire. The crowd cheered for twenty firefighters who were on the spot within minutes. But flames erupted from the building's roof. Some firefighters escaped by sliding down hoses and ropes. "Then followed a scene of horror such as few have ever witnessed." Some firefighters fell, while others dove onto the roof, eighty feet below; the last remaining fireman, swan dived into the flames. Twelve firemen died in the conflagration. "Tragedy at the 1893 World's Fair; Fire killed 16 while crowd watched." *Chicago Tribune,* Jul 28, 2018; see also "World's Columbian Exposition Fire, Chicago; Jul 10, 1893." www.ideals.illinois.edu/bitstream/handle/2142/84/World's%20Columbian%20Exposition%20Fire,%201893.pdf?sequence=2. Viewed Oct 17, 2020.
7. W.R. Woolrich, *The Men Who Created Cold: A History of Refrigeration* (New York: Exposition Press, 1967), 74.
8. "1892 Pacific Improvement Company $106.9 million." Stanford University Special Collections, PL17 B 1 F 19 PIC 1892.
9. "Establishment of Ice Plant and to Furnish Water and Electricity at The Needles," quit claim deed to D. Murphy, dated Jul 16, 1894.
10. "Contract 338 C.B.P. 35-2." Kansas Historical Society. MSS 789. Box 324. Folder "Dan Murphy."

11. "People Met in Hotel Lobbies." *Washington Post*, May 24, 1907.
12. "Needles." *Albuquerque Weekly Citizen*, Apr 21, 1894.
13. Thomas M. Gaffney, "Needles Ice Plant & Car Icing Station." *Ice & Refrigeration Illustrated*. Vol 50 No 3, Sep 1, 1916, 76.
14. "Fruit Season Closing," *Atchison, Topeka & Santa Fe Journal*, May 15, 1900; "Fruit Shipments, Santa Fe, Oranges" *Atchison, Topeka & Santa Fe Journal*, Apr 17, 1900.
15. Gaffney, "Needles Ice Plant…," 76.
16. Donald Duke, *Santa Fe: The Railroad Gateway to the American West* Vol 2 (San Marino, California: Golden West Books, 1997), 431.
17. "Justly Popular: The Firm of Monaghan & Murphy Known Far and Near." *Los Angeles Herald*, Jan 15, 1893. In 2020 dollars, the firm was making approximately $5.5 million per year (calculated using measuringworth.com).
18. *The Bazoo*, Jan 4, 1890.
19. *The Bazoo*, Jan 4, 1890.
20. The PLIC did not financially back these companies, but in some cases, granted facility sites adjacent to the rail lines.
21. John Steven McGroarty, *Los Angeles from the Mountains to the Sea: With Selected Biography* Vol 2 (Chicago and New York: The American Historical Society, 1921), 73.
22. As of 2020, the building was still standing.
23. "Will E. Keller 1868-" California Biography File. Western History-Material questionnaires, 1909–1910, undated, Los Angeles Public Library.
24. A.C.W. Bethel, "Edwin Tobias Earl and the Refrigerator Car." *The Branding Iron*. No. 29. Spring 2020, 14.
25. Oscar Edward Anderson, *Refrigeration in America: A History of a New Technology and Its Impact* (Princeton, New Jersey: Princeton University Press, 1953), 142–178
26. Woolrich, 74–75.
27. Murphy Water, Ice, and Light Company. "Articles of Incorporation." Feb 23, 1904.

CHAPTER 10 Pages 127 to 135
1. "Shot by Sam. Murderer Ahvote Killed by a Piute…" *Los Angeles Times*, May 15, 1897.
2. "The Piute Murders, by James Gardiner" *Los Angeles Times*, May 18, 1897.
3. "The Piute Murders …"
4. "The Piute Murders …"
5. "Murder Most Foul. Ahvote, a Piute Indian Kills Seven Men. A Fiend Runs Amuck." *Kingman Daily Miner*, May 15, 1897.
6. "The Piute Murders … "
7. "The Piute Murders … "
8. Donna Andress, *Eldorado Canyon and Nelson, Nevada Historical Documents, Reminiscences, Commentary* (Nelson, Nevada: D. Andress, 1997), 70.
9. Andress, 70.
10. Thomas "Tommie" R. Lee, "Deacon Dan" *Petroleum World*, May 1940, 118.
11. L. Burr Belden, "Vanderbilt Ranks High on List of Rich, Wild Camps." *San Bernardino Daily Sun*, Nov 30, 1952; see also, *Bowen v. Needles National Bank*, 94 F 925. Abner T. Bowen, Plaintiff, vs. The Needles National Bank, Defendant; Daniel Murphy, Receiver of the Needles National Bank, Interve-

Endnotes

nor. Circuit Court of the United States, Ninth Circuit, Southern District of California.
12. James A. Goff, "A Triumph Over Blindness." *Santa Fe Employee Magazine*, Vol 5, No 1, Dec 1910, 41–43
13. Jay Berman, "The Rise and Fall of a Candy Empire, Downtown Bishop & Co, Thrived for 43 Years, but Then the Cookie Crumbled." *Los Angeles Downtown News*, Dec 22, 2008.

CHAPTER 11 *Pages 137 to 142*
1. "A Great Oil Strike." *Los Angeles Herald*, Dec 17, 1899.
2. Margaret L. Davis, *Dark Side of Fortune: Triumph and Scandal in the Life of Oil Tycoon Edward L. Doheny* (Berkeley: University of California Press, 1998), 14, 23.
3. Howard J. Nelson, *The Los Angeles Metropolis* (Dubuque, Iowa: Kendall/Hall Publishing Co. 1983), 180.
4. Martin R. Ansell, *Oil Baron of the Southwest: Edward L. Doheny and the Development of the Petroleum Industry in California and Mexico* (Columbus: Ohio State University Press, 1998), 25.
5. "Map of the former oil wells of the Los Angeles City Oil Field overlaid on modern Los Angeles. https://www.reddit.com/r/MapPorn/comments/4cai7o/map_of_the_former_oil_wells_of_the_los_angeles/
6. Ansell, 38.
7. Ansell, 30.
8. Keith Bryant, *History of the Atchison, Topeka & Santa Fe Railway* (New York: Macmillan Publishing Company, Inc., 1974), 224.
9. Glen D. Bradley, "The Santa Fe's Great California Oil Fields." *Santa Fe Magazine*, Vol X. No 12, Nov 1916, 32.
10. Donald Duke, *Santa Fe: The Railroad Gateway to the American West* Vol 2 (San Marino, California: Golden West Books, 1997), 432.
11. Ansell, 49.
12. In typical corporate style, Santa Fe's obituary of Maginnis in 1917 read: "He asked to be relieved from the Land and Claims Department [PLIC]." While that wasn't true at all, it was the company's way of politely honoring a dead man.
13. Ansell, *43*.
14. Letters from E.P. Ripley to A.F. Walker, Jun 10, 1898 and Jun 20, 1899. Kansas Historical Society, RR Collection 789. Box 1: "Board and Executive Committee Meetings."
15. "Large Real Estate Deals." *Fullerton News Tribune*, Jul 28, 1899.
16. Nevin was the new manager at PLIC, replacing Wade who had died the year before.
17. Orange County Book of Deeds. Book 44, 144, 146, 162. These pages show both Dan Murphy's purchase of the oil field and his later sale of the property to Brea Cañon Oil Co.
18. "In the Oil Field: Magnificent Well Struck in Fullerton District." *Los Angeles Herald*, Dec 17, 1899.
19. Davis, 35.

CHAPTER 12 *Pages 143 to 151*

1. Western Union Telegram from San Francisco, Feb 25, 1900, 8:38 a.m.; Antoinette Murphy's Scrapbook. Ryan, Joseph Francis. Joseph Francis Ryan Research Collection on Daniel Murphy and Family, Approximately 1900–2012. 1900. Bancroft Library, Berkley, CA.
2. "Miss Antoinette Sinnott Marries Dan Murphy, a Capitalist of Los Angeles." *San Francisco Examiner,* Mar 3, 1900. Saved as a clipping in Antoinette Murphy's Scrapbook. Ryan, Joseph Francis. Joseph Francis Ryan Research Collection on Daniel Murphy and Family, Approximately 1900–2012. 1900. Bancroft Library, Berkley, CA.
3. Letter from W.H. Bonsall, Jan 28, 1900. Ryan, Joseph Francis. Joseph Francis Ryan Research Collection on Daniel Murphy and Family, Approximately 1900–2012. 1900. Bancroft Library, Berkley, CA.
4. *Carbonate Chronicle,* Aug 13, 1900.
5. *Mosher vs. Sinnott.* No. 2431 Stipulation. Court of Appeals of the State of Colorado, 1898. Famous Consolidated Gold Mining Company. Line 1273.
6. "Enjoining a Sale of Famous Stock." *Leadville Daily and Evening Chronicle,* Jul 14, 1898. Featured on page 1.
7. *Mosher vs. Sinnott.* Court of Appeals of the State of Colorado, 1898. Line 1273
8. *Carbonate Chronicle,* Aug 13, 1900.
9. *Mosher vs. Sinnott.* Line 1180–1183
10. *Mosher vs. Sinnott.* Line 1284
11. *Mosher vs. Sinnott.* Line 1516
12. "Attorney Burchard Won the Case." Ryan, Joseph Francis. Joseph Francis Ryan Research Collection on Daniel Murphy and Family, Approximately 1900–2012. 1900. Bancroft Library, Berkley, CA.
13. Letter from Delia Sinnott to Charles Weber. Leadville, Colorado, Apr 17, 1899. Weber Family Papers, BANC MSS 40:7. CB289. The Bancroft Library, University of California, Berkeley.
14. *Mosher vs. Sinnott.* Line 1521
15. "California's First Swell Summer Resort: White Sulfur Springs." *San Francisco Call,* Sep 2, 1900. "Mrs. Dan Murphy and her sister" were listed as early visitors to this resort. Founded in 1852, White Sulfur Springs was California's oldest resort; it was almost destroyed in the Glass Fire of 2020.
16. *Kathryn Sinnott, Respondent, v. J.F. Colombet, Treasurer of the City of San Jose, Appellant,* Apr 29, 1895, No. 15721, 187.
17. "Articles of Inc.," Cocopah Copper Company. Territory of Arizona, May 19, 1906.
18. "Mines and Mining, Southwest Miners Association to Quit, Will Turn Exhibits Over to Chamber of Commerce." *Los Angeles Times,* Mar 5, 1903.

CHAPTER 13 *Pages 153 to 159*

1. Howard King Bagley. Death Certificate 1966.
2. *Fullerton News Tribune,* Aug 28, 1902.
3. "Fullerton Producer Best in America." *Los Angeles Times,* Jul 18, 1903.
4. "Fullerton Producer Best in America." *Los Angeles Times,* Jul 18, 1903.
5. Gerald T. White, *Formative Years in the Far West; A History of Standard Oil Company of California and Predecessors through 1919* (New York: Appleton-Century-Crofts, 1962), 263.
6. Thomas "Tommie" R. Lee, "Deacon Dan" *Petroleum World,* May 1940, 120.

Endnotes

Some say Murphy is, by default, the founder of the town of El Segundo.
7. White, 465.
8. These 1920 leases have proven to be a very profitable investment that has added to the large endowment of the Dan Murphy Foundation, more than eight decades after Murphy's death.
9. In July 2020, the US Supreme Court upheld the Native American rights to this territory.
10. Because of the Cherokee alliance with the Confederacy during the Civil War, the US government required a new treaty in 1866. This treaty allowed the US to sell the land in the Cherokee Strip (a two-mile-wide strip of land along the northern border of Oklahoma, created by a surveying error) to non-Natives. After the war, Texas cattlemen drove their herds across this land into Kansas for market. By 1883, the cattlemen negotiated a five-year lease of the land from the Cherokee Nation. After the lease was up, Congress denied any further leasing and authorized the purchase of the land at $1.25 per acre. The Native Americans protested, since they had turned down $3.00 per acre from the cattlemen; their complaints were in vain, however. No payment was made to the Cherokee until 1964, when they settled their claims against the US government.
11. Since Murphy and Ball first met, Ball had become the owner of his hometown baseball team, the Saint Louis Browns. In 1909, PDC rebuilt Sportsman's Park in Saint Louis, the nation's third all-concrete-and-steel stadium.
12. "Who's Who In Oil and Gas." *Fuel Oil Journal*, May 1916, Vol 7, 120–121.
13. The Indian Territory became the state of Oklahoma on Nov 16, 1907.
14. "Getty, Jean Paul (1892–1976)." Oklahoma Historical Society. "https://www.okhistory.org/publications/enc/entry.php?entry=GE013
15. "Is Paying Fancy Prices." *Paul's Valley Sentinel*, Vol 1, No 1, May 19, 1904.
16. "Gusher in Brea Cañon Looks Like a Big Well." *Los Angeles Times*, Feb 6, 1916.
17. "Gas Roaring From Brea Cañon Well" *Los Angeles Times*, Feb 7, 1916.
18. "Big Oil Gusher Tapped." *Fullerton News Tribune*, Nov 3, 1904.
19. "Brea's Outlook Is Unpromising." *Los Angeles Times*, Jun 13, 1921.
20. *Fuel Oil Journal* Vol 7, May 1916 (Houston: H. Reavis, 1916), 112

CHAPTER 14 *Pages 161 to 167*
1. "Small Farms at Freemen: Important Plans for Settlement on Redondo Electric Line—260 Acres Bought for $50,000." *Los Angeles Herald*, Oct 29, 1905.
2. The Jessie Benton Fremont House was found extant at 3117 S. Raymond, Los Angeles, by Laura Meyers, a preservationist with West Adams Heritage Association. Fremont's funeral was one of the largest funerals held in the city at the time. She was cremated at Rosedale Cemetery. Her children never claimed her remains, which languished at the cemetery until the 1970s, at which time they were placed in a common pauper's grave in Rosedale.
3. David K. Randall, *The King and Queen of Malibu: The True Story of the Battle for Paradise* (New York: W.W. Norton, 2017), 76.
4. "Significance Statement." Los Angeles Cultural Heritage Commission. Case No. CHC-2015-237-HCM. Feb 5, 2015.
5. Restrictive covenants were prevalent throughout Los Angeles including the Western Addition. In the 1940s these contracts which forbid property owners from selling to Black people were challenged and ruled unenforceable by the Supreme Court case of *Shelly vs. Kraemer* (1948). Some of these contested

properties were in the Harvard Heights development, which became known as Sugar Hill by the Black homeowners.
6. Thirteen thousand volumes comprise the collection including a comprehensive collection of Oscar Wilde's works. Upon his death in 1934, the property, library, and a $1.5 million dollar endowment was granted to the University of California Los Angeles. UCLA continues to operate the library as a research source for scholars.
7. William D. Mangam, *The Clarks: An American Phenomenon* (New York: Silver Bow Press, 1939), 207–209. According to Mangam, W.A. Clark Jr. was under investigation and liable for "nuisance charges laid against his premises" because "he had held nude male parties in his own Italian gardens." In abeyance of any adverse publicity or litigation, Clark Jr. transferred his property at 2205 West Adams Blvd. "to the great commonwealth of California," in the name of University of California at Los Angeles on Jun 12, 1926. *The Pacific Historical Review* recorded that *The Clarks: An American Phenomenon* "treatment is appropriate, for besides its usefulness to the historian of the West, it will be of interest to the sociologist and the psychoanalyst." *Pacific Historical Review* 1941, 506.
8. Western Union Telegram from Dan Murphy to Mrs. Murphy, 2858 Orchard Street., Los Angeles, dated Oct 9 1902. Hays, Kansas. Ryan, Joseph Francis. Joseph Francis Ryan Research Collection on Daniel Murphy and Family, Approximately 1900–2012. 1900. Bancroft Library, Berkley, CA.
9. "Thomas Murphy Dead." *Ellis County News,* Oct 17, 1902.

CHAPTER 15 *Pages 169 to 179*
1. How Sue Sinnott came to be involved with Enrico Ruspoli is a somewhat mysterious tale, and not all the details can be documented. As best it can be determined, here is the chronology: Jennie Berry, age twenty-eight of Rome, Georgia, married tobacco-heir Henry Bruton, age forty-three, in 1889. Four years later, Henry died, making thirty-two-year-old Jennie a rich widow. A year after her husband's death, Jennie adopted her orphaned niece Florence, in Alameda, California. On Mar 2, 1901, forty-year-old Jennie married Prince Enrico Ruspoli, a twenty-three-year-old Italian who was attached to the Italian embassy in Washington, D.C., and to sound more "continental," Jennie changed her first name to Eugenia. Prince Ruspoli did not want to share "their" estate with Eugenia's adopted child, so in 1903, the couple paid Florence $6,000 to rescind her adoption, after an uncontested court case was settled in 1903 in San Jose, California (near the Sinnott family home, where Sue Sinnott often visited her sisters). This court case more than likely brought Prince Ruspoli to California in 1903, the same year that Sue conceived her female child, Bernardine, who was born on Jun 2, 1904. Coincidentally, and perhaps unrelated, a local Bay Area author, Fremont Older, wrote a novel in which a main character, Prince Ruspoli, visits Monterey in 1903. Although it cannot be confirmed that Sue Sinnott and the prince met in San Jose, Sue and Bernardine were welcomed as "family" by the Ruspolis when they went to Italy. See: "She Barters Away Her Heritage: Heiress of Italian Countess Accepts Coin To Give Up Her Claim." *Oakland Tribune,* Jan 19, 1903; "Prefers Gold to Noble Rank: Miss Bruton Renounces Right as Heiress To Count." *San Francisco Chronicle,* Jan 7, 1903; Fremont Older, *The Socialist and the Prince,* a novel written in 1903, includes a character named Prince Ruspoli who visited Monterey, California, in 1903.

Endnotes

2. The word "wayward" had a broad meaning when it came to women; a wayward woman could be unmarried and pregnant, sexually promiscuous, vagrant, charged with petty crimes, or frequently drunk in public. Any of these "offenses," among many others, could make a woman eligible for a stint of undetermined length at a Magdalene Laundry.
3. *History of the Good Shepherd Sisters*, (Los Angeles, undated). Typewritten manuscript in three-ring binders. Copied on location on Jan 27, 2014.
4. "Bishop Dedicates New Home of the Good Shepherd." Sisters of the Good Shepherd Archives, 1904.
5. Barbara Welter, "The Cult of True Womanhood: 1820–1860." *American Quarterly* Vol 18 No. 2 (1966), 152.
6. Nancymarie Phillips, "Education for Girls in the House of the Good Shepherd, US 1940–1980" (2008). Dissertation. Cleveland State University. ETD Archive, 241. https://engagedscholarship.csuohio.edu/etdarchive/241
7. *History of the Good Shepherd Sisters ....*
8. *History of the Good Shepherd Sisters ....*
9. "To Honor Madame Modjeska." *Los Angeles Herald*, Mar 5, 1905.
10. *Carbonate Chronicle*, Aug 13, 1900.
11. Delia Sinnott letter to Dan Murphy, Mar 6, 1906. Bancroft Library. Weber Family Papers. BANC MSS C-B 829. Box 40. Folder 7
12. Delia Sinnott letter to Dan Murphy, Mar 6, 1906.
13. Delia Sinnott letter to Dan Murphy, Mar 7, 1906.
14. Delia Sinnott letter to Dan Murphy, Mar 7, 1906.
15. Sinnott/Weber families held onto these claims until the early twenty-first century when they were advised to sell in case environmental issues arise. Interview with Helen Cahill, Feb 2, 2011.
16. "Filed for Record: Deeds." *Fairplay Flume*, Jan 14, 1907.
17. Antoinette Murphy telegram to Dan Murphy, Aug 25, 1907. Ryan, Joseph Francis. Joseph Francis Ryan Research Collection on Daniel Murphy and Family, Approximately 1900–2012. 1900. Bancroft Library, Berkley, CA.
18. "The Insider." *San Francisco Call*, Jan 13, 1909.
19. *Los Angeles Herald*, Jun 5, 1886, advertisement.
20. Jack Beardwood, *"From Browns to Greens: A History of the Los Angeles Country Club 1898–1973* (Los Angeles: Los Angeles Country Club, 1973), 31. This was the second location of the famed Los Angeles Country Club, the first being on sixteen acres at Alvarado Terrace (bounded by Pico Boulevard, Iowa, Alvarado, and Sixteenth Streets.). Large tomato cans were used for golf cups. The Wilshire Boulevard site is the country club's third location.
21. 202 Quotation: James Miller Guinn, *A History of California and an Extended History of Its Southern Coast Counties: Also Containing Biographies of Well-known Citizens of the Past and Present* (Los Angeles: Historic Record Company, 1907), 986.
22. "Real Estate Transfers." *Los Angeles Times*, Jul 20, 1901, 13.
23. "Three Great Banks Joined by Merger." *Los Angeles Herald*, Aug 4, 1905.
24. "Who's Who—And Why. Noted Men and Women of the Southwest." *Illustrated Weekly*, Sep 7, 1912.
25. "Local Capitalists Invest at San Diego." *Los Angeles Herald*, Apr 18, 1907.
26. Also see more information on the SS *Pasadena*: Jack McNairn and Jerry MacMullen, *Ships of the Redwood Coast*, (Stanford, California: Stanford University Press, 1946).

CHAPTER 16 Pages 181 to 183

1. Hazel E Olson, *"As the Sand Shifts" in Colton, California* (Colton, California: Hazel E. Olson), 1989.
2. *California Journal of Mines and Geology* Vol 15, 879–880.
3. Hubert Howe Bancroft, *The Book of the Fair; an Historical and Descriptive Presentation of the World's Science, Art, and Industry, as Viewed through the Columbian Exposition at Chicago in 1893* (Chicago and San Francisco: Bancroft Company, 1893), 480
4. "Articles of Incorporation" (State of California). California Portland Cement Company, Sep 15, 1891.
5. "Inferior Cement Contractor Has Trouble." *Los Angeles Times*, Jan 28, 1900.
6. "Commercial: California Cement." *Los Angeles Times*, Jun 15, 1896.
7. *Certificate of the Creation of Bonded Indebtedness of the California Portland Cement Company* (State of California), May 21, 1901.
8. "Chicago and Michigan Parties Options on California Portland Cement." *Cement and Engineering News*, Jul 1899, 13.
9. "People Met in Hotel Lobbies." *Washington Post*, May 24, 1907.
10. "Bigger Plant for Cement." *Los Angeles Times*, Jan 20, 1906.

CHAPTER 17 Pages 185 to 193

1. *Who's Who in the Pacific Southwest: A Compilation of Authentic Biographical Sketches of Citizens of Southern California and Arizona* (Los Angeles: The Times-Mirror Printing & Binding House, 1913), "Frank Dale Hudson," 186.
2. *Sanborn Insurance Maps of Los Angeles, California* Book 46 (New York: Sanborn Map,1906), 35.
3. "Guasti Villa." *Western Architect* Vol 18, Jan 1912.
4. "Villa Home is Charming–Dan Murphy Combines Beauty of Design and Setting." *Los Angeles Times*, May 8, 1910.
5. Letter from T.A. Riordan, Apr 19, 1909, Flagstaff, Arizona. Ryan, Joseph Francis. Joseph Francis Ryan Research Collection on Daniel Murphy and Family, Approximately 1900–2012. 1900. Bancroft Library, Berkley, CA.
6. "1909 Holterhoff Letters." Apr 20, 1909; Jun 4, 1909; Jun 29, 1909. Ryan, Joseph Francis. Joseph Francis Ryan Research Collection on Daniel Murphy and Family, Approximately 1900–2012. 1900. Bancroft Library, Berkley, CA.
7. Steven M. Avella and Jeffrey Zalar. "Sanctity in the Era of Catholic Action: The Case of Saint Pius X." *US Catholic Historian*.15, No. 4 (1997), 57–80.
8. Booth Tarkington. "A Vatican Sermon." *Harper's Monthly Magazine*, Vol 109, Jun 1904, 69.
9. David I. Kertzer, *The Pope and Mussolini: The Secret History of Pius XI and the Rise of Fascism in Europe* (New York: Random House, 2014), 83.
10. Msgr. Francis J. Weber, "Notes with Sir Daniel Donohue." Notes taken during conversation between Weber and Donohue, Nov 20, 2002.
11. "Grand Hotel de la Minerve Rome." Taken from a plaque outside the Grand Hotel Minerve, Rome, 2012.
12. Maestro del Sacro Ospizio. *Curia Romana*. Annuario Pontificio. L' Anno 1912 (Roma: Tipografia R.C.A., 1860, 1871), 437, 472.
13. Interview with Helen Cahill, Nov 4, 2011.
14. "Architectural Lines Effectively Combined with Attractive Landscaping Setting." *Los Angeles Times*, May 8, 1910.

Endnotes

15. "Kept Busy Dodging Cyclones and Snows." Newspaper clipping annotated as May 11, 1911, no source noted. Ryan, Joseph Francis. Joseph Francis Ryan Research Collection on Daniel Murphy and Family, Approximately 1900–2012. 1900. Bancroft Library, Berkley, CA.
16. "Success Meets Work of Fund Committee." *Tulsa Daily World*, Apr 15, 1911.
17. "Kept Busy Dodging Cyclones and Snows."

CHAPTER 18 Pages 195 to 199
1. Torsten A. Magnusion, "History of the Beet Sugar Industry in California." *Annual Publication of the Historical Society of Southern California* Vol 11, No. 1 (1918), 77.
2. News clipping: "Suit by Director." Jan 9, 1910, no source noted. Launer Room, VF, Fullerton Public Library.
3. *The Needles Eye*, Jun 6, 1908, 1.
4. "Capitol Group Sold." *Needles Eye*, Mar 7, 1908.
5. "T.J. Murphy Weds." *Mohave County Miner*, Jul 3, 1915; Los Angeles Department of Building & Safety, Public Records: 635 S. Muirfield Road.
6. "Bond Election Victorious Here." *Needles Nugget*, Apr 24, 1925
7. "Brother Frank Monaghan." Historical Record and Souvenir (Los Angeles: Times-Mirror Press, 1929), 170.
8. Fairhaven Memorial Park, section "Lawn K," Santa Ana, California.
9. "Yesterday Today and Tomorrow." *The Weekly Courier,* Jan 24, 1960.
10. "Angelenos Get Warm Welcome." *Los Angeles Times*, Nov 8, 1908.
11. "New Phase in Cement Issue Cruelty to Animals to Feed 'em Dusty Alfalfa." *Los Angeles Times*, Jul 27, 1910.
12. *A. Hubert vs California Portland Cement Company*. Superior Court of the State of California, Apr 17, 1911, 11–12.
13. "Cement Company Buys Dust-Blighted Zone." *Los Angeles Times*, Jul 9, 1914.
14. "Cement Company Buys ..."
15. Luke 12:58. *New American Standard Bible.*(La Habra, California: J.B. McCabe Company, 1977).
16. "Cement Company Buys ..."
17. "Cement Company Buys ..."

CHAPTER 19 Pages 201 to 205
1. "B. Cooper Corbet." *Who's Who in the Pacific Southwest* (Los Angeles: The Times-Mirror Printing & Binding House, 1913), 102; "A.H. Denker Dead." Los Angeles Public Library. California Biography File A, Nov 14, 1892.
2. Hammel died in 1890, and two years later, Andrew Denker dropped dead on a downtown street at the age of fifty-two and at the peak of his career. He was survived by Louise Denker, their four daughters, and a son, Louis. The men owned a large 3,500-acre Spanish rancho west of downtown called Rodeo de Las Aguas. Their widows sold it, and a few years later it was developed into what is now Beverly Hills and Trousdale Estates. Three years after the Murphys moved into their new home on West Adams, Louise Denker built a home at 3820 West Adams. A native of France, she imported all of the grand home's furnishings and decorative items from France—from the hardware to the Lalique lighting fixtures. The family members were all devoted Catholics. In later years, one of the daughters, Leontine, married Bernard Giannini, the brother of A.P. Giannini, founder of Bank of America. Louis Denkers had

one daughter, Louise, who married John DeMille, son of Cecil B. DeMille. By the 1980s, the Denkers were the only original family remaining on West Adams Boulevard
3. "A Debutante's Letter." Newspaper clipping, dated Jun 22, 1917, no source noted. Antoinette Murphy's Scrapbook. Ryan, Joseph Francis. Joseph Francis Ryan Research Collection on Daniel Murphy and Family, Approximately 1900–2012. 1900. Bancroft Library, Berkley, CA.
4. "A Debutante's Letter."
5. Later in life, Catherine Coffin Phillips wrote the book *Jessie Benton Fremont: A Woman Who Made History* (San Francisco: John Henry Nash, 1935). Fremont passed away at her West Adams home in 1902.
6. "A Debutante's Letter."
7. "To Honor Madame Modjeska." *Los Angeles Herald*, Mar 5, 1905.
8. "Musical Mention." *Evening Star,* Jan 21, 1917; James A. Goff, "A Triumph Over Blindness." *Santa Fe Employees Magazine*. Vol 5 No 7, Jun 1911, 41–43.
9. "Good Shepherd Home Benefit." *Los Angeles Herald*, Feb 19, 1905.
10. Margaret L. Davis, *Children's Hospital and the Leaders of Los Angeles: The First 100 Years* (Los Angeles: Children's Hospital, 2002), 236.
11. "Saint Bernardine Cottage." *Fifth Annual Report of the Barlow Sanatorium*, 1909, 3; "Life Members." *First Annual Report of the Barlow Sanatorium*, 1904.
12. Letter from Mrs. Coleman to Antoinette Murphy, May 10, 1910. Ryan, Joseph Francis. Joseph Francis Ryan Research Collection on Daniel Murphy and Family, Approximately 1900–2012. 1900. Bancroft Library, Berkley, CA.

CHAPTER 20 *Pages 207 to 214*
1. Letter from Most Rev. Thomas Conaty to Most Rev. Thomas Kennedy. Pontifical North American College, Rome. Murphy Family Papers, Apr 11, 1912.
2. Letter from Daniel J. Donohue to Msgr. Francis J. Weber regarding benefactions of the Dan Murphy Foundation. Archdiocese of Los Angeles Archival Center. Undated.
3. Thomas "Tommie" R. Lee, "Deacon Dan" *Petroleum World*, May 1940, 118.
4. "Santa Fe De-Luxe for Classy Folks." *San Francisco Call*, Aug 26, 1911.
5. Letter from. Dan Murphy to Rev. Frederick Ruppert S.J., Oct 11, 1923. Ryan, Joseph Francis. Joseph Francis Ryan Research Collection on Daniel Murphy and Family, Approximately 1900–2012. 1900. Bancroft Library, Berkley, CA.
6. Ruth Ben-Ghiat. "An American Authoritarian." *The Atlantic*, Aug 12, 2016.
7. Ben-Ghiat, "An American Authoritarian."
8. Carl Smith. "Pullman Strike." *The Electronic Encyclopedia of Chicago* (Chicago Historical Society: 2005).
9. Pius X. Encyclical letter: *Singulari quadam*: on labor organizations, Sep 24, 1912.
10. Curiously this gazebo remained at that location for nearly forty-five years before being airlifted by helicopter to Bernardine's new home after her marriage. It is extant at Villa San Giuseppe in the Los Feliz-area hills, overlooking Interstate 5.
11. Letter of Introduction from Most Rev. Conaty to Sister Mary Reeves, Assistant Superior General, Sisters of Charity, Apr 9, 1912.
12. "Congregation of Our Lady of Charity of the Good Shepherd." *Wikipedia*. Viewed Sep 27, 2020.
13. Letter from Bernardine Murphy to her aunt, Kathryn Sinnott, Jul 6, 1912.

Endnotes

Ryan, Joseph Francis. Joseph Francis Ryan Research Collection on Daniel Murphy and Family, Approximately 1900–2012. 1900. Bancroft Library, Berkley, CA.
14. Page & Turnbull Inc. (Ruth Todd, et al.). *Pebble Beach Historic Context Statement.* Monterey County, Jul 15, 2013, 44.
15. Fred Flint, owner of a large real estate company, was the son of California Senator Frank P. Flint, who had established the town of Flintridge, near Pasadena, California.
16. *Directory of Monterey, Pacific Grove, Carmel, Del Monte, Pebble Beach and Seaside for 1922–1923* (Peninsula Directory Company, 1923).
17. Neal Hotelling. "Early Days at Pebble Beach." *Forest News*, Apr–Jun 2013.
18. Letter from Dan Murphy to Sue Sinnott. Nov 30 1925. Sue Sinnott was in Rome with Bernardine Murphy.

CHAPTER 21 *Pages 215 to 221*
1. Letter from Gustar Zinnow to Antoinette Murphy, Mar 27, 1917. Ryan, Joseph Francis. Joseph Francis Ryan Research Collection on Daniel Murphy and Family, Approximately 1900–2012. 1900. Bancroft Library, Berkley, CA.
2. "Los Angeles Shipbuilding and Dry Dock Company." *Moody's Manual of Railroad and Corporation Securities.* Vol 23., 1922, 1375.
3. *United States Shipping Board Emergency Fleet Corporation: Hearings Before the United States Senate Committee on Commerce*, Sixty-Fifth Congress, 1918–1919. United States: US Government Printing Office, 1918. 2251
4. "Another San Pedro Launching." *Railway & Marine News.* Vol XVI No 1, Jan 1918, 24.
5. "House Resolution No. 267." *Assembly Daily Journal. California Legislature. Fifty-Fifth Session*, Apr 21, 1943, 3388. Bernardine was slated to christen the SS *Dan Murphy* in 1943. The order was forwarded to Rear Admiral E.S. Land to be carried out. But the ceremony never happened, most likely out of respect for Murphy's lifelong desire to remain out of the limelight.
6. Cholly Angeleno, "All Women Together." Newspaper clipping, no annotations as to date or source. Ryan, Joseph Francis. Joseph Francis Ryan Research Collection on Daniel Murphy and Family, Approximately 1900–2012. 1900. Bancroft Library, Berkley, CA.
7. "World War I: Wasted Lives on Armistice Day." *MHQ: The Quarterly Journal of Military History.* Winter, 2005
8. Nettie was honored for her donation after World War I when a letter of commendation and a brass plaque that read: "1918 Ambulance #613" were sent to her from France. Ryan, Joseph Francis. Joseph Francis Ryan Research Collection on Daniel Murphy and Family, Approximately 1900–2012. 1900. Bancroft Library, Berkley, CA.
9. "Soldiers and Sailors." *Los Angeles Times*, Apr 1, 1917.
10. Letter from Sergeant Lyman McFie to Antoinette Murphy, Nov 19, 1918, Ryan, Joseph Francis. Joseph Francis Ryan Research Collection on Daniel Murphy and Family, Approximately 1900–2012. 1900. Bancroft Library, Berkley, CA.
11. "Hope Held for Dan Murphy's Recovery." *Evening Herald and Express*, Dec 1, 1918.
12. "Dan Murphy Rallies; Condition Improved." *San Francisco Examiner*, Dec 1, 1918.

13. "Dan Murphy Is Seriously Ill with Pneumonia." Newspaper clipping, no annotation as to date or source. Ryan, Joseph Francis. Joseph Francis Ryan Research Collection on Daniel Murphy and Family, Approximately 1900–2012. 1900. Bancroft Library, Berkley, CA.
14. "Influenza Encyclopedia: American Epidemic of 1918–1919, Los Angeles." https://www.influenzaarchive.org/cities/city-losangeles.html.
15. "Inquiring for Mr. Murphy." *Evening Herald and Express*. Newspaper clipping, annotated "Dec 1918." Ryan, Joseph Francis. Joseph Francis Ryan Research Collection on Daniel Murphy and Family, Approximately 1900–2012. 1900. Bancroft Library, Berkley, CA.
16. "Ice Plant to Cost $1,000,000." *The Economist*, Vol 61, Mar 22, 1919.
17. Oscar E. Anderson, *Refrigeration in America: A History of a New Technology and Its Impact* (Port Washington, New York: Kennikat, 1972), 213.
18. "Bond Election Victorious Here." *Needles Nugget*, Apr 24, 1925.

CHAPTER 22 *Pages 223 to 236*
1. Letter from Bernardine Murphy to Antoinette Murphy, Rome, Apr 3, 1921. Ryan, Joseph Francis. Joseph Francis Ryan Research Collection on Daniel Murphy and Family, Approximately 1900–2012. 1900. Bancroft Library, Berkley, CA.
2. "Luxury In Italian Ship." *New York Times*, Feb 14, 1922.
3. David I. Kertzer, *The Pope and Mussolini: The Secret History of Pius XI and the Rise of Fascism in Europe* (New York: Random House, 2014). Kertzer writes: "Fascism, he [Mussolini] pledged, to the shock of many who knew him, would help bring about the restoration of Christian society. It would build a Catholic state befitting a Catholic nation." 27.
4. Kertzer, 27.
5. Clipping and ticket keepsake, undated. Ryan, Joseph Francis. Joseph Francis Ryan Research Collection on Daniel Murphy and Family, Approximately 1900–2012. 1900. Bancroft Library, Berkley, CA.
6. Dan Murphy letter to Fr. Frederick Ruppert S.J., dated Oct 11, 1923. Murphy Family Papers
7. "Holterhoff, Godfrey, Jr., 1860–" California Biography File. Western History-Material questionnaires, 1909–1910, undated, Los Angeles Public Library; see also J.M. Guinn, *Historical and Biographical Record of Los Angeles and Vicinity: Containing a History of the City from Its Earliest Settlement as a Spanish Pueblo to the Closing Year of the Nineteenth Century; Also Containing Biographies of Well-Known Citizens of the Past and Present* (Chicago: Chapman Pub., 1901), 262; "Death of G. Holterhoff Jr." *Santa Fe Magazine* Vol 17, Jun 1923, 49.
8. Letter from Antoinette Murphy to Bernardine Murphy, Sep 22, 1923. Ryan, Joseph Francis. Joseph Francis Ryan Research Collection on Daniel Murphy and Family, Approximately 1900–2012. 1900. Bancroft Library, Berkley, CA.
9. Wm. Holmes McGuffey, *McGuffey's New Juvenile Speaker: Containing More Than Two Hundred Exercises* (Cincinnati: Van Antwerp, Bragg & Co., 1860), 39.
10. Letter from Bernardine Murphy to Mr. and Mrs. Murphy, Rome, Nov 9, 1922. Ryan, Joseph Francis. Joseph Francis Ryan Research Collection on Daniel Murphy and Family, Approximately 1900–2012. 1900. Bancroft Library, Berkley, CA.
11. "Society. Dainty Bud Introduced in Society." *Los Angeles Times*, Jan 27, 1924.
12. "Bernardine Murphy Entertains Before Departure for Europe." Society and

Endnotes

Clubs. *San Francisco Examiner*, Feb 1, 1925.
13. Letter from Bishop John J. Cantwell to Antoinette Murphy, Feb 10, 1924. Murphy Family Papers
14. *Papal Indult*, Feb 8, 1924, signed by Cardinal Gasparri, Secretary of State, Vatican City. Murphy Family Papers
15. Letter from Bernardine Murphy to Antoinette Murphy, Nov 16, 1925. Hotel Russie Rome. Ryan, Joseph Francis. Joseph Francis Ryan Research Collection on Daniel Murphy and Family, Approximately 1900–2012. 1900. Bancroft Library, Berkley, CA.
16. "Captain A.H. Wilcox in Dying State." *Los Angeles Herald*, Mar 31,1874.
17. Charles Lockwood, "Seminarians Live Where Stars Slept: Mansion on Adams was Home to Film Celebrities." *Los Angeles Times,* Sep 20, 1987.
18. Letter from Bernardine Murphy to Antoinette and Dan Murphy. Rome, Nov 27, 1925. Ryan, Joseph Francis. Joseph Francis Ryan Research Collection on Daniel Murphy and Family, Approximately 1900–2012. 1900. Bancroft Library, Berkley, CA.
19. "These Fascinating Ladies." Newspaper clipping, no annotation as to date or source. Bernardine Murphy's Scrapbook. Murphy Family Papers
20. Bernardine Murphy's Diary entry: "Friday December 25 XMAS Hotel Russie, Rome, Italy." Dec 1925. Ryan, Joseph Francis. Joseph Francis Ryan Research Collection on Daniel Murphy and Family, Approximately 1900–2012. 1900. Bancroft Library, Berkley, CA.
21. The siege of the fortress was beautifully portrayed in *The Borgias* with Jeremy Irons, Francois Arnaud, and Holliday Grainger. Television series 2011–2013.
22. "Rome **Dons** Nothing. By One Who Knows." Bernardine Murphy's Diary entry: Dec 1925. Ryan, Joseph Francis. Joseph Francis Ryan Research Collection on Daniel Murphy and Family, Approximately 1900–2012. 1900. Bancroft Library, Berkley, CA.
23. "Rome **Dons** Nothing. By One Who Knows."
24. "Rome **Dons** Nothing. By One Who Knows."
25. "Rome **Dons** Nothing. By One Who Knows."
26. "Rome **Dons** Nothing. By One Who Knows."
27. Unposted Letter from Dan Murphy to Lelio Orsini, Jan 22, 1926. Ryan, Joseph Francis. Joseph Francis Ryan Research Collection on Daniel Murphy and Family, Approximately 1900–2012. 1900. Bancroft Library, Berkley, CA.
28. Lelio Nicolaas Orsini (1877–1952). https://www.myheritage.com/names/laura_rowan%20%20orsini. Viewed Oct 25, 2020.
29. "Princess Laura Orsini of Pioneer Family Dies." *Los Angeles Times*, Jan 17, 1957.
30. "Rome **Dons** Nothing. By One Who Knows."
31. "Rome **Dons** Nothing. By One Who Knows."

CHAPTER 23 *Pages 237 to 242*
1. Thomas "Tommie" R. Lee, "Deacon Dan" *Petroleum World*, May 1940, 119–120.
2. Lee, 118.
3. Lee, 115–118.
4. Lee, 118.
5. Lee, 120.
6. Dan Murphy's breast-pocket ring binder of investments. Ryan, Joseph

Francis. Joseph Francis Ryan Research Collection on Daniel Murphy and Family, Approximately 1900–2012. 1900. Bancroft Library, Berkley, CA.
7. Lee, 118.
8. "Jury Designates Notable Examples of Architecture." *Southwest Builders & Contractor Magazine,* Apr 16, 1920, 11.
9. Robert Smaus, "Gardens: California Essence: Seventy Years Ago, Florence Yoch Brought Us European Landscape Design." *Los Angeles Times Magazine,* Aug 20, 1989; see also: James J. Yoch, *Landscaping the American Dream: The Gardens and Film Sets of Florence Yoch 1890 to 1972* (New York: Abrams/Sagapress, 1989).
10. Jules Lecarine Bied, *Chaux Hydranliques et Cement.* Library of the Murphy Family.
11. Letter from Archbishop Nikola, Primate of Serbia, Sep 18, 1927. Ryan, Joseph Francis. Joseph Francis Ryan Research Collection on Daniel Murphy and Family, Approximately 1900–2012. 1900. Bancroft Library, Berkley, CA. Nikola would later be noted for his efforts in smuggling Jews out of Croatia during World War II.

CHAPTER 24 *Pages 244 to 248*

1. Prince Pignatelli, "Bernardine Murphy May Marry Prince." *Los Angeles Examiner,* Oct 9, 1929.
2. Telegram from Dan Murphy to Leo Gradenigo, Italian Consul, Oct 10, 1929. Paris. Ryan, Joseph Francis. Joseph Francis Ryan Research Collection on Daniel Murphy and Family, Approximately 1900–2012. 1900. Bancroft Library, Berkley, CA.
3. "Founder of World's Largest Vineyard Dies at Los Angeles." *Chino Champion,* Aug 30, 1927. Secundo Guasti passed away just two months after this event, leaving his fifty-five-year-old wife Louisa alone at the family home on West Adams.
4. Letter from Count Leo Gradenigo to Bernardine Murphy. Undated. Ryan, Joseph Francis. Joseph Francis Ryan Research Collection on Daniel Murphy and Family, Approximately 1900–2012. 1900. Bancroft Library, Berkley, CA.
5. Rose Bank letter, undated and unsigned. White Plains, New York. Ryan, Joseph Francis. Joseph Francis Ryan Research Collection on Daniel Murphy and Family, Approximately 1900–2012. 1900. Bancroft Library, Berkley, CA.
6. Letter from Margherita Borromeo, in English. "Borromeo Letters." Milan. Date unknown, signed "Margaret." Ryan, Joseph Francis. Joseph Francis Ryan Research Collection on Daniel Murphy and Family, Approximately 1900–2012. 1900. Bancroft Library, Berkley, CA.
7. To this day, tourists vie for tickets to visit the fabled gardens. Limited access is allowed as the Borromeo family continues to live there in splendor.
8. Newspaper clipping. *Paris Tribune,* 1933. Bernardine Murphy's Scrapbook. Ryan, Joseph Francis. Joseph Francis Ryan Research Collection on Daniel Murphy and Family, Approximately 1900–2012. 1900. Bancroft Library, Berkley, CA.

CHAPTER 25 *Pages 249 to 253*

1. "Six Listed for Honors at Loyola." *Los Angeles Times,* Jun 5, 1931.
2. "Ten Will Get Church Honor." *Los Angeles Times,* Feb 13, 1931. Antoinette Murphy's Scrapbook. Ryan, Joseph Francis. Joseph Francis Ryan Research

Endnotes

Collection on Daniel Murphy and Family, Approximately 1900–2012. 1900. Bancroft Library, Berkley, CA.
3. "Ten Will Get Church Honor."
4. Wm. Joe Simmonds, "The Boulder Canyon Project: Construction History Investigations." https://www.usbr.gov/history/hoover.html. Viewed Oct 1, 2020.
5. Leonards, R.J., "Enemies of the Republic." *Los Angeles Times*, Feb 13, 1927.
6. "Cement Men To Meet Here." *Los Angeles Times*, May 8, 1934.
7. Six companies were: Utah Construction, Morrison-Knudsen, Kaiser, Bechtel, Pacific Bridge, and MacDonald & Kahn.
8. "California Portland Cement." 1934. Dan Murphy's Dividend Ledger. Ryan, Joseph Francis. Joseph Francis Ryan Research Collection on Daniel Murphy and Family, Approximately 1900–2012. 1900. Bancroft Library, Berkley, CA.
9. Clippings of Princess Conchita Sepulveda Pignatelli, "Mrs. Daniel Murphy Hostess to Nina Koshetz Recital." *Los Angeles Examiner*, Jan 22, 1934. Antoinette Murphy's Scrapbook. Ryan, Joseph Francis. Joseph Francis Ryan Research Collection on Daniel Murphy and Family, Approximately 1900–2012. 1900. Bancroft Library, Berkley, CA.
10. Antoinette Murphy's Scrapbook. Ryan, Joseph Francis. Joseph Francis Ryan Research Collection on Daniel Murphy and Family, Approximately 1900–2012. 1900. Bancroft Library, Berkley, CA.

CHAPTER 26 *Pages 255 to 260*
1. "Personal." *The Argonaut*, Sep 3, 1937.
2. "Wynanspray." Inventory Appraisal, 1939. Ryan, Joseph Francis. Joseph Francis Ryan Research Collection on Daniel Murphy and Family, Approximately 1900–2012. 1900. Bancroft Library, Berkley, CA.
3. "Personal." *The Argonaut*, Sep 3, 1937.
4. Letter from Antoinette Murphy to Bernardine Murphy at Wynanspray, Apr 17, 1936. Ryan, Joseph Francis. Joseph Francis Ryan Research Collection on Daniel Murphy and Family, Approximately 1900–2012. 1900. Bancroft Library, Berkley, CA.
5. Princess Conchita Pignatelli, "Daniel Murphy Chrysanthemum Garden." *Los Angeles Examiner*, Nov 12, 1936.
6. Interview with Allan P. Bruttig, Aug 22, 1991.
7. "Southland Homes—Italian Garden Vista." Newspaper clipping, no annotations as to source and date. Ryan, Joseph Francis. Joseph Francis Ryan Research Collection on Daniel Murphy and Family, Approximately 1900–2012. 1900. Bancroft Library, Berkley, CA.
8. Jessica A. Sheetz, "Margit Slachta and Early Rescue of Jewish Families 1934–1942." Electronic Journal of Annual Holocaust Conference Papers, 1996, 1.
9. "Beauty of Pasadena Flower Show Told." Newspaper clipping, no annotations as to source and date. Ryan, Joseph Francis. Joseph Francis Ryan Research Collection on Daniel Murphy and Family, Approximately 1900–2012. 1900. Bancroft Library, Berkley, CA.
10. Letter from Virginia Milbank to Antoinette Murphy c/o Metabolic Clinic, La Jolla, California, Apr 4, 1938. Ryan, Joseph Francis. Joseph Francis Ryan Research Collection on Daniel Murphy and Family, Approximately 1900–2012. 1900. Bancroft Library, Berkley, CA.
11. Letter from Dr. Groedel to Bernardine Murphy. Los Angeles, Apr 7, 1937.

Ryan, Joseph Francis. Joseph Francis Ryan Research Collection on Daniel Murphy and Family, Approximately 1900–2012. 1900. Bancroft Library, Berkley, CA.
12. Telegram from Dr. Groedel to Bernardine Murphy, New York City, Apr 8, 1937. Ryan, Joseph Francis. Joseph Francis Ryan Research Collection on Daniel Murphy and Family, Approximately 1900–2012. 1900. Bancroft Library, Berkley, CA.
13. "Wife of Oil Man Daniel Murphy Dies." *Los Angeles Examiner,* Jul 17, 1938; Death Notice. *Los Angeles Times*, Jul 18, 1938.
14. "Wife of Oil Man Daniel Murphy Dies."
15. Upon completion of the Cathedral of Our Lady of the Angels in 2002, the remains of the Murphy family (Daniel, Antoinette, Bernardine, Sue Sinnott, and Kathryn Sinnott) were transferred from the family crypt at Doheny Memorial Mausoleum at Calvary Cemetery to Central Mausoleum, under the main altar at the Los Angeles cathedral.
16. "List of Pallbearers." Sep 16, 1939. Ryan, Joseph Francis. Joseph Francis Ryan Research Collection on Daniel Murphy and Family, Approximately 1900–2012. 1900. Bancroft Library, Berkley, CA.
17. Interview with Cardinal Roger Mahony, Sep 19, 2016.

EPILOGUE *Pages 261 to 265*
1. Msgr. Francis J. Weber, *His Eminence of Los Angeles: James Francis Cardinal McIntyre* (Mission Hills, California: Saint Francis Historical Society, 1997), 47.
2. Clipping of "Brother Makes Solemn Vows." *Tidings*, Jul 19, 1946. Bernardine Murphy's Scrapbook. Ryan, Joseph Francis. Joseph Francis Ryan Research Collection on Daniel Murphy and Family, Approximately 1900–2012. 1900. Bancroft Library, Berkley, CA.
3. "The Murphy Site." *Stand – LA*. http://www.stand.la/murphy.html. Viewed Jul 8, 2017.
4. Letter from Daniel Donohue to Clair Peck, president of California Club, Jun 28, 1966. Donohue Letters. Ryan, Joseph Francis. Joseph Francis Ryan Research Collection on Daniel Murphy and Family, Approximately 1900–2012. 1900. Bancroft Library, Berkley, CA.
5. One year after Bernardine Murphy Donohue's passing, the Tate-LaBianca murders by the "Manson Family," occurred next door to the Waverly Drive home on Aug 10, 1969,
6. "Dan Murphy Foundation." www.insidephilanthropy.com.
7. "Disputed convent will be vacated." *Los Angeles Times*, Sep 17, 2015.

Acknowledgments

It was in 2011, nearly ten years after the dedication of the Cathedral of Our Lady of the Angels in Los Angeles. that I first became aware of Dan Murphy. I vividly recall gazing at the dedication wall (actually a massive glass panel overlooking the Hollywood freeway). At the top, etched in giant letters is the largest donor, the Dan Murphy Foundation. When I discovered that same year that Archdiocese Chief Historian Monsignor Francis J. Weber knew only a brief history of Dan Murphy, I became intrigued. The Dan Murphy Foundation preferred to be true to Dan Murphy's humble preference for anonymity, so out of pure curiosity, I decided to do research. My curiosity resulted in this book.

Although it would be impossible to name each of the people I have turned to over nearly a decade that it took to research this man and his legacy, I am first and foremost grateful to Julia Donohue Schwartz (a past board member of the Dan Murphy Foundation and niece, by marriage, to Bernardine Murphy Donohue) who graciously gave me unlimited access to the Murphy Family Papers. These papers were largely those preserved by Murphy's wife Antoinette and his daughter Bernardine, and the trove includes documents from the last half of Dan Murphy's life. Amongst this collection is a remarkable album of photos taken by Dan during his earliest days in Needles.

Additionally, I will always be grateful to Nick Curry, who provided me with vital records and biographical information on Dan Murphy and the co-incorporators of his numerous companies (see Appendix B), in addition to providing consolation and encouragement when I needed both. My heartfelt thanks to Cheryl Mangin the past curator at the Needles Museum who was the only person I found who actually knew who Dan Murphy was. She generously shared her research into Murphy, but also read early drafts and offered suggestions. I am very appreciative that Walt Bethel took the time to read a first draft and made astute comments; I relied upon him for accurate facts regarding Los Angeles's early transportation. And I am also grateful to my local colleagues Jack San Filipo and Pete Kelly who listened to my endless tales of Murphy and gave me support when I needed it the most.

Three California repositories yielded the most information on the reconstruction of Murphy's life. First were the remarkable librarians at the California State Archives in Sacramento, which preserves all of the "Articles of Incorporation" for the state. In particular were Karen Paige and her colleagues, who retrieved nearly forty files of Murphy's companies and even sought after and found companies of which I was unaware. Many thanks go to David Kessler at the Bancroft Library at University of California at Berkeley, who provided the Sinnott/Weber letters that gave insight into life in the mining town of Leadville, Colorado, and the legal trials in which the Sinnott women were appellants. I am grateful to the volunteers in the Arda Haenszel California Room of the Feldheym Library in San Bernardino, who have tirelessly clipped and filed years of historical articles regarding Needles from the local newspapers and have provided information I would not have otherwise found.

I am especially thankful to Special Collections Librarian Polly Armstrong at Stanford University, who responded to my numerous calls for Pacific Improvement Company records. She was particularly patient with my calls for partially burned record books (and the mess they made) from the 1906 San Francisco Earthquake and the resulting fires. Local History Archivist Cheri Pape at the Albert Launer Memorial History Room in the Fullerton Public Library was most helpful in providing essential history on Brea Cañon Oil Company. The name Dan Murphy was rarely found in any library, but many librarians provided historical background for which I am most thankful: Collections Manager John M. Cahoon at the Seaver Center for Western History Research; History Room Librarian Kevin Cabrera at the Santa Ana Public Library, who enlightened me about Orange County's sugar beet industry; John Hawk, who heads the Special Collections at Gleeson Library at the University of San Francisco furnished information on the Bernardine Murphy Donohue Rare Books Room; Archivist Kevin Feeney of the Los Angeles Archdiocese Archival Center San Fernando Mission; Archivist Kathryn Santos of the California State Railway Museum and Library Sacramento; Reference Librarian Monique Matta of the San Luis Obispo Library, who obtained from the California State Library the microfilm rolls of Needles local newspapers *The Bazoo* and *The Needles Eye*; Manuscript Curator Dr. Clay Stalls of the William Hannon Library at Loyola Marymount University, who furnished Lester Donahue's papers for my research; Librarian Viltis Jatulis at St. Bernardine of Siena Library at St. Thomas Aquinas College, who gave me access to the Murphy/Donohue Libraries donation; and Archi-

Acknowledgments

vist Jennifer Albin of the National Archives and Records Administration at Riverside, California.

In 2013, I took a road trip to four western states and visited various university special collections, historical societies, as well as county and state public records departments, culminating at the vast Atchison, Topeka & Santa Fe archive held by the Kansas Historical Society in Topeka. Each provided essential information for this book, but only one had a newspaper clipping that actually mentioned the enigmatic Dan Murphy by name. However, my special thanks to these diligent searchers of their collections: Librarian Kay Ellerman, Mohave Museum of History and Arts, in Kingman, Arizona; Archivists Sean Evans and Samantha Meier of Special Collections and Archives at Cline Library, Northern Arizona University in Flagstaff; Center for Southwest Research and Special Collections, Zimmerman Library University of New Mexico, Albuquerque; Local History Coordinator Janice Fox at the Lake County Public Library of Leadville, Colorado; Stephan H. Hart Library and Research Center in Denver, Colorado; Archivist Katie Rudolph of the Denver Public Library found a last minute reference for an important Leadville quote; and finally my thanks to Digital Services Librarian Irene Berry of the Dudley Knox Library and to Greta Marlatt who together helped me track down an important historical photograph at the last minute.

Special thanks and my sincere appreciation to literary editor Harry Dewulf whose expertise and talent gave the manuscript its structure and historical framing. To my, now-deceased sister Pat Ryan who encouraged me to write the book in the first place and who spent innumerable hours searching digitized newspapers in search of many of the characters. My gratitude goes to historian Tom Sitton, whose words of introduction to this book reflect not only his understanding of the time period in which Dan Murphy lived, but also of his appreciation for the importance of the many unsung heroes like Murphy who contributed to shaping the California we know today. And most importantly of all, to my dear editor Paddy Calistro at Angel City Press. We locked down for the Covid-19 pandemic as we edited this manuscript over many months of isolation. In our up to five-hour phone conversations, she questioned and guided me through the process, during which we became close friends and confidants. She provided the most insightful phrasing and just the right words to turn my stilted manuscript into a delightful tale.

And last, but far from least, there is Chuck Roche, my life partner who has been with me every step of the way, and who knows as much about Dan Murphy as I do. His perception and insights into the character of Dan Murphy were without doubt what made the difference not just in this book, but in my life.

BIBLIOGRAPHY

BOOKS

Ambrose, Stephen. *Nothing Like It in the World: The Men Who Built the Transcontinental Railroad, 1863–1869.* New York: Touchstone, 2000.

Anderson, Oscar E. *Refrigeration in America: A History of a New Technology and Its Impact.* Princeton, New Jersey: Princeton University Press, 1953.

Andress, Donna. *Eldorado Canyon and Nelson, Nevada: Historical Documents, Reminiscences, Commentary.* Nelson, Nevada: D. Andress, 1997.

Ansell, Martin R. *Oil Baron of the Southwest: Edward L. Doheny and the Development of the Petroleum Industry in California and Mexico.* Columbus: Ohio State University Press, 1998.

Bancroft, Hubert Howe. *The Works of Hubert Howe Bancroft Vol XXIV: History of California, Vol. VII, 1860–1890.* San Francisco: The History Company, Publishers, 1890.

———. *The Book of the Fair: An Historical and Descriptive Presentation of the World's Science, Art, and Industry, as Viewed through the Columbian Exposition at Chicago in 1893, Designed to Set Forth the Display Made by the Congress of Nations, of Human Achievement in Material Form, so as the More Effectually to Illustrate the Progress of Mankind in All the Departments of Civilized Life.* Chicago and San Francisco: Bancroft Company, 1893.

Bellows, Henry W. *Historical Sketch of the Union League Club of New York: Its Origin, Organization and Work, 1863–1879.* New York: Club House, 1879.

Berkman, Pamela. *The History of the Atchison, Topeka & Santa Fe.* Greenwich, Connecticut: Bonanza, 1988.

Bettmann, Otto, and James Harvey Young. *The Good Old Days: They Were Terrible!* New York: Random House, 1974.

Birnbaum, Charles A., Lisa E. Crowder, and Sally Boazberg. *Pioneers of American Landscape Design: An Annotated Bibliography.* Washington, D.C.: US Department of the Interior, National Park Service, Cultural Resources, 1993.

Brigandi, Phil. *A Hundred Years of Yesterdays: A Centennial History of the People of Orange County and Their Communities.* Santa Ana, California: Orange County Historical Commission, 2004.

Brushey, Stuart (editor). *Preliminary Report of the Inland Waterways Commission: Message from the President of the United States, Transmitting A Preliminary Report of the Inland Waterways Commission.* New York: Arno Press, 1972.

Bryant, Keith L. *History of the Atchison, Topeka & Santa Fe.* New York: Macmillan Publishing Company, Inc, 1974.

Burdette, Robert J. *American Biography and Genealogy California Edition.* Vol. II. Chicago and New York: Lewis Publishing 191-.
Carroll, Francis M. *American Opinion and the Irish Question, 1910–23: A Study in Opinion and Policy.* Dublin: Gill and Macmillan, 1978
Catalog of Tenth Annual Exhibition of Painters and Sculptors. Moore, Nancy D.W. Directory of Art & Artists in Southern California before 1930. Glendale, California: Dustin Publications, 1975.
Chittenden, Newton H. *Health Seekers', Tourists' and Sportsmen's Guide to the Sea-Side, Lake-Side, Foothill, Mountain, and Mineral Spring Health and Pleasure Resorts of the Pacific Coast.* San Francisco: C.A. Murdock, 1884.
Clark, Judith Freeman. *America's Gilded Age: An Eyewitness History.* New York: Facts on File, 1992.
Cramer, Esther R. *Brea: The City of Oil, Oranges, and Opportunity.* Brea, California: The City, 1992.
Cross, Ira B. *Financing an Empire; History of Banking in California,.* Chicago: S.J. Clarke Pub., 1927
Crump, Spencer. *Ride the Big Red Cars: How Trolleys Helped Build Southern California.* Los Angeles: Crest Publications, 1962.
Daggett, Stuart. *Chapters on the History of the Southern Pacific.* New York: Ronald Press Co., 1922.
Davis, Margaret L. *Children's Hospital and the Leaders of Los Angeles: the First 100 Years.* Los Angeles: Children's Hospital, 2002.
———. *Dark Side of Fortune: Triumph and Scandal in the Life of Oil Tycoon Edward L. Doheny.* Berkeley: University of California Press, 2001.
Ducker, James H. *Men of the Steel Rails: Workers on the Atchison, Topeka & Santa Fe Railroad, 1869–1900.* Lincoln: University of Nebraska, 1983.
Duke, Donald. *Santa Fe: the Railroad Gateway to the American West.* Vol. 2. San Marino, California: Golden West Books, 1997.
Dumke, Glenn S. *The Boom of the Eighties in Southern California.* San Marino, California: Huntington Library, 1944.
Giddens, Paul H. *The Birth of the Oil Industry.* New York: Macmillan, 1938.
Glimpses of the World's Fair: a Selection of Gems of the White City Seen through a Camera. Chicago: Laird & Lee, 1893.
Gould, Stephen. *Orange County: A Bibliography of Historical, Geographic, Political, Economic, Agricultural, Archaeological, Ethnic, Environmental, Biographic, and Other County Sources.* Anaheim, California: Publisher Not Identified, 1989.
Grinnell, Joseph. *A Bibliography of California Ornithology.* University of California. Santa Clara, California: Cooper Ornithological Society, 1909.
Guinn, J.M. *Historical and Biographical Record of Los Angeles and Vicinity: Containing a History of the City from Its Earliest Settlement as a Spanish Pueblo to the Closing Year of the Nineteenth Century.* Chicago: Chapman Publishing Company, 1901.
———. *Historical and Biographical Record of Southern California: Containing a History of Southern California from Its Earliest Settlement to the Opening Year of the Twentieth Century.* Vol. 2. Chicago: Chapman Publishing Company, 1902.
Guinn, James Miller. *A History of California and an Extended History of Its Southern Coast Counties: Also Containing Biographies of Well-known Citizens of the Past And Present.* Los Angeles: Historic Record Company, 1907.
Hammond, George P., and Dale L. Morgan. *Captain Charles M. Weber: Pioneer of the San Joaquin and Founder of Stockton, California.* Berkeley, California: Friends of the Bancroft Library, 1966.

Bibliography

Harper, Franklin. *Who's Who on the Pacific Coast: A Biographical Compilation of Notable Living Contemporaries West of the Rocky Mountains*. Los Angeles: Harper, 1913.

Harper, Jane C., Craig W. Leavitt, and Thomas J. Noel. *Colorado Newspapers: A History & Inventory, 1859–2000* (Westminster: Colorado Press Association Foundation & Center for Colorado and the West at Auraria Library, 2014)

Harvey, Tim. *Brea, Then and Now: A Pictorial History*. Brea Historical Society, 2012.

Historical Record and Souvenir. Los Angeles: Times-Mirror, 1923.

Hodge, Hiram C. *Arizona as It Is, or, The Coming Country: Compiled from Notes of Travel during the Years 1874–1875, and 1876*. New York: Hurd and Houghton, 1877.

Holterhoff Jr., Godfrey. *Historical Review of the Atchison, Topeka & Santa Fe Railway Company (With Particular Reference to California Lines): as Furnished to the Railroad Commission of the State of California in Compliance with Its General Order No. 38*. Los Angeles: Railroad Commission of the State of California, 1914.

Humphrey, Arthur Luther. *Autobiography of Arthur Luther Humphrey 1860–1937*. Pittsburgh, Pennsylvania: privately printed, 1911.

Hunter, Eileen Curry. *El Segundo, Seventy-five Years: A Pictorial History of El Segundo, California*. El Segundo, California: H2 Ltd., 1991.

Ingersoll, Luther A. *Ingersoll's Century Annals of San Bernardino County, 1769 to 1904: Prefaced with a Brief History to the State of California, Supplemented with an Encyclopedia of Local Biography and Embellished with Views of Historic Subjects and Portraits of Many of Its Representative People* Vol 1. Los Angeles: L.A. Ingersoll, 1904.

Ives, J.C., and A.A. Humphreys. *Report upon the Colorado River of the West: Explored in 1857 and 1858 by Joseph C. Ives, Corps of Topographical Engineers, under the Direction of the Office of Explorations and Surveys, A.A. Humphreys, Captain Topographical Engineers, in Charge: by Order of the Secretary of War*. Washington, D.C.: Government Printing Office, 1861.

Kertzer, David I. *The Pope and Mussolini the Secret History of Pius XI and the Rise of Fascism in Europe*. Oxford: Oxford University Press, 2014.

Lewis, Oscar. *The Big Four; the Story of Huntington, Stanford, Hopkins, and Crocker, and of the Building of the Central Pacific*. New York: A.A. Knopf, 1951.

Llorente, Segundo. *Memoirs of a Yukon Priest*. Washington, D.C.: Georgetown University Press, 1990.

Mangam, William D. *The Clarks: an American Phenomenon*. Silver Bow Press, 1941.

Marshall, James. *Santa Fe the Railroad That Built an Empire*. New York: Random House, 1945.

McGroarty, John Steven. *Los Angeles from the Mountains to the Sea : With Selected Biography of Actors and Witnesses of the Period of Growth and Achievement*. Chicago and New York: The American Historical Society, 1921.

McGuffey, William Holmes. *McGuffey's New Juvenile Speaker: Containing More than Two Hundred Exercises, Original and Selected for Reading and Speaking*. Cincinnati: Van Antwerp, Bragg & Co., 1860.

McHugh, Tom, and Victoria Hobson. *The Time of the Buffalo*. New Jersey, New Jersey: Castle Books, 2004.

Men of the Pacific Coast; Containing Portraits and Biographies of the Professional, Financial and Business Men of California, Oregon and Washington. San Francisco: Pacific Art, 1902.

Myrick, David F. *Railroads of Arizona*. Glendale: Trans-Anglo Books, 1984.

———. *Railroads of Nevada and Eastern California*. Vol. 2. Reno: University of Nevada Press, 1992.

Nadeau, Remi A. *City-Makers: The Story of Southern California's First Boom, 1868–*

76. Corona del Mar, California: Trans-Anglo Books, 1977.
Nelson, Howard J. *The Los Angeles Metropolis*. Kendall/Hunt Pub. Co., 1983.
Nunis, Doyce B. *The Founding Documents of Los Angeles: a Bilingual Edition*. Los Angeles: Historical Society of Southern California, 2004.
Olson, Hazel E. *"As the Sand Shifts" in Colton, California*. Colton, California: Hazel E. Olson, 1989.
Orange County History Series. Vol. 2. Santa Ana, California: Orange County Historical Society (California), 1932.
Orsi, Richard J. *Sunset Limited the Southern Pacific Railroad and the Development of the American West 1850–1930*. Berkeley: University of California Press, 2007.
Peterson, Richard H. *The Bonanza Kings: The Social Origins and Business Behavior of Western Mining Entrepreneurs, 1870–1900*. Lincoln: University of Nebraska Press, 1977.
Phillips, Catherine Coffin. *Jessie Benton Frémont: A Woman Who Made History*. Lincoln: University of Nebraska Press, 1995.
Plat Book of Washington County, Kansas ; Containing Carefully Prepared Township Plats, Village Plats, Analysis of US Land System, Leading Farmers Directory. Des Moines, Iowa: Brown-Scoville Publishing, 1906.
Press Reference Library: Notables of the West, Being the Portraits and Biographies of the Progressive Men of the West Who Have Helped in the Development and History Making of This Wonderful Country. New York: International News Service, 1913.
Randall, David K. *The King and Queen of Malibu: The True Story of the Battle for Paradise*. New York: W.W. Norton & Company, 2017.
Redpath, Lionel V. *Petroleum in California a Concise and Reliable History of the Oil Industry of the State ...* Los Angeles: L.V. Redpath, 1900.
Rintoul, William. *Spudding In: Recollections of Pioneer Days in the California Oil Fields*. San Francisco: California Historical Society, 1976.
Robbins, Lloyd M. (San Francisco), and Bernardine M. Murphy (Los Angeles). *Laws of Community Property – Laws of Toro 1505*. Lausanne, Switzerland: Imprimerie Des Arts et Metiers S.A., 1929.
Robertson, Donald B. *Encyclopedia of Western Railroad History*. Caldwell, Idaho: Caxton Printers, 1986.
Sanborn Insurance Maps of Los Angeles, California. New York: Sanborn Map. Book 46. 1906.
Savage, A.H. *Dog-Sled Apostles*. Savage Press, 2007.
Sitton, Tom. *Grand Ventures: The Banning Family and the Shaping of Southern California*. San Marino, California: Huntington Library, 2010.
Smythe, William E. *History of San Diego, 1542–1908 an Account of the Rise and Progress of the Pioneer Settlement on the Pacific Coast of the United States*. San Diego: The History Company, 1908.
Starr, Kevin. *Inventing the Dream: California through the Progressive Era*. New York: Oxford University Press, 1985.
Talbert, Thomas B., Mildred MacArthur Yorba., and Don Meadows C. *The Historical Volume and Reference Works: Orange County*. Whittier, California: Historical Publishers, 1963.
The National Cyclopedia of American Biography.V. 21. 160. New York: James T. White, 1931
Thorndike, Joseph J. *Their Fair Share: Taxing the Rich in the Age of FDR*. Washington, D.C.: Urban Institute Press, 2013.
van der Poel, J.M.G.. *Gospel Hill: a History of St. John the Baptist Church, Hanover,*

Washington County, Kansas, 1868–1978. John M. Poell, 1978.
Vredenburgh, Larry M., and Gary L. Shumway. *Desert Fever: an Overview of Mining in the California Desert*. Canoga Park, California: Living West Press, 1981.
White, Gerald T. *Formative Years in the Far West: a History of Standard Oil Company of California and Predecessors through 1919*. New York: Appleton-Century-Crofts, 1962.
Who's Who in the Pacific Southwest. a Compilation of Authentic Biographical Sketches of Citizens of Southern California and Arizona. Los Angeles: The Times-Mirror Printing & Binding House, 1913.
Wilson, Neill Compton, and Frank John. Taylor. *Southern Pacific. The Roaring Story of a Fighting Railroad*. New York: McGraw-Hill Book Co., 1952.
Wolfe, Wellington C. *Men of California: 1900–1902*. San Francisco: Pacific Art, 1900.
Woolrich, W.R. *The Men Who Created Cold: a History of Refrigeration*. New York: Exposition Press, 1967.
Yenne, Bill. *The History of the Southern Pacific*. New York: Bonanza Books, 1985.
Yoch, James J. *Landscaping the American Dream: The Gardens and Film Sets of Florence Yoch, 1890–1972*. New York: Abrams, 1989.

NEWSPAPERS
Albuquerque Weekly Citizen. Albuquerque, New Mexico
Aspen Daily Times. Aspen, Colorado
Arizona Weekly Citizen. Tucson, Pima County, Arizona Territory
Bazoo. Needles, California
Booth' Bazoo. Needles, California
Carbonate Chronicle. Leadville, Colorado
Chino Champion. Chino, California
Daily Alta California. San Francisco
Ellis County News. Hays, Kansas
Evening Herald and Express
Evening Star. Washington, D.C.
Fairplay Flume. Fairplay, Colorado
Forest News. Del Monte Forest, Pebble Beach, California
Fullerton News Tribune. Fullerton, California
Hays Daily News. Hays, Kansas
Kingman Daily Miner. Kingman, Arizona
Leadville Daily and Evening Chronicle. Leadville, Colorado
Leavenworth Weekly Times. Leavenworth, Kansas
Los Angeles Downtown News
Los Angeles Examiner
Los Angeles Herald
Los Angeles Times
Los Angeles Times–Mirror
Mohave County Miner. Kingman, Arizona
Needles Desert Star
Needles Nugget. Needles, California
Needles Eye. Needles, California
New York Daily Tribune
The New York Times
Oakland Tribune. Oakland, California
Paul's Valley Sentinel. Paul's Valley, Oklahoma

Reformatory Press. Anamosa, Iowa
San Bernardino Daily Sun. San Bernardino, California
San Francisco Call
San Francisco Examiner
Tulsa Daily World. Tulsa, Oklahoma
Washington Post. Washington, D.C.
The Weekly Courier. San Bernardino, California
The Weekly Examiner (Bartlesville Indian Territory). Bartlesville, Oklahoma

JOURNALS
American Global Investors Magazine
American Quarterly
Annual Publication of the Historical Society of Southern California
Assembly Daily Journal
The Atlantic
Atchison, Topeka & Santa Fe Journal
Bankers Magazine
Catholic Historian
Cement And Engineering News. Chicago
The Centennial 1840–1940 (Published by Archdiocese of Los Angeles, 1940)
The Commercial and Financial Chronicle
Commercial & Financial Chronicle
Electronic Journal of Annual Holocaust Conference Papers
The Economist
Fortune
Harper's Monthly
Harvard Business Review
Historic American English Record
Ice & Refrigeration Illustrated.
Illustrated Weekly
Los Angeles Westerners' Branding Iron
Oil Journal
The Nation
Nebraska History
Petroleum World
Railway and Marine News
Santa Fe Employees' Magazine
Southwest Builder and Contractor
Western Architect

BIBLIOGRAPHY

INTERVIEWS
Helen Kennedy Cahill, Villa Marin; San Rafael, California. Jan 17, 2012
Julia Donohue Schwartz; B-flat Ranch, Oregon. August 5, 2011, Sep 18, 2012
Brother Patrick Corr, O.H. and Brother Stephen de la Rosa, O.H., St. John of God Retirement and Care Center, Los Angeles. Jan 20, 2014
Sister Anne Kelly, R.G.S.; Sister Mary Christopher Mullan, R.G.S.; Sister Mary Charlotte Kirst, R.G.S.; Convent, Los Angeles. Jan 27, 2014
His Eminence Roger Cardinal Mahony; Los Angeles. Sep 19, 2016
David Gunther; Alta Loma, California. Mar 14, 2017
Dennis Casebier, Mojave Desert Archives; Goffs, California. Oct 29, 2012
Edward Landry, Musick Peeler & Garrett; Los Angeles. May 23, 2011
Renata Ortega, St. John of God Retirement and Care Center; Los Angeles.
John Dandola, 2010
Larry Burgess, Smiley Library; Redlands, California. Jan 24, 2012
Charles Weber IV, Cathedral of Our Lady of the Angels Conference Center; Los Angeles. Dec 16, 2014

DISSERTATIONS
Phillips, Nancymarie, "Education for Girls in the House of the Good Shepherd, US 1940–1980" (2008). Dissertation. Cleveland State University. https://engagedscholarship.csuohio.edu/etdarchive/241
Surmiller, Jason M. BA, MTh. "The Conflicted Relationships of the American Catholic Church with European Fascism." Doctor of Philosophy in Humanities—History of Ideas. University of Texas at Dallas. Dec 2016.

THESES
Altergott, Alexander Jr. "An Economic History of the Valley of the Mohaves." A Thesis Presented to the Department of Economics, University of Southern California. December, 1930.

UNPUBLISHED MANUSCRIPTS
History of the Good Shepherd Sisters. Los Angeles, California. Typewritten manuscript in three ring binders. Copied on location on Jan 27, 2014.

INDEX

35th Parallel Route, 40-42, 55, 62

Ahere, J., 74
Ahvote, 127, 128
Albuquerque, NM, 40, 46, 60, 88, 118
Alexander VI, 233
American Ambulance Field Service, 217-218
American Bridge Co., 183
American Equal Rights Assoc., 163
American Oil & Asphalt, 183
American Refrigerator Transit, 125
Ammons, T., 101
Amtrak, 226
Angeleno, Cholly, 244
Anger, France, 211-212
Anthony, Earle C., 262
Anthony, Susan B., 163
Apple, John, 128
Arapaho Indians, 23
Arg, Jose, 231
Argenta, AR, 124
Argentine, KS, 122
Arizona Garden, 45
Arizona Territory, 12, 21-22, 39, 48-49, 52, 60, 62, 68, 80, 91, 97, 102, 162
Arkansas River, 124
Armour & Co., 125
Armour, Philip, 124
Askeet, Chief, 81-83
AT&SF Journal, 119

Atchison, Topeka & Santa Fe Railway (AT&SF; see also Santa Fe), 12-13, 17, 27, 40, 44, 68, 87, 90-94, 97, 99, 101, 111-116, 119, 122-125, 133, 137-142, 151, 155, 156, 157, 164, 174, 176-177, 188, 193, 226, 227
Atlantic & Pacific Express, 95
Atlantic & Pacific Railroad (A&P), 22, 35, 40-43, 60-62, 78, 87-90, 93, 95, 116, 118-119
Atlantic & Pacific Sonora Railway, 87
Avery, William H., 183

Bad Nauheim spa/clinic, Germany, 223, 225, 240-241, 243, 256, 258
Bagley, Howard King, 18, 131, 153, 192, 239, 260
Bakersfield, CA, 124, 179
Balch, Alan C., 179
Ball Ice and Cold Machine Co., 112, 124
Ball, Philip De Catesby (PDC Ball), 112-113, 116, 124-125, 157, 192-193, 220
Banning, Phineas, 12
Barlow Sanatorium, 204, 259
Barlow, Jarvis, 204
Barlow, Marion, 172
Bartlesville, OK, 157, 193
Beau-Rivage Palace Hotel, Lausanne, 210-211, 225, 255
Benedict XV, 224
Benton, Thomas Hart, 164
Berkeley Square, Los Angeles, 203, 229
Beverly Hills, CA, 165, 261

Index

Bigheart, OK, 193
Biondi, Pietro, 229
Bishop & Co., 133
Bishop, Harriett Schaeffer, 133
Bishop, William, 133
Black Canyon, NV/AZ, 72-74, 250-252
Black Metal Mine, 80, 99, 106-107
Black Nobility, 189, 190, 224-225, 246
Blake, Isaac, 132
Bonsall, Col. W.H., 143
Booth, Dr., 78, 120
Borgia, Cesare, 233
Borgia, Giovanni, 233
Borromeo, Federico, 231, 243, 247-248, 261
Borromeo, Margherita, 247-248
Borromeo, Saint Charles, 243
Boston Safe Deposit & Trust Co., 92
Boulder Dam, 19, 73-74, 250-252
Bowen, Abner T., 132
Brea Canyon, CA, 237
Brea Cañon Oil Co., 17, 135, 140-141, 153, 155, 156, 158-159, 166, 175, 177, 179, 188, 226, 237-238, 242
Briggs, George, 220
Brothers of Saint John of God, 261, 262
Brunswig, Lucien, 216-218, 260
Brunswig, Marguerite, 217
Bryant, Susanna, 229
Bunnell, Dan, 82
Burlington Northern Railroad, 65

Cajon Pass, CA, 90, 193
California Club, Los Angeles, 156, 177, 219, 240, 263
California Institute of Technology (Caltech), 166, 241, 249
California Portland Cement Co., 13, 16, 182-183, 185, 188, 197-199, 240, 251-252, 260-262
California Southern Railroad, 40, 89, 91-92, 133, 137-138, 176, 226
Call, Asa, 260
Calvary Cemetery, 259-260, 264
Canfield, Charles, 136, 141, 179, 241
Cantwell, John Joseph, Bishop, 229-230, 244, 249, 259
Canyon Diablo, AZ, 40-41

Cape Horn, 48
Capitol (mine), 250
Captain Joe, 84-85
Case-Hinze, 195
Castle Bracciano, Italy, 232-233
Castletown, Ireland, 190
Central Pacific Railroad, 12, 35-38, 40, 49, 64
Chaffey, George, 140
Chambers, Robert, 260
Chandler, Elizabeth, 216
Chandler, Harry, 260
Chandler, Lenore, 217
Chaplin, Charlie, 203
Charles VIII, 233
Chemehuevi Indians, 107
Chemehuevi Mountains, CA, 79
Cheney, Anna, 203
Cheney, Katherine, 203
Chester Place, Los Angeles, 161, 162, 163, 185, 201, 214, 217, 229, 231
Cheyenne American Indians, 23
Chicago World's Fair (World's Columbian Exposition), 109-119, 181, 183
Chicago, IL, 16-17, 23, 65, 68-69, 88, 90, 92-93, 109-119 122-125, 139, 164, 177, 181, 182, 193, 207, 208, 220, 252
Childs, Emeline, 172
Childs, Suzanne, 172
Chinese laborers, 37, 47, 52, 55-57, 59, 60-63, 66, 74, 76
Chisholm Trail, 23, 26
Cincinnati, OH, 91
Clark Memorial Library, Los Angeles, 166
Clark, Eli, 176
Clark, Miriam, 229
Clark, William Andrews Jr., 166
Claypool General Store, 196
Claypool, William A., 196
Cleveland Faucet Co., 177
Cochran, George Ira, 165
Cocopah Copper Co., 151, 165
Cody, Buffalo Bill, 26
Cold Machine Co., 124
Coleman, Frances, 204-205

Colorado River, 13, 16, 38, 39, 42-43, 52, 60, 62-63, 71-74, 76, 89, 105, 120, 128, 165, 183, 249, 252
Colorado Steam Navigation, 68, 231
Colton Marble and Lime Co., 181, 185
Colton, CA, 110-112, 119 197-199, 240
Comstock Lode, 33, 37, 104, 105
Conaty, Thomas J., Bishop, 169-171, 187-189, 196, 207, 211
Concours d'Elegance, 45
Connell, Agnes, 203
Cook, Wilbur David Jr., 185-186, 188, 240
Cosmopolitan Hotel, Los Angeles, 57, 201
Crane & Co., 65, 177
Crocker, Charles, 12, 36-37, 45-46, 53, 55, 76, 88, 106-108, 177, 183, 212, 252
Crookshank, A.J., 195
Custer, George, 26

Dan Murphy Co., 153, 183, 239, 247, 263
Dan Murphy Foundation, 17, 183, 259, 263-264
de Lafarge, Auguste Pavin, 242
de Lafarge, Joseph Pavin, 242
de Medici, Isabella, 233
de Paul, Saint Vincent, 166, 211
Del Valle, R.F., 140
Delia Sinnott Lode, 105
DeMille, Allan, 257
DeMille, Cecil B., 257
Denker, Andrew, 57, 201
Denker, Louise Ruellen, 201, 216, 257
Denver City Railroad, 30, 32
Diaz, Melchor, 72
Dill, R.G., 101
Dillon, Henry Clay, 132
Dillon, Richard J., 239
Dockweiler, Gertrude, 172
Dodge City, KS, 26, 41
Doheny Memorial Mausoleum, 259-260, 264
Doheny, Carrie Estelle Betzold, 163
Doheny, Edward L., 136, 139-142, 163, 179, 230, 249, 263
Doheny, Estelle, 230, 231, 249, 263

Dolly B Mine, 105, 146, 172, 173
Donahue, Lester, 204
Donohue, Daniel J., 262-264
Duque, Ernest E., 252
Durant, T.C., 37

Earl, Edwin Tobias, 124, 125
Earp, Wyatt, 26, 101
Easton, Robert, 183
Echo Park, Los Angeles, 136
Edwards, W.A., 219
El Segundo, CA, 155-156, 176, 220
Eldorado Canyon, 74, 127-128, 131, 196
Elting, Julian, 203
Elysian Park, Los Angeles, 136, 204
Emergency Fleet Corp., 215-216
Enlisted Men's Club, 216-217
Equestrian Order of the Holy Sepulchre, 249
Eternal City (see Rome)

Fairbanks, Douglas, 203
Famous (mine), 144-146, 174
Farrand, Bill, 237
Fatherless Children of France, 217
Federal Ice & Refrigerating Co., 220-221
Federal Reclamation Dept., 250
First Nat'l Bank of Los Angeles, 156, 176, 183, 201, 214, 241
First Unitarian Church, Los Angeles, 163
Flagler, Henry, 107, 135
Fleming, T.J., 183, 197
Flint, Frank P., 201
Flint, Frederick Jr., 185, 214, 260
Flint, Katharine, 185, 201, 216-217, 229
Flint, William, 260
Forest Lawn Great Mausoleum, Glendale, CA, 226
Fort Hays, KS, 23
Fort Kearny, KS, 23, 31
Fort Mohave, AZ, 72, 74, 81
Fort Yuma, CA, 39, 72
Franzen, Lee, 128
Freeport-McMoRan Inc., 263

INDEX

Fremont, Elizabeth, 164
Fremont, Jessie Benton, 164
Fremont, John C., 164
Friday Morning Club, 163
Fullerton Oil Co., 153, 155-156
Fullerton, CA, 139, 153, 166, 237, 238

Gallup, NM, 51, 96
Garden Club of America, 253
Garland, Blanche, 203
Garland, William, 260
Getty, George, 157
Getty, J. Paul, 157
Ghirardelli, Joe, 213
Giannini, Dr. Attilio H., 257
Gila River, 39
Gila Trail, 39
Gilmore, Edward W., 183
Globe Grain and Milling, 122, 124
Godshall, Dr., 151
Golden Spike, 35, 37
Grace Henderson Elementary School, 262
Gradenigo, Count Cesare, 245-247
Grand Canyon, 74, 208
Grand Central Station, 108
Grand Hotel de la Minerve, Rome, 189, 209, 224, 231, 235, 263
Great Northern Railway, 214
Great White City (see Chicago World's Fair)
Grinnell, Joseph, 91
Groedel, Dr. Franz, 223, 241, 258
Guasti, Louisa, 187, 216-217, 229, 245, 249
Guasti, Secundo, 185, 187
Guggenheim Exploration Co., 165
Gulf of California, 38, 120
Guthrie, Mary Eudora, 49
Guthrie, Robert Burns, 50

Hammel & Denker, 57, 201
Hampton, Frances, 171
Hancock Park, 19, 165, 197, 261
Hancock, W.S., 82
Hanna, Edward Joseph, Archbishop, 230
Hanover, KS, 17, 21-31, 71, 106, 227

Harrison, Benjamin, 157
Harvard Heights, 165-166
Hastings, NE, 31
Hayes, Rutherford B., 39
Hays, KS, 25, 26, 106, 166, 196
Hell Street, Canyon Diablo, AZ, 41
Hemingway, Ernest, 217
Heyn, Bernard, 224
Hickok, Wild Bill, 26
Hill, James, 214
Hill, Lewis, 214
Hollenberg, G.H., 23
Holliday, Doc, 101
Holiday Stage Line, 23
Hollywood, 176, 240, 257
Holterhoff, Godfrey, 17, 87-88, 90-93, 113-115, 125, 137-141, 156-157, 179, 195, 202, 208, 217, 224, 226-227, 239, 241, 256
Holterhoff, Leila, 133, 202, 204, 224
Holterhoff, Louise, 133, 217, 256
Hoover Dam (see Boulder Dam)
Hopkins, Mark, 36, 37, 52
Horowitz, Vladimir, 252
Hotel de Russie, Rome, 230-233
Hotel Del Monte, Pebble Beach, 45-46, 81, 97, 108, 212-214, 252
House of Murphy, 245, 246
Hudson & Munsell, 187
Hudson, Frank, 185, 188
Humphrey, Arthur Luther, 63, 78, 89, 95
Huntington Beach, CA, 159
Huntington Gardens, San Marino, CA, 240
Huntington, Collis P., 36, 41, 43, 54, 61, 87
Huntington, Henry, 240
Hutchinson, KS, 27, 106

Ida Nice Shaft (mine), 172
Illinois Central Railroad, 23
Independence (mine), 108
Interstate Commerce Commission, 125
Irvine, James, 195
Isola Bella, Lake Maggiore, Italy, 247
Ives, Lt. Joseph C., 72

John XXIII, Saint John XXIII, 263
Johnny Sinnott Lode, 105
Johnson, Hiram, 216
Jones, Edward, 21, 98
Josephine (mine), 22, 80-81, 97-99, 102, 153, 165
Judah, Theodore, 35
Juniata (mine), 108
Juvenile (mine), 227

Kall, Dr. Alexis, 252
Kansas City, MO, 93, 169, 208
Kansas Pacific Railroad, 113
Katie Sinnott Lode, 105
Keller, Gertrude H., 197
Keller, Will E., 122, 124, 200
Kennedy, John F., 260, 263
Kennedy, Rose Fitzgerald, 263
Kennedy, Thomas F., Bishop, 207
Kerckhoff, Louise, 172, 179, 185
Kerckhoff, William, 179, 223, 241
Kerckhoff-Cuzner Mill & Lumber, 179
Kingman County, AZ, 108
Kingman, Arizona Territory, 21-22, 80, 97, 108, 128
Koshetz, Mme. Nina, 252
Krakatoa, Indonesia, 89

La Junta (mine), 108
Laboure, Saint Catherine, 211
Lagegren, Marquis Leo, 231
Laughlin, Homer, 153
Le Petit Trianon, Versailles, 201
Leadville, CO, 21, 99, 101-106, 143-150, 165, 172-174
Lee, Thomas R., 237-238
Lewis, Louise Schaeffer, 133
Lewis, Silas J., 68, 118, 219-220
Lincoln, Abraham, 23
Lippincott, J.B., 74
Little Blue River, 23-24, 27
Little Flower of Jesus (see Thérèse of Lisieux, Saint)
Little, S.W., 182
London Consolidated Mining, 104
Long Beach, CA, 159
Longstreet, Mamie Wilcox, 231

Los Angeles & San Pedro Railroad, 48-49
Los Angeles Chamber of Commerce, 151, 177
Los Angeles Cherokee Oil, 157-159, 173, 188, 192
Los Angeles City Council, 136, 138
Los Angeles City Historical Society, 19
Los Angeles Country Club, 176
Los Angeles County, 12, 151, 197, 264
Los Angeles County Museum of Natural History, 151
Los Angeles County Pioneer Society, 69, 197
Los Angeles County Superior Court, 264
Los Angeles Cultural Heritage Commission, 19
Los Angeles Electric Railway, 176
Los Angeles Nat'l Bank, 176, 201
Los Angeles oil field, 136-137
Los Angeles Philharmonic, 166
Los Angeles Shipbuilding and Dry Dock, 215-216
Los Angeles Symphony, 259
Los Feliz, Los Angeles, 262
Loyola High School, Los Angeles, 166
Loyola University, Los Angeles, 249-250

MacDonald, Genevieve, 257
MacDonald, J. Wiseman, 260
MacGowan, Eleanor, 229
MacGowan, Lillie, 229
Magdalene Laundry, 170-171, 176
Magellan, Ferdinand, 48
Maginnis, Almon P., 113-115, 120, 137-142
Mahony, Roger Cardinal, 259
Maier, Genevieve, 201, 229
Maier, Isabel Denker, 201, 257
Manchester, 89, 137
Marlborough School, 201
Marshall Field Dept. Store, Chicago, 65, 177
Masterson, Bat, 101
Mathieson, Kenneth, 145
Maybeck, Bernard, 262
Mayer, Louis B. 257, 257

INDEX

McDermott, Anna Marie, 196
McFadden, James, 195
McFie, Lyman, 217
McIntyre, James Francis Cardinal, 262-263
McLaughlin, Eugene, 260
McLaughlin, Hortense, 203, 214, 229
Meinhardt, Ms., 201, 209
Merchants Nat'l Bank, 183
Methodist Episcopal Church College, 161, 165
Mexican Central Railroad, 141
Midwick Country Club, 156
Milbank, Frances, 216
Milbank, Phila, 217
Milbank, Virginia, 258
Minahaha (mine), 108
Miner, Randolph Huntington, 231
Miner, Tulita Huntington, 230-231
Modjeska, Mme. Helena, 172, 203-204
Mogollon Rim, 40
Mohave County, 22, 99, 196
Mohave County Miner, 98-99, 116, 196
Mojave Desert, 59
Mojave Line, 42-43, 57, 59-69, 87-90, 93, 95, 151, 201
Mojave Nation, 71, 118
Mojave people, 15, 16, 19, 60-63, 71-85, 107, 117-119, 121-122, 130-131, 213
Mojave Railroad Division, 46, 57, 63-64
Mojave, CA, 42-43, 55, 59, 63-64, 68
Monaghan & Murphy, 16, 60, 65-69, 71, 75-76, 78-79, 93, 99, 106, 118, 120, 130-131, 145, 162, 176, 196-197, 250, 261
Monaghan & Murphy Bank, 197
Monaghan & Murphy Co., 68, 176, 196-197, 261
Monaghan & Murphy General Merchandise, 16, 60, 65-67, 71, 76, 78-79, 93, 130, 162, 196
Monaghan, Charlie, 106, 127-132, 196
Monaghan, Dora, 49, 56, 128, 195
Monaghan, Frank, 16, 48-49, 56, 66, 68, 76, 94, 99, 111, 120, 125, 127, 131, 144-145, 151, 181, 195, 197-198, 201, 217, 226, 241, 249-250
Monaghan, Gertrude, 217

Monterey Express Railroad 45
Moore, Charles I.D., 165
Moore, Fred, 143
Morgan, J.P., 107
Morrell, Mary Murphy, 80, 99, 102, 104, 146-148, 174
Morrell, Winters, 102, 146-148, 174
Morrison, M.H., 219
Mosher, William, 145
Mount Slover, 185, 198
Mountain Ice Co., 124
Mudd, Harvey, 165-166
Mudd, Seeley W., 165
Munday, M.E.C., 140
Munday, Walt, 237
Munsell, William, 185
Murphy Water, Ice and Light Co., 121, 196-197, 221
Murphy, Anna Rafter (Dan's mother), 23-26
Murphy, Antoinette "Nettie" Sinnott, 103-104, 143-144, 146, 148-151, 162, 164-165, 167, 169-170, 172, 178, 185, 188, 201, 203, 209, 213, 216-218, 229, 240-241, 243-244, 249, 252-253, 257, 260, 264
Murphy, Bernardine, 18, 170, 174-175, 187, 190-191, 201-205, 207, 209-214, 216, 219, 223-235, 239, 241-248, 253, 255-265
Murphy, Margaret, 26, 95, 196, 264
Murphy, Pat, 219
Murphy, Thomas (Dan's father), 26, 30-33, 166-167, 190
Murphy, Tom, 106-107, 125, 131, 144, 166, 175, 188, 196, 198, 199, 221
Murphy-Briggs Saloon, 99
Mussolini, Benito, 209, 224, 225, 245

Needles (The Needles), 42-43, 55-56, 59-69, 71-85, 87-89, 114-125, 127-133, 143, 151, 196-197, 221, 261-262
Needles Division, 87-88, 115
Needles Ice Co., 122, 125, 135
Needles Machine Works, 68, 118
Needles Nat'l Bank, 19, 132-133, 176
Nevada Southern Railway, 132
Nevin, William George, 140, 176
New Mexico, 21, 39, 49, 66, 96, 136

New Orleans, 12, 16, 23, 38, 87, 171
New York City, 16, 17, 37, 39, 42, 48, 69, 84-85, 107, 164, 174, 193, 207, 224, 245, 258, 262
Niel, Marechal, 104
Noble Guard (see Black Nobility)
Notre Dame de Namur, 103
Nutt, Henry C., 42, 60,
Nuttall Ornithological Club, 91

O'Sullivan, Guy, 231
Oakley, Annie, 257
Olinda Ranch, Orange County, 139
Orange County, 49, 50, 139-140, 153, 172, 195
Orange County Fruit Growers Assoc., 50
Oregon Trail, 23-24, 31
Orsini Villa, 232
Orsini, Domenico, 235
Orsini, Domina Isabella, 232
Orsini, Don Lelio, 232-236
Orsini, Frances, 233
Orsini, Paolo, 233
Otoe North American Indians, 29
Ox Bow Trail, 104

Pacific Coast Oil Co., 155
Pacific Grove, CA, 201
Pacific Improvement Co. (PIC), 43-44, 68, 78, 87, 213
Pacific Land Improvement Co. (PLIC), 43-46, 56, 63-64, 71, 76, 88, 93-94, 99, 113-116, 122, 124-125, 132, 138, 140, 151, 157
Pacific Light and Power, 179
Pacific Mutual Life Insurance Co., 165
Pacific Railroad, 36, 38, 164, 196
Paiute Indians, 128-129, 130, 213
Palace Hotel, San Francisco, 83
Palazzo Ruspoli, 190
Pandemic of 1918, 219-220
Papal Countess, 263
Parkinson, John, 153
Pasadena Flower Show, 1939, 258
Pasadena, CA, 179, 240, 249, 258
Patton, George S., 156

Pebble Beach, CA, 46, 108, 212-214, 219, 252-253, 255-256
Pennsylvania, 22, 33, 68
Perry, Katy, 264
Petroleum World, 19, 208, 237
Pfaehler, Frau, 215
Philadelphia, 113, 157
Phillips, Catherine Coffin, 202-203
Phillips, Kathryn, 203
Pico Blvd., 170
Pignatelli, Conchita Sepulveda, 244, 256
Pignatelli, Valerio, 244
Pius X, 187-189, 207, 209-210
Pius XI, 224-226, 230, 234, 224, 248
Pius XII, 262
Plaza Hotel, NYC, 224
Pontifical North American College, 207, 209
Portland Cement Co., 110, 133, 182, 185, 197
Pullman, 65, 95, 124, 142, 208, 210

Rancho San Juan Cajon de Santa Ana, 140
Red Cross, 215-217, 231, 242
Redondo Beach Development Co., 162
Redondo Beach, CA, 155
Reeves, Sister Mary, 211
Reinhart, J.W., 116
Rindge, Frederick Hastings, 165
Rio Grande, 39
Riordan, T.A., 188, 260
Ripley, E.P., 92, 139, 151
Riverside, CA, 125, 198
RMS *Berengaria,* 226
RMS *Lusitania,* 215
Robinson, A.A., 141
Robinson, D.B., 116
Robinson, J.W., 156
Robinson, Louise Chandler, 156
Rockefeller, John D., 107, 135-136
Rocky Mountains, 40, 74, 89
Rome, 187, 189, 190, 192, 207-209, 210, 223-226, 230-235, 241, 243-248, 263
Roosevelt, Franklin, 250, 255
Root, R.T., 145
Rosedale Cemetery, 165

INDEX

Rowan, Laura, 235
Ruspoli, Alessandro, 190
Ruspoli, Lelio, 263

Sacramento Valley Railroad Co., 35
Sacramento, CA, 24, 35-37, 52-53, 63-65, 89
Saint Agnes Church, 166
Saint Agnes Orphanage, 174
Saint John the Baptist Catholic Church, 25
Saint Joseph's Church, Hays, KS, 106, 166-167
Saint Joseph's Church, San Jose, CA, 143
Saint Peter's Basilica, 224, 230, 232
Saint Peter's Square, 190
Saint Vibiana, Cathedral of, 47, 249, 259
San Antonio, TX, 39, 42
San Bernardino County, CA, 76, 92
San Bernardino, CA, 17, 38, 40, 76, 83, 89-90, 92, 94, 137-138, 181, 193, 198
San Diego Bank of Commerce and Trust Co., 179
San Diego, CA, 38-40, 89-91, 258
San Francisco Mint, 80, 97
San Gabriel Electric Co., 179
San Gabriel Valley Railroad, 90
San Jose Normal School, 150
San Jose, CA, 102-105, 143-144, 148, 150-151, 164, 167, 169-170, 173-174, 187, 190, 204, 212
San Marino, CA, 156, 185, 224, 253
San Pedro, 12-13, 48, 50
San Pedro Railroad, 48
Santa Ana, CA, 49, 68, 125, 132, 181, 195, 197
Santa Barbara, CA, 252, 263
Santa Fe de-Luxe, 207-208
Santa Fe Depot, 207-208
Santa Fe Railway (see Atchison, Topeka & Santa Fe)
Santa Fe Refrigerator Dispatch, 125
Santa Fe, NM, 39, 215
Sartori, Joe F., 256, 260
Scott, Joe, 249, 260
Seventeen Mile Drive, 45

Severance, Caroline Maria Seymour, 163
Sheridan, Philip, 27
Sherman, William Tecumseh, 27
Sierra Nevada Mountains, 35-37
Silent, Charles, 162
Silver City, NM, 21, 136
Sinnott, Delia Ela, 102, 104
Sinnott, Delia Elizabeth, 102, 105, 145-148, 150, 173-174
Sinnott, John, 102-105, 144-146
Sinnott, Kathryn, 103, 150, 190, 191, 210, 212, 261, 264
Sinnott, Sue ("Aunt Sue"), 150, 164, 169-170, 172, 174, 178, 190-191, 198, 207, 225, 248, 259-260, 264
Sisters of Charity, 211
Sisters of Mercy, 169
Sisters of Notre Dame de Namur, 103
Sisters of Saint Joseph, Los Angeles, 171
Sisters of Social Service, 257-259
Sisters of the Good Shepherd, 169, 170, 171, 172, 203, 211, 242, 261
Sisters of the Immaculate Heart, 264
Slachta, Margit, 258
Slover Mountain, 181-182, 185, 198, 252
Smith, F.W., 60
Smokestack, 71, 72, 118
Sonoran Desert, 48
Southern California Railway, 137
Southern California Sugar Co., 195
Southern Pacific Railroad, 11-13, 15-16, 38-39, 43-45, 47-48, 53-54, 56, 60-62, 64, 80, 87, 90, 93, 108, 111, 115, 181, 231
Southwest Museum, 213
Southwestern Miners Assoc., 151, 241
Spellman, Francis J. Cardinal, 262
SS *Conte Rosso*, 224
SS *Moltke*, 187
SS *Pasadena*, 179
SS *Rotterdam*, 208
St. Joseph & Denver City Railroad, 30, 32, 47
St. Joseph & Western Railroad, 26, 32
St. Joseph, MO, 16, 30, 47, 68, 106
St. Louis World Exposition, 125

St. Louis, MO, 16, 68, 112-113, 124-125, 157, 169, 193
Standard Oil Co., 68, 107, 132, 135, 139, 153, 155, 176-177, 220
Standard Oil Co. of California, 108, 155, 177, 188
Stanford, Leland, 36-37, 44, 54
Sterry, C.N., 140
Sterry, Norman, 260
Stetson, John B., 65
Stewart, Lyman, 137, 155, 179, 237
Stimson Auditorium, Los Angeles, 203
Stolle, Antoine, 203
Sullivan, Dennis C., 21, 80, 98, 102, 269
Sunset Limited, 171
Sunset Route, 38, 87
Supreme Court of the United States, 19
Susie Sinnott Lode, 105
Swift, Gustavus, 124
Switzerland, 204, 210-211, 255

Taconia, 216
Temecula Canyon, CA, 89
Texas & Pacific Railroad, 39
The Alameda, San Jose, 103, 143, 150, 167, 174, 187, 191
Thérèse of Lisieux, Saint, 224, 225, 226
Throop College of Technology (see California Institute of Technology)
Toberman, J.R., 182
Tolono, IL, 22, 23, 30
Tombstone, AZ, 21, 41
Topeka, KS, 17, 68
Tulsa, OK, 156-158, 173, 193

Union Club, NYC, 17, 107-108, 177
Union Oil Co., 137, 155, 179, 237-238
Union Pacific Railroad, 25, 35-36
Univ. of Southern California, 161, 165
US Army Corps of Topographical Engineers, 40, 72
US Geological Survey, 183
US Open Golf Championship, 45

Vail, Nathan, 162-163
Valentine, Louise, 224
Valentine, Susan, 229

Valentine, William, 155-156, 185, 220, 224, 260
Vanderbilt, Cornelius, 107
Vatican City, 187-190, 224-225, 229-230, 243, 245, 246, 247, 263
Villa d'Este, Tivoli, Italy, 187

Wade, K.H., 137-138
Walker, Aldace F., 92, 139
Wallapai District, 98
Washington, D.C., 19, 23, 35, 37, 39, 177, 216, 229
Waverly Drive, Los Angeles, 262-264
Weber, Charles II, 105, 148-149
Weber, Charles III, 144, 149, 151, 229
Weber, Charles M., 105
Weber, Grace Mae, 144, 149
Weber, Helen, 144
Weber, Julia, 149, 151
Wells, A.G., 151
West Adams District, Los Angeles, 133, 161-162, 165-166, 175, 179, 185-187, 216, 226, 228-230, 252, 257, 261-262
West, J.H., 82
Western Development Co., 43, 54
Westinghouse Air Brake Co., 48, 65
Westinghouse, George, 107
Whipple, Lt. A.W., 62, 85
White Plains, NY, 174, 246, 261
White Sulfur Springs Spa, CA, 150, 164
White, Gerald T., 155
Wilcox, Alfred Henry, 231
Wilmington, 48-50, 122, 166
Wilson, Benjamin D., 12
Workman, William, 260
World War I, 159, 217, 219, 223, 224, 225
World War II, 15
Wynanspray, 212-214, 219, 253, 255-256

Yoch, Florence, 240-241
Yuma Crossing, 39
Yuma Line, 15, 39, 42, 48, 50, 52, 54-55, 66, 70, 110-111, 181
Yuma, AZ, 15, 38-43, 48, 52-53, 54-55, 62-63, 66, 87, 231

www.iceandoil.com

www.ingramcontent.com/pod-product-compliance
Lightning Source LLC
Chambersburg PA
CBHW070128080526
44586CB00015B/1609